Japanese Philosophies of Education

Bloomsbury Introductions to World Philosophies

Series Editor:
Monika Kirloskar-Steinbach
Assistant Series Editor:
Leah Kalmanson
Regional Editors:
Nader El-Bizri, James Madaio, Ann A. Pang-White, Takeshi Morisato, Pascah Mungwini, Mickaella Perina, Omar Rivera and Georgina Stewart

Bloomsbury Introductions to World Philosophies delivers primers reflecting exciting new developments in the trajectory of world philosophies. Instead of privileging a single philosophical approach as the basis of comparison, the series provides a platform for diverse philosophical perspectives to accommodate the different dimensions of cross-cultural philosophizing. While introducing thinkers, texts and themes emanating from different world philosophies, each book, in an imaginative and path-breaking way, makes clear how it departs from a conventional treatment of the subject matter.

Titles in the Series:

A Practical Guide to World Philosophies, by Monika Kirloskar-Steinbach and Leah Kalmanson
Daya Krishna and Twentieth-Century Indian Philosophy, by Daniel Raveh
Māori Philosophy, by Georgina Tuari Stewart
Philosophy of Science and The Kyoto School, by Dean Anthony Brink
Tanabe Hajime and the Kyoto School, by Takeshi Morisato
African Philosophy, by Pascah Mungwini
The Zen Buddhist Philosophy of D. T. Suzuki, by Rossa Ó Muireartaigh
Sikh Philosophy, by Arvind-Pal Singh Mandair
The Philosophy of the Brahma-sūtra, by Aleksandar Uskokov
The Philosophy of the Yogasūtra, by Karen O'Brien-Kop
The Life and Thought of H. Odera Oruka, by Gail M. Presbey

Mexican Philosophy for the 21st Century, by Carlos Alberto Sánchez
Buddhist Ethics and the Bodhisattva Path, by Stephen Harris
Contextualizing Angela Davis, by Joy James
Yorùbá Art and Aesthetics, by Barry Hallen
Phenomenology of Tea, by Adam Loughnane
The Philosophy of No-Mind, by Nishihira Tadashi

Japanese Philosophies of Education

Watsuji Tetsurō and Mori Akira

Anton Sevilla-Liu

BLOOMSBURY ACADEMIC
LONDON • NEW YORK • OXFORD • NEW DELHI • SYDNEY

BLOOMSBURY ACADEMIC

Bloomsbury Publishing Plc, 50 Bedford Square, London, WC1B 3DP, UK
Bloomsbury Publishing Inc, 1359 Broadway, New York, NY 10018, USA
Bloomsbury Publishing Ireland, 29 Earlsfort Terrace, Dublin 2, D02 AY28 Ireland

BLOOMSBURY, BLOOMSBURY ACADEMIC and the Diana logo are trademarks
of Bloomsbury Publishing Plc

First published in Great Britain 2026

Copyright © Anton Sevilla-Liu, 2026

Anton Sevilla-Liu asserted his right under the Copyright, Designs and Patents
Act, 1988, to be identified as Author of this work.
For legal purposes the Acknowledgements on p. ix constitute an extension
of this copyright page.

Series design by Louise Dugdale
Cover image: © bgblue / Getty Images

All rights reserved. No part of this publication may be: i) reproduced or transmitted in any form, electronic or mechanical, including photocopying, recording or by means of any information storage or retrieval system without prior permission in writing from the publishers; or ii) used or reproduced in any way for the training, development or operation of artificial intelligence (AI) technologies, including generative AI technologies. The rights holders expressly reserve this publication from the text and data mining exception as per Article 4(3) of the Digital Single Market Directive (EU) 2019/790.

Bloomsbury Publishing Plc does not have any control over, or responsibility for, any third-party websites referred to or in this book. All internet addresses given in this book were correct at the time of going to press. The author and publisher regret any inconvenience caused if addresses have changed or sites have ceased to exist, but can accept no responsibility for any such changes.

A catalogue record for this book is available from the British Library.
A catalog record for this book is available from the Library of Congress.

ISBN: PB: 978-1-3505-7277-5
HB: 978-1-3505-7276-8
ePDF: 978-1-3505-7279-9
eBook: 978-1-3505-7278-2

Typeset by RefineCatch Limited, Bungay, Suffolk
Printed and bound in Great Britain

For product safety related questions contact productsafety@bloomsbury.com

To find out more about our authors and books visit www.bloomsbury.com
and sign up for our newsletters.

Contents

List of Illustrations　　viii
Series Editor's Preface　　ix
Acknowledgments　　x

Introduction　　1

Part I
Watsuji Tetsurō

1　Confucianism and Finding Your Place　　27

2　Relation without an Other?　　57

3　Buddhism and Awakening to Self　　81

Part II
Mori Akira

4　The Practical-Pragmatic Nexus　　111

5　The Rhythm of Life　　137

6　Learning to Live　　167

Conclusion　　197
Notes　　205
Bibliography　　227
Index　　235

Illustrations

1.1	The tensional view of the human being.	54
4.1	Yin and Yang.	111
4.2	The mutual negation of *ningen*.	112
4.3	Non-duality of subject-object.	127
5.1	Two non-dualities in emptiness.	137
5.2	Tensions within.	147
5.3	Shifting emphasis.	148
5.4	Layers of personality.	149
5.5	Stages of human development through personal needs and social needs.	153
5.6	The rise and fall of life.	163
5.7	Multi-generational bridges.	164

Series Editor's Preface

Bloomsbury Introductions to World Philosophies offers plural, hitherto unexplored pathways into the study of world philosophies. Instead of privileging a single philosophical approach as the basis of comparison, the series provides a platform for diverse philosophical perspectives to accommodate the many different dimensions of cross-cultural philosophizing. While the choice of terms used by the individual volumes may indeed carry a local inflection, they do not foreclose critical thinking about philosophical plurality. The individual volumes strike a balance between locality and globality.

Drawing from insights of Watsuji Tetsurō (1889–1960) and Mori Akira (1915–1976), *Japanese Philosophies of Education* offers an account of transformatory education that centers human cultivation. Bringing Watsuji's *ningen sonzai* (人間存在, philosophy of human existence) together with Mori's understanding of *ningen seisei* (人間生成, philosophy of becoming a human being), Anton Sevilla-Liu illustrates how students and the teachers can develop relationships that guide students in wrestling the tensions that come with facing challenges in their daily lives. As students learn to meet these challenges, they can co-develop with their teachers pathways or 'arched bridges' that connect to the creative development of their communities.

Japanese Philosophies of Education will serve as a valuable guide to those who seek for a pedagogy for change instead of continuing the market-oriented model of education that shapes students to fulfill market needs.

Monika Kirloskar-Steinbach

Acknowledgments

I would like to thank my research group, the Kyushu University Clinical Pedagogy Team, for being my main impetus to grow as an educator, learning with me, helping me refine my ideas, challenging me, and cooperating in research projects that shaped this book. I would especially like to acknowledge members Catherine Sevilla-Liu (who read and discussed this book from the earliest draft), Honda Teruhiko, Mizokami Atsuko, Himori Sakiko, Ikubo Rin, Tokutsu Kensuke, and Kataoka Yūri, and two guests, Dr. Takaya Shōko and Dr. Tezuka Chizuko, who joined a reading group to read and refine the first draft of this book. I am also grateful to my education teachers, Prof. Nishihira Tadashi and Prof. Saito Naoko, who guided my journey into Clinical Pedagogy at Kyoto University and continue to support my intellectual growth. Finally, I would like to thank the Department of Philosophy at the Ateneo de Manila University, Philippines. It seems despite all these years in Japan, I keep coming back to cura personalis and the other values we lived by.

This book was written with the aid of funding from Japan Society for the Promotion of Science (JSPS), project numbers JP17K13988 and JP21K13525.

Introduction

This is a book in Japanese philosophy of education. I have written this for researchers in education and philosophy, school teachers and counselors, educators of all levels, future educators, even parents—anyone who is interested in thinking deeply about what it means to be part of the process of forming people and accompanying them as they grow. I wrote this book because life is *complicated*, and that means taking any responsibility for the formation of someone else's life is hard work. Students are pulled in all directions, with the needs and expectations of their families, their peers, the market, the state, with different standards of what it means to be competent or successful. At the same time, students also feel a deep need to make sense of who they are and their own direction in life. There are practical demands in life as an employee, a citizen, a family member, but there is also the need to make personal sense of what it all *means*. Being pulled in different directions is literally the definition of "stress."

Many books might try to resolve this confusion—to distill the recipe of life to one principle, be it success, authenticity, meaning, or connection. I do not blame them; the mind likes cognitive efficiency. But I am going to do something different. In this book, I talk about two Japanese philosophers who begin with the *paradoxes* of life, bring some clarity to the different tensions that we experience, and build a whole vision of education on the basis of contradiction—in hopes that we might better sit with these dilemmas and find our ways to walk with them.

But why *Japanese* philosophy of education? People in the English-speaking world often have hyperbolized ideas of Japan. One common question I get in conferences is "Isn't Japanese education all just testing and pressure and uniformity? Why would I want to learn their philosophy of education?" There is this stereotypical image of Asian collectivism, which seems far removed from the needs of more pluralist, individualist societies. On the other end of the spectrum, there are those who have a very positive image of Japan—of Zen, *wabi-sabi*, and *ikigai*, a Studio Ghibli or Hayao Miyazaki view of Japan with its openness to the present moment and the beauty of small things. (I am leaving out a third common view of Japan, of video entertainment of both wholesome and unwholesome varieties, since most conference-goers have been kind enough not to ask me about that!)

This exoticization of Japan has grains of truth and indeed there is a lot of collectivist uniformity *and* spiritual depth in "real Japan." But let us look at some examples of Japanese students, especially in moments of struggle, when the vulnerability of being human comes to the fore. (I refer to them as "*-kun*" and "*-san*" where the former is an honorific used for junior males and the latter for females. One occasionally drops the honorific, but this usually indicates a much more personal relationship.)

> Jin-*kun* is a sharp and enthusiastic young man. But he is so accustomed to competing for grades that when I teach him a new lesson, he seems to focus on how to ace it and not how this lesson might be personally meaningful. He also struggles with groupwork, giving others the impression that he is always trying to prove his superiority.
>
> Junko-*san* is a quiet and agreeable student, always liked by her groupmates. But when she misses an assignment, she gets terrified of my disappointment. And she seems directionless, struggling with knowing what she herself wants to do with her studies.
>
> Taro-*kun* is genuinely interested in educational counseling. But the deeper he engages it, the more it brings out his fundamental doubts about education and life as a whole. He tries to learn in an experientially rich way, but he finds that what he is trying to learn often conflicts with how he views the world.
>
> A research group is trying to learn ideas together in a real, experiential way. To make space for personal experience, they value having the team be a safe space for personal growth. However,

sometimes, people use this "safe space" to stay in their comfort zones and avoid academic challenges.

Do any of these examples strike you as familiar? These are real examples from my experience in Japan that I will be discussing in the chapters of this book. My point is that despite cultural difference, Japanese people are *human*. I have taught in Japan and closely engaged students for over a dozen years, and I find that when I deal with Japanese students and teachers in a deep, personal way, the challenges they face in education are quite recognizable and have much to teach anyone from any culture.

I learned to start with paradox because of the particular Japanese philosophy I use in this book—that of the Kyoto School of Philosophy. During Japan's rapid modernization in the Meiji period, many Japanese philosophers focused on importing western philosophy. However, the Kyoto School countered this trend to draw from Japan's wisdom traditions—Buddhism, Confucianism, Shintoism—and bring them to critical dialogue with western ideas. They tried to push beyond textual critique to see philosophy as a matter of self-cultivation that leads to personal realization.[1] The result was a philosophy that heavily focused on "nothingness" (*mu* 無) or "emptiness" (*kū* 空) that unlike a philosophy of being is much more comfortable with embracing contradiction and the non-rational. I believe this philosophy of emptiness can help us—educators of all sorts—as we try to face the complexities of becoming human.

However, a quick caveat before we explore these ideas in greater depth. First, due to the growing recognition of the Kyoto School in international research, some people misconceive of the Kyoto School as "traditional" and "representative" of Japanese philosophies. Like the famed Philosopher's Path in Kyoto, it seems "essentially" Japanese. But as we see above, the Kyoto School emerged as a critique against the mainstream way of doing philosophy in Japan—translation and textual critique of western philosophy. And despite the rise of the Kyoto School of Philosophy and its increasing recognition in world philosophy, text critique of foreign philosophy is *still* the dominant approach in departments and associations of philosophy.

These suggest that the Kyoto School has never been a "representative" of Japan in a statistical sense. It has always been a critical response, a minority in relation to the main trend of Japanese philosophy. Their critique uses traditional sources that are distinct from that of western philosophy, but these sources are not unique to Japan, often shared by many Asian countries. Nor do these wisdom traditions exclusively define Japan. And the Kyoto School's use of these traditions is hardly traditionalist—mixing Zen with William James or Confucianism with Hegel ... I argue that thinking of the Kyoto School as traditionally and representatively Japanese results in misunderstanding the reality of Japan, over-exoticizing the Kyoto School, or both.

Second, this mixing indicates that the ideas of the Kyoto School do not exclusively belong to Japan. The Kyoto School is merely one avenue to seeing things in a deeper way, fruitfully connecting with other philosophers like Nel Noddings, George Herbert Mead, or Erik Erikson. This research is an attempt to open doors rather than to close them via cultural essentialism.

The Kyoto School of Philosophy and Education

Who were the Kyoto School, and what is this "philosophy of emptiness?" To briefly introduce the Kyoto School of Philosophy, there is no better person to begin with than Nishida Kitarō (1870–1945). James Heisig, Thomas Kasulis, and John Maraldo go as far as to say that he is "generally considered Japan's greatest philosopher."[2] He taught in Kyoto Imperial University from 1910 until 1928, and his influence on various people— Tanabe Hajime, Nishitani Keiji, Miki Kiyoshi, Kōyama Iwao, Kimura Motomori, and Watsuji Tetsurō—would result in the founding of the Kyoto School of Philosophy and its gradual extension into education.

Nishida began his career publishing *An Inquiry into the Good* (1911). Nishida criticized European philosophy's tendency to separate subject and object and build a philosophy purely on the basis of subjective thinking (as idealism tends to) or purely on the basis of objective things (as empiricism and natural science tends to). Instead, he took as his starting point "pure experience."³ This pure experience arises when, for example, you completely lose yourself in the moment as you play a musical instrument—an experience beyond words. In such an experience, rather than the subject thinking about the object, you have the subject losing itself in the object—a non-duality of subject and object. This inaugurated a radically new way of philosophizing, not merely interpreting western sources but transforming them through his personal religious experience (particularly Zen meditation), and also combining eastern and western sources (like Buddhism with James). His subsequent career would span various topics—neo-Kantianism, the logic of locus, absolute nothingness—various ideas excellently introduced in Heisig's *Philosophers of Nothingness*.

What is less known is that Nishida was involved in education all his life, both as a teacher and as a consultant of the Ministry of Education.[4] On the ministry's request, he gave a talk, "On the Scholarly Method" (1937, available in English).[5] He also wrote directly about education *once*, in an article simply entitled "On Education" (1933, no translation).[6] Here, Nishida's primary aim was to criticize the Herbartian idea (which was, and arguably still is a dominant approach to education in Japan) that sees education as forming students in an abstract way towards universal ethical values like autonomy. In contrast, Nishida writes:

> Education, I believe, can be thought of as a kind of formative process. The educator forms the human being as a sculptor forms a sculpture. To form is to objectively create something by means of an idea, to realize an idea-like thing. In this sense, the act of formation may be considered subjective, but true formation is not merely the objective manifestation of the subject, but the self-manifestation of the object. The imagination in the mind of the sculptor is not directly the sculpture itself. In artistic creation, the artist himself does not know what kind of work will be created. There must be a creative action of subject-object unity.[7]

Nishida begins with a decidedly teacher-centric Herbartian image of carving down students like a block of wood, only to turn the metaphor on its head.[8] If you consider the actual experience of sculpting or calligraphy (Nishida's art form), you realize that in the artistic process, formation is *not* a one-sided affair in which the subject is imposed on the object. You may have an idea of what you want to sculpt or write, but as your hand interacts with the unique density of the medium, as the brush interacts with the fibers of the paper, art develops in unexpected directions—and a key part of the artistic process is how we listen to that response of the object and harmonize with it.

Similarly, we may have an idea of what students ought to be, but when we interact with the actuality of this particular student before us, in this unique encounter, formation *happens* with a non-duality of subject and object. It is not I-form-the-student, but that the student-takes-form-with-me. And in this *happening*, there is something larger than the teacher and the student at play. Nishida saw this student as a concrete person who both stands in a particular place and time (Japan and its culture) but at the same time can transcend to the eternal now and take part in the reconstruction of society and history, the self-aware determination of nothingness (*mu no jikakuteki gentei* 無の自覚的限定). Thus, formation is not of an abstract student but of a dynamic singularity that itself forms history.

"On Education" is often seen as part of a dialogue between Nishida and Kimura Motomori, when Nishida was encouraging Kimura to move from the field of aesthetics to education—a move that would give rise to the Kyoto School of *Education*.[9] This school resulted in the growth of the very theory of the Kyoto School itself through its encounter with the realities of forming actual human beings.

Kimura Motomori (1845–1946) took up the very idea that Nishida had given him and, using the Greek idea of *poeisis*, he recast human nature as "formative/expressive awareness" (*keiseiteki jikaku*). In *Culture and Education within the Nation State* (1946), he wrote, "What, especially, is the existence called human (*ningen*)? It is an existence that expresses itself formatively, and by so doing acquires concrete awareness of itself."[10] Just as an artist does not now her style beforehand but discovers it as she struggles with the process of self-expression, teachers understand themselves as teachers as they form students, and a nation understands itself as it forms citizens.

Education forms not only individuals but through individuals forms society as a whole:

> Educative activities shoulder the infinite tradition of the past and look forward to infinite creation in the future. And while doing so, educative activities sublate the former [tradition] within the latter [the future], and thus are tradition-*soku*-creativity, creativity-*soku*-tradition, and from such a standpoint of the dynamic present, they subjectively raise the foundation of culture. This is where education's particular cultural mission lies.[11]

Beyond teachers shaping students, tradition and culture shape themselves. Nishida and Kimura both bestow on this movement an ontological importance:

> Historical life, which is intrinsically an existence with formative and expressive awareness, manifests through education its function of active self-formation—one in which it cultivates within itself the basis of objective self-formation. If so, then education in itself means an ultimate form of formative awareness within this formative and self-aware life. Suppose the essential meaning of the person's cultural activities as a self-aware individual should consist in being in absolute life, and in shedding light on such life from within and helping and cultivating it in a self-aware way. Then, education that aims to cultivate such a self-aware individual is none other than the ultimate form of formative awareness, one that helps and cultivates what helps the cultivation of heaven and earth.[12]

Education is about the self-formation of historical life as a whole, and thus part of the self-awakening of reality itself: the very meaningfulness of reality as a whole is formed as people come to terms with how to face reality meaningfully through education.[13]

All in all, the work between the Kyoto School of Philosophy and Education includes work by Nishida himself, other members of the Kyoto School like Watsuji Tetsurō, Kōyama Iwao, and Kōsaka Masaaki, educationalists like Kimura, Mori Akira, and Kido Mantarō. These figures are introduced in English by Paul Standish and Naoko Saito's *Education and the Kyoto School of Philosophy* (2012).[14] These thinkers all elaborated these ideas of non-dualism and formation, giving the philosophical basis for an approach to education that begins with paradox. Research on this school continues in Japanese, such as in Yano Satoji's extensive research into the historical influence of the Kyoto School on Japanese education,[15] Takaya Shōko's research on Nishida's philosophy of education,[16] and Monzen Ayaki's research on Kimura's philosophical anthropology.[17]

However, at this level of abstraction, it is difficult to address problems of people like Jin-*kun*, Junko-*san*, and Taro-*kun*, actual students whose struggles we share with in education. For such, we go deep into two particular and very practical thinkers—Watsuji Tetsurō and Mori Akira.

Watsuji's Ethics of Education

Nishida's penchant to invite people to Kyoto University was one of the driving forces that led to the Kyoto School of Philosophy and Education. One of the people he invited to teach at Kyoto University was Watsuji Tetsurō (1889–1960).

Author's Note

The inclusion of Watsuji in a book on the Kyoto School might not sit well with some purists, because technically Watsuji never studied under Nishida. He is thus usually seen as a "peripheral member" of the Kyoto School. However, given the less historical focus of this book, I will define the Kyoto School *broadly* as those directly influenced by

Nishida and who, in relation with each other, critically contributed to this philosophy of nothingness. Watsuji was heavily influenced by Nishida, and as he developed into Japan's best-known modern ethicist, his work in turn influenced many in the Kyoto School—including Kimura and Mori. His work was also very close to other members of the Kyoto School like Tanabe Hajime and Kōyama Iwao.

Popularly, Watsuji is best-known for his book *Climate and Culture* (1961 [1935]), which is widely-researched as in Johnson's *Watsuji on Nature* or Berque's *Thinking Through Landscape*. I was pleased to find out that this book is widely-read even by some high school students in Japan! In this work, he drew from his experiences of traveling to Europe for an entertaining philosophical journey through various monsoon, desert, and meadow climates. The main insight of this work is that the human being does not exist in isolation from their milieu (*fūdo*, literally wind and earth). Rather, human life is one wherein meaning (language, culture, and religion) is fundamentally tied to our responding to the material environment, resulting in a non-dualism between the subjective and objective world. This book set up insights that would lead to *Ethics as a Study of Ningen* (1934, a book he had hand-signed for Kimura and whose influence Kimura credits[18]) and eventually his magnum opus, the three volumes of *Ethics* (1937, 1946, 1949; first volume available in English, 1996). Philosophically, this is what he is best-known for—systematic ethics.

Allow me to recapitulate the key points of *Ethics* in some detail to prepare for their application to education. (I apologize for the density of the following explanations, but the essential points are further unpacked in each chapter.)

Watsuji begins *Ethics I* (1937) writing, "The essential significance of the attempt to describe ethics as the study of *ningen* consists in getting away from the misconception, prevalent in the modern world, that conceives of ethics as a problem of individual consciousness *only*."[19] Most modern western approaches to ethics think about the good life in terms of various individual factors—individual happiness (utilitarianism), individual rationality (deontology), and individual virtue (virtue ethics). This is similar to the world view of Jin-*kun* that we will see in Chapter 1. However, if you are happy but the people around you are miserable, what kind of happiness is that? (Utilitarianism looks at the *sum total* of happiness of people, but Watsuji's point is that you could not even have a quantity for individual happiness separate from that of others.) If you are able to be rational, but your community punishes every moral act you do, while this may be morally heroic, do we really want to make this tragic state the ideal of ethics? For Watsuji, ethics is relational, and thus includes both individual and social aspects. Thus, for Watsuji, a good life is one wherein your happiness connects to that of others, your rationality is contributive to and supported by community, and your virtues are in harmony with the virtue around you.

Watsuji's insistence on this relational approach to ethics came from a unique way of seeing the human being. On one hand, he was critical of individualistic views that take the individual as the starting point, because many of the things we take as the boundaries of the individual—the body, sensations, consciousness—are actually relational. But at the same time, he did not think that substantializing society was a good idea either. Examining sociological theory, he looked at examples like the family, a business, and a nation-state, and saw that while the totality is not reducible to the sum of its parts, communities cannot exist without the unity and commitment of its members. If all members quit a community or even merely refuse to act like members of the community, that community dies.

Therefore, instead of choosing one side and reducing the other to it, Watsuji began with a fundamentally tensional approach to the human being (*ningen*):

> The Japanese language, therefore, possesses a very significant word; namely *ningen*. On the basis of the evolved meaning of this word, we Japanese have produced a distinctive conception of human being. According to it, *ningen* is the public and, at the same time, the individual human beings living within it.... *Ningen* denotes the unity of these

contradictories. Unless we keep this dialectical structure in mind, we cannot understand the essence of *ningen*.[20]

On one hand, what he did here is heavily influenced by the non-dualism of Nishida and Buddhist philosophy, wherein reality is made up of inseparable aspects, like yin and yang. However, Watsuji wanted to stress that despite this unity, it is a tensional and non-reductive unity, and we are always tempted to take things from one side and not the other. In an attempt to be ethical, if you try to be authentic, to listen to what your conscience calls you to do, you might find yourself at odds with more conventional ways of seeing a problem. The clearer your own way of viewing things, the more distant you might get from what others see as "common sense," making it difficult to engage others effectively. But in the same way, if you prioritize engaging and connecting with others, you might find that you are drawn to more conventional ways of seeing, losing your unique personal realization. His view of ethics thus articulates a very palpable *tension* that students like Junko-*san* and Taro-*kun* struggled with, and perhaps you yourself have experienced in your attempt to live well.

Watsuji thus considered individuality and totality as both part of human existence (*ningen sonzai*) but in a *negative* relationship with each other. Allow me a fairly lengthy quote:

> Now that *ningen's sonzai* is, fundamentally speaking, a movement of negation makes it clear that the basis of *ningen's sonzai* is negation as such, that is, absolute negation. The true reality of an individual, as well as of totality, is "emptiness," and this emptiness is the absolute totality. Out of this ground, from the fact that this emptiness is emptied, emerges *ningen's sonzai* as a movement of negation. The negation of negation is the self-returning and self-realizing movement of the absolute totality that is precisely social ethics ... [T]he basic principle of social ethics involves two moments. One of these is the establishment of the individual as the other, over against totality. What is at stake here is the taking of a first step toward self-awareness. Apart from the self-awareness of an individual, there is no social ethics. The other moment

is the individual's surrender to the totality. This is what has been called the *demand of the super individual will*, or of total will. Without this surrender, there is also no social ethics.[21]

Just as we see out students struggling with balancing their own wishes and hopes and the expectations of family and society, ethics is not a simplistic single-principle endeavor, but a back-and-forth movement. Everyone has a double challenge to let go of egotism to connect with the whole, but at the same time to go beyond conformism to creatively contribute. This letting-go of one-sided principles is expressed via the word "emptiness" (or "nothingness") which is a Buddhist idea shared by the Kyoto School. Ethics is about learning to realize the emptiness of all things.

While the focus of Watsuji's ethics was the tension of individuality and totality, he also continued the idea of the non-duality of subject and object, via his idea of a "practical act nexus" (*jissenteki kōiteki renkan*)— the mesh we live in as we live cooperatively in communities. In this nexus, we see a combination of the subjective and the objective: people connect via *meaningful action*, that is, both practical responses to the objective world (as learning to live in one's climate) and the symbolic meanings in the subjective world (like summer harvest celebrations). This conception allowed him to analyze ethical challenges holistically—he would look at both its individual and its group side, and simultaneously, he would look at both the objective actions and expressions and what they subjectively meant to people.

The book above is available in English, and I heartily recommend it. But Watsuji wrote two more volumes, which unfortunately remain untranslated. In *Ethics II* (1946), Watsuji expands this view of human existence to an overall theory of society, not merely in the abstract, but in the different levels of complexity of human organization. People are not part of only one community but of various *finite* organizations of ethical life (*jinrinteki soshiki*). For example, the family is a finite organization, wherein one has roles (son, daughter, brother, sister, etc.). Furthermore, certain things that are shared mediate that relation (ex.

blood ties in a family). A larger organization like the local community would include but sublate these smaller organizations, both allowing the family its space, but also creating different connections at a higher level. Communities also have flows, connections, and boundaries, as seen in economics. And finally, there are virtues (loyalty in the family, consideration in the local community, mutual service in economics) that sustain these relationships, meaning the shape of ethics depends on the kind of relationship you are considering.

The key level of organization of ethical life that Watsuji highlights is cultural community. He defines culture as symbolic forms—language, art, religion, science—that bind people together over time and across a territory. As different individuals, families, villages, and cities relate with each other through a shared history of economic and political activity, they begin to share in their experiences and responses to their common milieu.[22] Of course, much of education has to do with teaching people these elements of culture, and we see that education plays a key role in allowing people to connect with each other in socio-ethical life.

In *Ethics III* (1949), after Japan's defeat in the Second World War, Watsuji was forced to contend with the broadest senses of community—humankind as a whole and the changes of history. But he does not merely juxtapose his ethics onto the world stage. On one hand, he builds a theory of relational time, seeing how different groups have their own shared histories (like a family tree) and their own shared futures (like the long-term plan of a school). On the other hand, he builds a theory of relational space and his original idea of milieu, showing how different groups relate with each other in a way mediated by the space they share. However, the combination of history and milieu become the here-and-now of groups, especially the nation-state. He thus considers what it means for nation-states to encounter each other, to learn from each other, and to undergo *social change*—hopefully toward a world where nations are able to contribute to each other instead of being locked in endless conflict.

Above, we see an overview of the "ethics of emptiness"—a uniquely relational view of ethics, a tensional model of human existence, a profound vision of social ontology, and a consideration of social change in international history. I wrote a book detailing Watsuji's ethics and its potential contributions to contemporary philosophy—*Watsuji Tetsurô's Global Ethics of Emptiness* (2017).[23] However, Watsuji's insights were closely related to *education*. In *Ethics I*, Watsuji already suggested that education forms *relational* cognition and used education to explain how relationships are always mediated by roles. In *Ethics II*, he gave schooling the central role of building this "spiritual connection" between citizens by teaching them the culture that binds them to each other. And in *Ethics III*, he wrote about how education can also become the site of cultural change. Furthermore, he has other books such as *Purifying Zen* (1926) and *Confucius* (1938) that showed the specifics of education, explored via Buddhism and Confucianism.

In other words, Watsuji not only has a relational ethics, but the fragments of an *ethics of education*. Furthermore, Watsuji also directly influenced education. He was part of the Ministry of Education's committee for the renewal of education and scholarship (*Kyōgaku sasshin hyōgikai*, 1935) with Nishida, and supported Nishida when he criticized the committee for its insular thinking.[24] Around the same time, he was also part of the committee that drafted the *Cardinal Principles of the National Polity of Japan* (*Kokutai no hongi*, 1937), which laid the ideals for Japan's wartime education.[25] He also wrote articles in *Encyclopedia of Education* (*Kyōikugaku jitten*) on national morality.

In English, most of the research directly linking Watsuji to education is in my own work, but you can see glimmers of his educational thought in recent research by Graham Mayeda and Kyle and Sayaka Shuttleworth on his relationship with his teachers.[26] In Japanese, there is some research connecting Watsuji to geography education and moral education.[27]

Given that Watsuji had these fragments of a philosophy of education and was deeply involved in education, I will try to draw from these fragments, in order that we may see his view of education as a whole, and how it handles key tensions between individuality and community, and between subjectivity and objectivity.

Mori Akira's Philosophy of Human Becoming

Even with merely a fragmentary view of education, Watsuji has already influenced educational philosophy in Japan. His disciple Katsube Mitake (founder of the Japanese Moral Education Society) used Watsuji's ideas to consider moral education. However, a more broadly influential figure who took up Watsuji's ideas was Mori Akira (1915–1976), the other focal point of this book.

Mori was a disciple of Tanabe Hajime (the co-founder of the Kyoto School with Nishida), studied under Kimura Motomori, and was tutored by Nishitani Keiji (both Kimura and Nishitani being Nishida's disciples), and is thus properly a member of the second generation of the Kyoto School. However, Tanaka Tsunemi suggests that he did not deliberately position himself as a representative of the Kyoto School in order to have critical distance from the various academic controversies in the post-war.[28] Mori moved from philosophy to philosophy of education, expanding beyond the Kyoto School and writing extensively on existential education, pragmatism, and the human sciences. This made him one of the most important post-war philosophers of education in Japan, becoming president of both the Japan Educational Research Association and the Philosophy of Education Society of Japan.

Unfortunately, none of Mori's work is translated. But in this book, I will introduce his ideas in detail, ensuring that one can follow along without reading the Japanese originals. Loosely following Tanaka's categorization of Mori's work,[29] I will focus on five main phases of Mori's work: existentialism, pragmatism, moral education, educational science, and integration. Again, let the descriptions function as a teaser and an overview—we will see the details of Mori's work all throughout this book.

The first phase of Mori's work starts with his first book, *The Philosophical Quest for Educational Ideals* (1948). Japan had just been defeated in the Second World War, and the values that had grounded the wartime education system—the Japanese empire, the divinity of the emperor, the absolute obedience of imperial subjects—had been thrown into question. Mori took this particular national-historical crisis as an essential feature of education—an *antinomy* of education. On one hand, education is about helping students grow into better people, to realize "true human being." But all teachers have experienced moments of doubt: Do we *really* know what is good for students? Do I really have the right, as a fallible human being, to shape students into better human beings? Mori writes, "[I]n the ideal of 'true human being', there is a harshness (*kibishisa*) included here that lies beyond our abilities.... In this way, we are forced to reflect if we even have the power *as human beings to educate in a way that forms true human beings*."[30]

In a time of social meaninglessness, there is a deep temptation to abandon education altogether. But at the same time, human beings need education. As Kant says, human beings are the only animals that need education to become what they are. Thus, we are put in an antinomy: We cannot educate, but we cannot *not* educate. The core existential attitude of Mori thus affirms our struggle as we face the paradoxes of confusion—these are an essential part of how education really is.

Furthermore, Mori explored the main philosophies of education—Rousseau's naturalism, Kant's idealism, Dewey's pragmatism, Dilthey's philosophy of life, Marx's materialism, and Jaspers's existentialism. In these different philosophies, we see different tensions. Just like Watsuji's *nin-gen*, there is a tension between valuing the freedom of the individual and in forming the individual to abide with the cultural community. And like the practical nexus, there is a tension between valuing subjective meaningfulness and practically responding to objective demands of material life. And like Watsuji, rather than "awakening to emptiness" in a way that resolves these tensions, he suggests a continuous process of living out these tensions, a "questing self-awareness" (*tankyūteki jikaku* 探求的自覚).[31]

In the second phase of Mori's work, he turned to pragmatism. He wrote *Empircism and Educational Principles* (1951), which became an important work in the world of Dewey research. In this book, he warns of the dangers of Japan's one-sided focus on German idealism as tending to be guided entirely by intellectual coherence without testing this coherence with its actual consequences in real life.[32] Against this, he argued for the importance of empiricism's grounding in facts. But rather than merely rejecting ideas in exchange for facts, pragmatism goes beyond early empiricism by showing how experience can build up into meanings and ideas (subjective), but at the same time how these ideas are still tested and refined via experiential engagement with life (objective).[33] This addresses the clash we feel even outside Japan, between seeking "practical" success in life and finding a personal sense of meaning, developing Nishida's and Watsuji's ideas of the unity of subject and object.

Mori was deeply influenced by John Dewey, who looked at the unity of subject-object not merely epistemologically or psychologically but socially. The separation of subject and object is not merely philosophical but comes from a social context where the intellectual class is separated from those who merely work with material labor—and thus ideals become divorced from embodied experience.[34] Thus, this non-duality implied not merely a philosophical change but a need for social change—to educate people in a way that subjective and objective life are connected and thus democratically overcome the divide between the intellectual class and the labor class. In what could be a veiled critique of the Kyoto School (which sometimes ended up siding with conservatives in Japan), Mori wrote:

> If philosophy were to be faithful to its social mission, solve the problems of social life, and build a system that is unified, coherent, and complete, it needs to aim for a unification of social life and the conflicting dualisms therein that have given rise to the dualist theories within philosophy itself. In other words, it needs to reach the praxis of transforming (*kaizō suru jissen*) traditional society that in some way includes feudal and undemocratic qualities.[35]

While some might think that Buddhist or mystical approaches means escaping the problems of the world to gaze at one's navel, Mori suggests a philosophy that is socially transformative.

In his third phase, Mori tied to combine the idealist side of existentialism with pragmatism as he focused on the theory of moral education. In these works, Mori took up Watsuji's non-dualities of individuality and totality (autonomy and solidarity) and subject-object (inwardness and practicality) in order to come up with a theory, a practice, and actual textbooks on moral education. In the theoretical book, *The Practicality and Inwardness of Education* (1955), he defined education as "human becoming, in relation to others."[36] He saw the human being as having an organic layer (objective), a conscious layer (subjective), and a self-aware layer (subjective-objective), each of these layers having an individual aspect and a collective aspect, building a much more sophisticated model of the tensions of human existence.

But at the same time, he saw these theories of human *being* as limited in that they were focused on a static image of the human being. Life does not begin and end in adulthood. Rather, human existence is a human *becoming*. Drawing from Erik Erikson's idea of identity development, he showed how the child develops, first through direct action and experience, then through cultural and social transmission, and then finally through reflective thought. This ensures that the model of human existence is useful given the changes that the human being goes through *in life*.

In the fourth phase of Mori's work, given that human becoming is not just about ideas but about pragmatic challenges and empirical facts, he focused on connecting philosophy to the sciences, writing *Philosophical Anthropology of Education* (1961). This is quite similar to Watsuji, who was deeply interested not only in philosophy but in social science theories. But Mori went beyond theory to the actual data and methodologies of various sciences. In this 850-page tome, Mori examined the foundations of human existence in evolutionary biology (standing upright, opposable thumbs, speech) and how these unfold in the process of infant and child development. He examined the psychology of learning and emotions, using them to consider philosophical questions like autonomy and reflective thought. He also considered anthropology, sociology, political science, and history to see how individuals are socialized into culture and how cultures transform over time. He ended this massive work with practical educational issues: educational materials, passive and active forms of learning, totalitarian vs. liberal forms of education, and the contradictions of capitalism.

One of the leading researchers on the Kyoto School of Education, Yano Satoji, considers Mori's bridging to the human sciences to be one of the greatest contributions to the Kyoto School's often abstract and idealized philosophy of awakening.[37] These ideas also had traction, leading to the formation of the School of Human Sciences at Osaka University, one of the first and most prestigious schools for interdisciplinary studies of the human person that continues until today.

At the end of his life, Mori integrated the different facets of his work. In his last, uncompleted work, *The Fundamental Principles of Human Formation* (1977), he attempts to build a view of education that can face the contingencies of life and death. He returns to the issue of educational nihilism, repeating his more processual view of awakening as "self-awareness of the 'quest for meaning.'"[38] But his return to existentialism now includes his forays into science, looking at the evolution of human beings and how our evolution, and thus human existence itself, has no telos and is thus "creative indeterminacy." In this indeterminacy, human beings try to come to terms with the tensions between the relationship to the world, the relationship to oneself, and the movement of transcendence. Furthermore, he looks at social sciences and suggests that socialization into impersonal institutions essentially leads into alienation and thus a tension between socialization and self-realization.

The need to overcome all these natural and social tensions requires what he calls "multiple self-awareness."[39] Unlike the mystical awakening of sages, Mori suggests an awakening that is not only never *completed*, but is never *unified* or closed on itself. And the image he gives of this "self-awareness" is not individual but of an "arched bridge of life." This arched bridge is one wherein one comes to terms with the rise and fall of life in its contingency and finitude. But this rise and fall is not completed within oneself but in linking generatively by taking up previous generations in one's own way and bridging them to future generations in one's creative contribution to the world.

Rather than something new, this "phase" pulled together all of the things he had struggled with from the very beginning of his career. And also, this phase was never completed—he died just as he had presented the idea of the arched bridge of life.

As we see above, Mori's philosophy directly brings the insights of the Kyoto School, the idea of facing tensional reality and awakening to emptiness to the pragmatic world of education—giving us a clear guide on how these seemingly abstract ideas might change the way we journey with students along this path of life.

In Japan, Tanaka Tsunemi has devoted several books explaining and developing the ideas of Mori into a "theory of clinical human formation."[40] Kawakami Hideaki has also contributed much on Mori's philosophy, especially in relation to Tanabe Hajime.[41] In English, Mori is discussed in *Education and the Kyoto School of Philosophy* and in several articles I published on moral education, narrative, and self-awareness.

Outline

Above, we see that Nishida's idea of non-duality and Kimura's idea of the formative self-awareness of *ningen*—fundamental insights of the Kyoto School of Philosophy and Education—are developed by Watsuji and Mori in their own ways. Taking the idea of non-duality, Watsuji and Mori present philosophies of education that rest not on a single principle like reason, knowledge, or experience, but on a paradox, a resistance-to-principle. Through the ethics of emptiness and an education for self-awareness, they both began with the dilemmas of education taken as *essential*—Is education about individual liberation or social belonging? Is education about subjective meaning or objective practicality? In wrestling with these questions, the formative self-awareness of *ningen* takes place: individuals learn their place in the practical nexus of society, but at the same time traditions are creatively transformed through individuals.

In this book, I will share with you a journey into this different view of education. Perhaps this paradoxical approach may have something to teach us, wherever in the globe we may find ourselves, and whatever part of the educational experience we may be undergoing.

*

Allow me to briefly outline the path our shared journey will take.

Part One focuses on Watsuji Tetsurō's educational ideas. In "Chapter 1. Confucianism and Finding Your Place," we will examine the case of Jin-*kun* and look at the dangers when students and teachers take a primarily individualistic and competitive approach to education. We will then examine Watsuji's ideas on learning, thinking, and education in *Ethics* and develop these via his *Confucius* (1938). These books argue for a fundamentally relational approach to education, where the objectives and process of learning are fundamentally social in character and where the virtues of students and of teachers are cultivated via their mutual call and response.

However, I acknowledge that a relational approach bears the danger of the opposite extreme of a loss of individuality. In "Chapter 2. Relation without an Other?," I turn to the case of Junko-*san* and explore times when teachers and students become mired in certain socially pre-given roles, ceasing to encounter each other as unique people. I explore the limitations of Watsuji via Nel Noddings's care ethics, which warns us about the danger of merely projecting expectations on other people (projective empathy). I deepen this via Mori Akira's existential education. These are not merely criticisms of Watsuji, but a way of thinking with Watsuji himself as he was trying to overcome these problems post-war.

In "Chapter 3. Buddhism and Awakening to Self," we ask: How can we educate people with *depth*, that awakens their own unique insights? I examine the work of Watsuji on Zen Master Dōgen in *Purifying Zen* (1926), but ground this deeply spiritual chapter in the more mundane realities of secular education via the case of Taro-*kun*. We shall explore the process of learning to question the status-quo, to let go of oneself via a personal relationship between master–disciple, but through this letting-go, awakening to one's unity with all reality. This awakening is not a generic enlightenment but one where each awakens in a unique way that is transformative of tradition. We end with Mori and the question of the teacher–student relationship—what kind of teachers are we called to be, if we are to help people learn in a deep way?

We then move to Part Two of the book, shifting our focus to Mori Akira. In "Chapter 4. The Practical-Pragmatic Nexus," we ask: If ethics involves being able to negate (check-and-balance) both totality and individuality, how can we distinguish between a "negation" that is helpful and one that is not? This is particularly clear in the case of leading our research team at Kyushu. Watsuji tried to consider objectivity via the idea of milieu and the practical nexus, but still lacked the pragmatic idea of learning from consequences. Through Mori, I show the importance of this pragmatism and how it functions in both individual learning and social change. This result in an education for a social nexus that is both practical (in the sense of realizing ideas in action) and pragmatic (in testing ideas via the fruits of action), reconciling connection and critical creativity. This concern for consequences also has important suggestions for how to understand science in education.

In "Chapter 5. The Rhythm of Life," I start with the question, "What's life?" Mori contributes a theory of life as *becoming* human. He explores the actuality of this becoming via Erik Erikson's developmental psychology, and how it leads to a personality that has distinct and irreconcilable layers—of organic growth, symbolic socialization, and self-awareness. This "continuity of discontinuity" leads to an inevitability of crisis that we see mirrored in the *social* development from primitive community, to functional society, and to existential communion. Finally, the question of life leads to the question of death, where we examine Mori's insight into life as an arch bridge, that rises and falls, but at the same time connects to the succeeding generation.

In "Chapter 6. Learning to Live," we examine how this rhythm of life might actually be supported in the practice of education. I introduce Mori's view of bottom-up life guidance against the idea of imposing moral education top-down. Mori starts with a holistic understanding of the lifestyle of each child, and building up from that to questions of morality as they appear within actual life. We then examine various methods like dialogue, discussion, and journaling, as we progress to formal moral education. We then examine four chapters written for children co-authored by Mori, seeing the stories, essays, and activities by which he helps students contend with the ethics of self, communication, the group, and creativity. Picking up from Chapter 4's discussion of science, I end with a critical discussion of evidence-based education as I examine the "evidence" in my own use of Mori's moral education theories.

Finally, in "Conclusion," I examine how the active side of the chapters above rest on a fundamentally receptive moment. Rather than a philosophy of mere learning, Watsuji and Mori require a moment of unlearning, of letting go. We end at the heart of it all, the core of the Kyoto School—the philosophy of emptiness.

Author's Note

I wrote this book in attempt to bridge the world of scholars and the world of practitioners. For scholars, I put detailed theoretical explanations and references in endnotes, including academic papers I wrote explaining similar issues in a more traditionally scholastic way. Some practitioners may prefer to gloss over the technical explanations in the text and notes, and instead focus primarily on the examples, which I have developed at length under the stylistic influence of Mori (see Chapter 6).

Part One

Watsuji Tetsurō

1

Confucianism and Finding Your Place

How can we help students find their place in the world and their own ways of contributing to society? I remember in my first year of teaching in Japan, I was tasked with teaching a project-based collaborative learning course. I had assigned work in groups of five on experiences of cultural difference. But when I asked them to begin discussing, many students were content to stare at each other. I tried several icebreakers, and after a few laughs, some students started discussing. Others needed further encouragement, only opening up when I reassured the class that for the initial brainstorming, there are no wrong answers. At this point, most were getting into their discussions. But I noticed that in one group, while four of the students were discussing with each other, one student was slouched back, fiddling with his phone—and as I went over to check what he was doing, I found he was playing video games, completely ignoring his group!

In this example, we see different forms of withdrawing into oneself that prevents people from connecting with others, and it can come from many causes: from a fear of being judged by others, to a lack of social skills, to discipline and entitlement issues. Even "collectivist" Japan is not immune to this. Culture shapes *how* people struggle with individuality or communality, not whether or not they will. In what ways have you seen this struggle? As educators, we are in a position to help these people. But how?

In this chapter, I want to think about the case of Jin-*kun* and our graduate team. Jin-*kun* was a very bright student, energetically taking on challenges. However, I noticed that despite his exuberance and competence at remembering various ideas and acing quizzes, he seemed to have difficulty connecting what he was learning to his own life. This made it difficult to have fruitful insights. Furthermore, Jin-*kun* tended to take on the work himself instead of cooperating with his groupmates, worried that others would do a mediocre job and harm his grade. Because he was in higher studies and was considering a doctorate, I found myself worried. Could he learn productively with others and become a collaborative member of our graduate team? Some of you might find that this kind of a problem is something best left for the student to work out alone. But if, like me, your research context requires that you address problems like these, we can examine what Watsuji's Confucianism offers.

> ### Author's Note
>
> All of the examples in this book are real, but I combine features from various cases and alter details to maintain the anonymity of each student.[1] My hope is that these examples help readers connect with the theories in a concrete way without drifting off into abstractions. However, cases are always partial examples looking at particular struggles and they do not exhaustively convey any theory. If the cases do not fit for you, please feel free to substitute them with an image of your own students who have similar problems. For example, if you find Jin-*kun*'s more aloof tendencies to be unrelatable, you could imagine instead a shy student who withdraws and disconnects from others.

To address problems of this sort, this chapter will begin with the implications of Watsuji Tetsurō's *Ethics I–III* for learning, education, and society. I will then make these abstractions more concrete by examining Watsuji's *Confucius*, focusing on its idea of virtues and relational learning. By concretizing these, I hope to show the first crucial element of Watsuji's vision of education—*finding one's place*.

Ethics of Education

As we have seen in the Introduction, the heart of Watsuji's ethics of emptiness is seeing that the good life is not something we go about alone, like some tragic moral hero in a corrupt world. A truly good life is one wherein the individual has their personal values that come from their uniqueness as individuals and contribute to the community, and at the same time these values are nurtured within relationships in society to which the individual can open oneself. While there may be tragic times where we need to educate students to rage against the tide, Watsuji suggests preparing them to go beyond rebellious rage to be able to *build communities* where one can cooperate, turning the tide as a whole to flow supportively toward moral life. What would this vision of ethics imply for education?

In *Ethics I*, Watsuji repeatedly explored how things that we think are the boundary of an individual—the individual body, individual sensations, individual thoughts—are actually thoroughly relational. But as Watsuji was building this argument about the "emptiness" of individuality, he constantly referred to quotidian examples in education. Watsuji writes,

> Originally, "to learn" meant "to imitate." In other words, it meant to follow another person who already had the ability to do something and learn how to do it by imitation. First of all, it is an action or an activity, but it is not concerned with noematic knowledge. Second, it is transacted with other persons, . . . not an isolated person's contemplation.[2]

Unlike some current individualist theories of learning and cognition, where the mind is seen as an individual processing unit for solving its own problems, Watsuji saw thinking and learning as ways of connecting with and learning from others and their own attempts to find their way in life. Thus, the results of learning—"knowledge," "noema," "information," "skills and competencies"—are not mere contents inside one's head, but are connections with others, not just individual consciousness but "the consciousness of *ningen*."[3]

Watsuji clarifies this by examining the linguistic character of thinking. "[W]riting is an expression of words, and words are what have come to shape themselves in anticipation of partners who live and talk together."[4] Even when one voices the most private of thoughts, like one's sense of meaninglessness and exclusion from the world, these thoughts take the form of *words* ("meaningless," "I'm all alone"). We did not invent these words! They are of social origin, a medium designed to bring people in contact with one another.

Furthermore, Watsuji points out that education does not happen between two isolated people. When you have a teacher and a student, it presumes a system of roles (where there are others who have this role "teacher" or "student"). While people can learn from anyone, when someone with the role of teacher enters the classroom, dressed in a certain way and speaking in a certain way, it smoothly prepares the learning of students. (I learned this the hard way. I used to teach wearing casual clothes and cursing like a sailor. Unsurprisingly, students were entertained but unwilling to take me seriously.) Furthermore, one does not just claim these roles for oneself. Rather, roles are made available and stable via institutions. "What is called a *school* is a composite of these relationships.... To become a student of this school, you are obliged to enroll. I also acquire the status of teacher by accepting a job at this school."[5]

This results in a key theoretical point for Watsuji:

> We can now confirm an obvious everyday fact, that we always act within a certain capacity and that this capacity is prescribed by something whole, further that this whole is the relationship we construct by means of possessing a certain capacity. Simply speaking, we exist in our daily life in the being in betweenness.[6]

And as human beings exist in this betweenness, learning and cognition is made possible relationally through roles and institutions.

In *Ethics II*, Watsuji developed his relational view of human existence to different levels of community. As mentioned in the Introduction, cultural community was the central community in *Ethics II*. Culture is a locus wherein people connect with one another by sharing in symbolic systems—speaking the same language, enjoying the same music, sharing a faith or ideals. For Watsuji, this sharing was key to "relatability," which he called "friendship" (*hōyū* 朋友). Unlike closed family ties, friendship is open and culture can be learned. He writes,

> [In friendship,] a stranger with no connection to the filial existential communion of one's family, through some opportunity, forms a spiritual existential communion (*seishinteki sonzai kyōdō* 精神的存在共同) with me. In this situation, it is *culture* that is the mediator. As I and thou, we converse about our views on life and we resonate with each other from the bottom of our hearts.[7]

It is in this cultural community that Watsuji gives a central position to education: "In school, people are taught the same knowledge and way of thinking and undergo the same spiritual training. This togetherness in itself can become the foundation to lead people to spiritual communion."[8] In a community, education connects people and gives them a certain shared base of presuppositions in a way that goes beyond direct formation between one person and another. Through informal education and formal schooling, students learn the basics of language, the scientific pursuits of a community, beliefs, aesthetic attitudes, and in so doing, "find their place."[9]

This view of culture may seem too narrow for those in individualist or multicultural contexts. But Watsuji's point, which resonates with global ethicists like Will Kymlicka, democratic theorists like John Dewey, and even psychologists like Jonathan Haidt, is that human connections do not form from universality without the aid of concrete things.[10] Even in an individualist or multicultural society, this mediation exists, albeit thinly, in the form of official languages and shared ideals like tolerance and diversity.

Watsuji had a particular model for this kind of education: "In China and Japan, Confucius's school has functioned for a long time as a model, and similarly Plato's Academy lives on as a model for Europe even today . . ."[11] However, Watsuji was by no means satisfied with the state of education in Japan:

The schools at present, as learning communities (*gakumon ni okeru kyōdōtai* 学問における共同体), are extremely deficient in many things. Instead, they can be said to betray a strong *Gesellschaft* (profit-society, *dasan shakai* 打算社会) character. Scholarship is becoming a means for livelihood, and school is becoming a place for business. Rather than trying to come together for the sake of scholarly inquiry, researchers compete for that position. Rather than trying to collaborate in their pursuit of knowledge, students do everything they can to get jobs. As a result, schools are even administered as profit-making enterprises. However, this shows that schools have lost their original meaning, and not that schools are originally as above.[12]

Against this kind of "egoistic" model of education, Watsuji suggests an education of socialization, akin to Emile Durkheim's "methodologic socialization."[13] Some readers might be uncomfortable with this collectivism and how it risks sacrificing individuality. I will focus on these criticisms next chapter, so hold on to those questions! But for this chapter, we will focus on the *positive* side of socialization as it addresses the dangers of egotism.

In *Ethics III*, written after Japan's defeat in the Second World War, Watsuji had to contend with the fact that societies are not static but subject to change. Amidst encounters with other cultures and various upheavals in history, cultures come to terms with certain *limitations* in how they see the world. Thus, he developed a theory of social critique, historical change, and leadership. In this, education was central as well. He wrote,

> Academe is not *memorizing* (*oboekomu* 覚え込む) pre-existing knowledge or given formulae but cultivating *the power to think for oneself*. If this simple idea were to spread throughout the nation, that would reform education as a whole, and restore the dignity (*menboku o arata ni suru* 面目を新たにする) of the everyday life and political activity of the nation. Citizens who have the power to think and decide for themselves will not fall into conventionalism (*fuwa raidō* 付和雷同) or thought control.[14]

Watsuji's message here deeply resonates with Nishita Kitarō's "On Education"—education must form students who can both let go of egoism to find their place, but at the same time be free and critical, taking part in the creative formation of a socio-historical whole.

Confucian Education

If the good life, ethics, is not to be lived solo, education has a key role in building relational learning and thinking (*Ethics I*), building cultural connections (*Ethics II*), and educating leaders of socio-historical change (*Ethics III*). But these fragments above only amount to ten pages in total. Is there somewhere we can get a more concrete view of his vision of education?

This can be found in a rarely researched book that Watsuji wrote in 1938 entitled *Confucius*.[15] This might easily be mistaken to be a mere side project unrelated to his other work. However, Watsuji's ethical system has been shown to be deeply influenced by Confucianism: the very idea of relationality, Mencius' five relations, the relationship between the family and state, virtues like filial piety and loyalty are all drawn from Confucianism.[16] Furthermore, *Confucius* was published between *Ethics I* and *II*. His mention of Confucianism in *Ethics II* quoted above can be read as bringing his book *Confucius* inside his systematic ethics. Rather than a merely historical commentary on an eastern thinker, *Confucius* can be seen as his own philosophical position on how ethics of education should function *in the present*, and *universally*.

At the start of the book, Watsuji names Confucius, Socrates, Buddha, and Jesus as four "teachers of humankind." Watsuji writes, "The most particular has the most universal significance. . . . It is so for the teachers of humankind."[17] He explains that these four teachers started by teaching small groups of people in China, Greece, India, and the middle east, but their teachings spoke so deeply to people that they drew capable disciples who then spread their ideas, shaping societies and entire civilizations. These ideas were so strong that often when the country was colonized by an empire, these ideas influenced the colonizers instead (as in the case of Rome and Mongolia). Thus "humankind" and "universal significance" do not refer to an abstraction of humanity without borders but the historical potential of an ideal to cross actual national and cultural borders and shape civilizations while adapting to other cultures.[18] Perhaps his reference to Confucianism in *Ethics II* meant to suggest that in addition to the field of ethics, education around the world could also learn from this teacher of humankind, giving us ideas on how to educate students to go beyond closed egoism.

Watsuji draws on the *Analects of Confucius,* beginning with the first analect. As Watsuji cited it in Chinese, I rely on the philosophical translation of Ames and Rosemont:

> The Master said: "Having studied, to then repeatedly apply what you have learned—is this not a source of pleasure? To have friends come from distant quarters—is this not a source of enjoyment? To go unacknowledged by others without harboring frustration—is this not the mark of an exemplary person (*junzi* 君子)?"[19]

Watsuji writes that this analect lists the "mottos of life in Confucius's school . . . [that] show the aims of the life of learning."[20] Watsuji explains these as three interlocking principles that guide education:

> [F]irst, the joy of learning (*gakumon* 学問), second, the joy of the community of friendship bound by learning, and third, the results one can achieve in this community. These [results] are autotelic and lie in elevating one's personality and life, and have nothing to do with fame and fortune. . . . Not only is this ideal shared by the Platonic Academy, Buddha's *sangha*, and Jesus Christ's church, it continues to be serviceable today. If the spirit of learning expressed in these three are lost, there can be no living learning (*ikita gakumon* 生きた学問).[21]

Watsuji suggests that the whole first book (of twenty books) of the *Analects* is arranged roughly according to the flow of these three principles. And Watsuji focuses on this first book of the *Analects*, clearly signaling to us that he is specifically highlighting the *education* part of

Confucianism in so far as it can be universalized today for anyone who aims at "living learning"—scholarship that is not merely abstract but vital and real.

1. Deconstructing Degreeocracy

Let me begin with the third part of the analect, "To go unacknowledged by others without harboring frustration—is this not the mark of an exemplary person?" This message repeats at the end of the first book of the *Analects*:

> Zigong said: "What do you think of the saying: 'Poor but not inferior; rich but not superior'?" The Master replied: "Not bad, but not as good as: 'Poor but enjoying the way (*dao* 道); rich but loving ritual propriety (*li* 禮)'"[22]

These analects warn against what Watsuji calls an education directed at "fame and fortune." If people think that the good life is merely individual (and not communal), then the goal is to attain success amidst social adversity. This results in a *Gesellschaft* (profit-society) wherein individuals compete for success rather than cooperate toward shared goals. In such a society, "Rather than trying to come together for the sake of scholarly inquiry, researchers compete for that position. Rather than trying to collaborate in their pursuit of knowledge, students do everything they can to get jobs." This is what is referred to in sociology of education as "education for social sorting," where education functions as a gatekeeper to sort who gets social standing (poor vs. rich) and acknowledgment.

The personal struggles of students like Jin-*kun* need to be seen within their social context of a lifetime of extrinsically motivated education in a culture where education has been used primarily for social sorting. Learning becomes about abstract data to be remembered and regurgitated in an exam. I had a student evaluation once that said, "I don't really care about all this philosophy of education stuff. I just want to get my degree and get a job." It was shocking to read it spelled out, but a lot of students are probably thinking the exact same thing. In Japan, universities are ranked according to "standard deviation" (*hensachi* 偏差値) which indicates the difficulty of passing each department of a university. And competition for the highest *hensachi* becomes a means for social sorting, by which students can secure their place in the job hunt. This is true even for graduate school, which is quickly becoming a place to gain additional points for one's CV in competing in the job market. Ronald Dore calls this "degreeocracy" (*gakureki shakai* 学歴社会, educational credentialism) and this is a genuine problem in Japan.[23]

Some may argue that degreeocracy is a form of meritocracy, resisting ascribed status (as in feudalism) with status that comes from achievement. However, does it create real democratic transformation of the social order? In *Ethics III*, we see that because "*memorizing* pre-existing knowledge or given formulae" is easily tested, education becomes about teaching these facts, resulting in the inability of students to think for themselves, making them susceptible to "conventionalism or thought control." If students are busy competing to memorize information better, they do not really have the room to *question* what they learn.

2. The Nature of Subject Matter

Education for social sorting in profit-society is not merely a social but an *epistemic* configuration. It changes the way students learn things. In the case of Jin-*kun*, because he was learning philosophy merely to show his superiority in learning, he was not connecting it to his experience, allowing his experience to deepen, enrich, and even question what he was learning. This is deeply influenced by a learning history of just memorizing things to be regurgitated in exams.

In contrast to this, Watsuji presents a different approach to learning: "Having studied, to then repeatedly apply what you have learned—is this not a source of pleasure?" What Watsuji is presenting here is a total attitude toward the subject matter that results in the "joy of learning." As we saw in *Ethics I*, thinking is not originally closed on the individual and learning is not fundamentally competitive. Human beings try to find their way in life. And in a relational process of learning, students learn to connect with how others have found their way in life. Thus, what is learned becomes real, and is something repeatedly applied in one's own life. In this way, learning is felt as something meaningful in itself rather than extrinsically motivated by exam scores. This realness is also what allows information to be relevant enough to put to question, and thus deepen in social change (*Ethics III*'s "the power to think for oneself").

This means that to resist degreeocracy, one practical task of education is to reframe the nature of the ideas that are taught. In an attempt to help Jin-*kun* and other students get beyond memorization, I try to show the human side of the philosophy. For example, when teaching Watsuji's ideas, I try to depict Watsuji as a human being struggling with problems of selfish individualism, and how his ideas form a real response to these problems. I also try to come up with concrete examples of egotism that are relatable to students, like freeloaders in groupwork. In discussions and activities, I do not merely ask them to define or discuss Watsuji's ideas but also ask them, "What experiences might these ideas connect to? What other things you've learned might these link up with?" This formative assessment allows me to both gauge the realness of their learning and help them push learning toward greater relevance.

Furthermore, *Ethics II* suggests that rather than merely using knowledge to compete, knowledge allows us to connect with others in culture and find our place within it. For example, when I teach Watsuji, Watsuji is not merely an individual thinker, but someone thinking within a real social context: Japan's hurried modernization and westernization, the importation of western ethics (particularly utilitarianism). Watsuji's ideas, while unique, were also inspired by both eastern thinkers (Confucianism) and western thinkers (Aristotle, Plato, Hegel). Learning about Watsuji is a way of connecting to the struggles of a nation as it tries to deal with the changes of modernization and globalization.

This way of teaching has much in common with the recent move for "active learning." For example, Fink's *Creating Significant Learning Experiences* suggests that learning should not be restricted to building foundational knowledge, but must include application, integration to other ideas, the human dimension (connecting it to one's own life), caring, and learning how to learn.[24] This "taxonomy of significant learning" can be used for any subject, be it explaining the context and application of a mathematical theory or connecting literature to one's own experience. However, while active learning tends to center on improving the quality of learning and the retention of ideas, Watsuji's reasons for this "active learning" are ethical. To move toward the good life that is both individual and communal, teachers need to present material in ways that are relevant to individual learners and their personal and cultural contexts.

3. The Learning Community

Education for social sorting does not only reduce knowledge to mere abstractions for future testing, but it also blocks any real relationship within a learning community. In the case of Jin-*kun*, his competitive approach to learning made it difficult to cooperate with his group mates, made him more aloof, to the point that his way of participating in class seemed like a weapon to display his superiority over others. This was irritating for his classmates, but it resulted in real social isolation for Jin-*kun* himself. What good is meritocratic liberation from "ascribed status," if it only leads to new forms of arrogance and oppression via "attained status," rather than genuine democratic community?

Against this, Watsuji presents a different view of the learning community. Confucius said, "To have friends come from distant quarters—is this not a source of enjoyment?" Watsuji's reading of this highlights that learning is done in a communal way, as a "community of friendship bound by learning." When one is able to let go of knowledge as a weapon of advancement and is able to see it as *ningen* learning from *ningen* about living life, one opens up to deeper relationships between teacher and student and between students themselves.

For example, as I teach Jin-*kun* philosophy as a real struggle of people making sense of life, I am at the same time demonstrating my own engagement as a human being with this philosopher we are reading. I care about the material and the author behind it, and I care about my students. And my hope is to bridge these two worlds. Thus, as Jin-*kun* begins deepening his academic knowledge, he is also modeling my approach and connecting with me (learning as imitation in *Ethics I*). In this way, the teacher–student relationship becomes a conduit for the realness of the subject matter—a realization that hopefully Jin-*kun* sees as possible not just for his relationship with me but with other teachers as well.

However, as we see in *Ethics II*, the relationship of learning is not restricted to teacher–student. As Jin-*kun* learns to see philosophical material as real and connects it to his own experience, he is able to contribute meaningful examples and ask helpful questions in class instead of merely grandstanding. And so other students start to listen to him. But also, this opens him up to listen to other students in a different way, seeing them not as competition but as people who are similarly trying to learn something real about life. Thus, he is able to resonate with their questions, share their doubts, and feel joy (instead of envy) at their moments of insight. In the *Analects*, it is written, The Master said: "Don't worry about not being acknowledged by others; worry about failing to acknowledge them."[25] Jin-*kun* is learning to acknowledge and genuinely connect with others.

Learning together, students find themselves in different roles. Some students who are more used to the way of learning of the team become "*sempai* 先輩" (seniors) and those who are new become their "*kōhai* 後輩" (juniors). When cooperative learning functions well, these roles are functional and flexible, with juniors learning from their seniors, seniors deepening their learning by teaching it, and both providing a sense of camaraderie. Furthermore, these roles are supported by institutions. While most English-speaking universities institutionally enable the teacher–student relationship, the Japanese educational system also deliberately cultivates *sempai–kōhai* relationships starting middle school.

In this process, we are not merely isolated cognitive boxes in a room together, using each other solely as sources of information. Instead, we become a learning *community*, connecting with the joys and sorrows of each in their path of learning and supporting each other.

Again, the active learning movement has pushed similar ideas via "collaborative learning." For example, Johnson and Johnson's *Circles of Learning* talk about the interrelation of roles above as "positive interdependence," where you can create accountability both on the individual level and the group level, creating "promotive interactions" that exceed the teacher's ability to assist learning alone.[26] Again, in active learning, the focus is primarily on outcomes:

> From the research, we know that cooperation, compared with competitive and individualistic efforts, typically results in (a) higher achievement and greater productivity, (b) more caring, supportive, and committed relationships, and (c) greater psychological health, social competence, and self-esteem.[27]

However, for Watsuji, the primary importance of learning communities is ethical—this is how we learn in a way that is true to our nature as relational beings, who learn about relational realities through a process that is in itself relational.

David Baruch Gordon did research on Watsuji's autobiography, and we see that this sense of connection was real in his personal experience. Nitobe Inazō (1862–1933), celebrated author of *Bushido: The Soul of Japan* (1900), was actually Watsuji's teacher. "Watsuji was greatly taken with Nitobe's lectures. 'I think that at no point in the rest of my life did I listen to lectures with such a powerful feeling of enchantment.'"[28] This openness to learn from his teachers connected to his openness to engage his classmates. Gordon continues,

> In an address that Nitobe gave in December 1906, he unveiled to his student listeners his concept of "*soshiarichii* (sociality)." . . . "the capacity

for 'spiritual sympathy' which brings two human beings together as friends; it was the ability to communicate on an idealistic level of 'pure' thought and emotion through letters and great books; it was the hallmark of the well-rounded gentleman who was 'inclusive in his attitude toward life.'"[29]

In *Confucius* and *Ethics II*, almost forty years after this, his view of the potential of education to allow for "spiritual communion" retains this very structure from Nitobe. And Watsuji's autobiography is full of reminiscences of his friends: Shimodoi Yoshiaki, who introduced him to novels that made a deep impression on his worldview, Haruyama Takematsu and Kurosaka Tatsuzō, who were classmates and fellow ardent fans of their teacher, Natsume Sōseki, and others.[30]

In *Ethics II*, this connection can spread broader throughout culture. Students like Jin-*kun* can learn to connect not merely to their classmates but to the academic community (locally and internationally), and to entire cultures (like Japan for Japanese philosophy, or western civilization as a whole, for those doing western philosophy). In my experience, learning about Watsuji was actually one of the most important keys to help me adapt to living in Japan and eventually becoming a Japanese citizen!

But there is a part of this that I genuinely struggle with. While I helped Jin-*kun* connect to his classmates, I did not really prepare him to connect to the academic community. Our very experiential approach to philosophy can be so removed from the abstract approach of mainstream Japanese academia that my students feel alienated in dealing with their peers. And Jin-*kun* often finds himself feeling like his hard-won personal engagement with philosophy is rendered socially meaningless. However, one time, Jin-*kun* went to a conference (interestingly *not* a philosophy conference but a practitioner's conference) where he found that his real understanding of philosophy allowed him to contribute to other graduate students in very fruitful ways. It was here where he found that what he was learning in our graduate team was able to connect to the broader society.

Watsuji discusses social change in various ways in both *Ethics I* and *Ethics III*. I think Jin-*kun*'s example points to the value of Watsuji's more modest approach to social change: Instead of tackling social change head on, Watsuji seems to recommend that we find our place, the right team, the right organization, so that what we personally believe in can be bridged to the society as a whole.[31]

*

Above, we have seen Watsuji's approach to philosophy of education as seen in *Confucius*. Rather than education for social sorting in a competitive society, he sought a way to educate in a way that builds a good life of both individual competence and communal connection. He thus suggested a relational approach to real learning that is a joy in itself and learning as a community in a way that broadens to connect to wider community. Building on this real learning and learning community effectively resist, even from the positionality of a single teacher, the whole culture of degreeocracy.

However there are times when these indirect approaches are not enough. At times I have to work around degreeocracy, telling my students that while having a good degree is advantageous, it is even more helpful in the long-term to have a genuine understanding of the subject matter. Other times, I challenge this competitive view of society head-on, showing philosophically the dangers of egoism, using the political theories of democracy to criticize social Darwinism, showing the data from Johnson and Johnson on the limitations of competitive learning, and so on. But we need work beyond the classroom—in teacher education, in public discourse, in politics—and my hope is that books like this and my work in interfacing with certain applied psychology organizations will do some of the work in creating systemic change.

The Virtues of Learning

For Watsuji, the approach to education above is via the *virtues* of teachers and learners. Virtues simply refer to behaviors and dispositions that have become habitual—like Jin-*kun*'s cooperation progressing from being a very deliberate control of his urge to withdraw to a more natural habit of openly engaging others. When Watsuji showed the expanding stages of human relationships in *Ethics II*, each of these stages had virtues to support that stage—like fidelity in the couple, filial piety in the family, mutual consideration in the local community, mutual service in economics, and friendship in culture.[32]

Recent research by Kyle Shuttleworth has pointed out the uniqueness of Watsuji's view of virtues in comparison to Aristotle, Confucius, and other virtue ethicists and theorists.[33] Okuda Kazuhiko compared Aristotle and Watsuji, suggesting that Watsuji's was unique in focusing on the dialectical unity of individuality and totality,[34] where a virtue both allows individuals to let go of their egoism to allow a relation to form, but also maintains the place of those individuals within the relationship. In other words, Watsuji's virtues of education are not individual virtues of learners or teachers but are *relational virtues*.

We begin first with the learner's side of the virtues, keeping in mind that these will be connected to the virtues of educators. First, as we have seen above, "Having studied, to then repeatedly apply what you have learned . . ." In another analect, Confucius writes, "[W]here you have erred, do not hesitate to mend your ways."[35] These lines suggest a certain willingness to learn, where the student opens up to what is learned, seeing these as things that are genuinely meaningful and part of connecting with others in society. Thus, one does not merely memorize things but lives what one learns.

Elsewhere, Confucius told Zigong, "With Yan Hui, learning one thing he will know ten; with me, learning one thing I will know two."[36] Here, Confucius is praising his favorite student, and we see that learning also requires a certain thoughtfulness, exploring the implications of what one has learned so that one can apply what one learns not just in immediately applicable scenarios but also in other more tangential situations.

However, learning is something that occurs in relation—between master and disciple, teacher and student, and also among friends. This means that learners also need interpersonal virtues in addition to intellectual ones. Watsuji highlights the following analect for the newcomer of the academy:

> Master You said: "It is a rare thing for someone who has a sense of filial and fraternal responsibility (*xiaodi* 孝弟) to have a taste for defying authority. And it is unheard of for those who have no taste for defying authority to be keen on initiating rebellion. Exemplary persons (*junzi* 君子) concentrate their efforts on the root, for the root having taken hold, the way (*dao* 道) will grow therefrom. As for filial and fraternal responsibility, it is, I suspect, the root of authoritative conduct (*ren* 仁)."[37]

As we saw above, Jin-*kun* struggled with this sense of responsibility, and thus his arrogant behavior blocked him from learning from both me and his other classmates. Watsuji writes, "We can avoid the danger of stubbornness [*ganko*] by cultivating a pliant, supple attitude. While it is important not to be fickle in one's opinion, there is no merit in being stubborn."[38] While learning philosophy in a real way, listening to me, and trying to learn with others, Jin-*kun* was also cultivating this pliant attitude, the virtue of responsibility.

This responsibility blossoms into other virtues:

> The Master said: "Exemplary persons (*junzi* 君子) lacking in gravity would have no dignity. Yet in their studies they are not inflexible. Take doing your utmost and making good on your word (*xin* 信) as your mainstay. Do not have as a friend anyone who is not as good as you are. And where you have erred, do not hesitate to mend your ways."[39]

Doing your utmost (忠) is literally written with "in the middle" of "heart-mind," and means trying to be loyal and sincere in your relations. In learning with others, Jin-*kun* was learning how to have a sincere connection with them as people. (I remember how happy I was when I heard that he and several of his teammates had gone on a trip together. I was worried this kid would never make friends!) This also allows him to be a trustworthy student (the character 信 is literally a man standing beside his words) both to me and to others.

These virtues of the learner—responsibility, earnestness, openness—connect to different social contexts, as seen in the following analect.

> The Master said: "As a younger brother and son, be filial (*xiao* 孝) at home and deferential (*di* 弟) in the community; be cautious in what you say and then make good on your word (*xin* 信); love the multitude broadly and be intimate with those who are authoritative in their conduct (*ren* 仁). If in so behaving you still have energy left, use it to improve yourself through study."[40]

Virtues are connected in time and across one's relationships. In a caring family, one learns virtues like filial piety. Thus, when one enters school, one is able to take that filial piety and transform it into responsibility—openness to one's teachers and seniors and to form caring relations with them. This flows beyond the school toward social and political life, learning trustworthiness and authoritative conduct. By learning more active virtues of teaching and leading from teachers and seniors, students learn to become leaders themselves. Watsuji calls this the bridging from family virtues to political (治国) virtues.[41]

When I see students who struggle with opening up to me or to their teachers, I find that often they have problems in the social context of where they learn these relational virtues. Some of them are traumatized from *sempai–kōhai* relations in clubs where their seniors lorded it over them. Others have learned to mistrust teachers for caring little for their learning and only about how their exam results reflect on the standing of the school. And for some, the trauma comes from home, where they faced relentless criticism from parents, were compared to other siblings, and generally learned that community is not where you grow but where you are measured and found wanting.

It is important that we understand the relational contexts that block virtue, rather than merely blaming students for being unvirtuous. (And it is dangerous to force students to be "virtuous" in a situation that does not properly value that virtue, like teaching a student to submit to an abusive senior.) Thus, learning virtue requires, on one hand, personal work. For traumatized students, helping them open up to the learning community requires much counseling (in cooperation with clinical psychologist colleagues) in order to help them recognize their closure, to validate the pain behind it, and open themselves up to learning in a way that initially feels thoroughly unfamiliar.[42] But on the other hand, learning virtue requires systemic work by the teacher and the classroom context.

The Virtues of Teaching

The virtues of the learner are made possible relationally, needing the virtues of the teacher.

> Ziqin asked Zigong: "When the Master arrives in a particular state and needs to learn how it is being governed, does he seek out this information or is it offered to him?" Zigong replied: "The Master gets all he needs by being cordial, proper, deferential, frugal, and unassuming. Perhaps this way of seeking information is somewhat different from how others go about it."[43]

What we see here is governance via virtue. Watsuji writes, "[E]ducation (*kyōka* 教化) should come from virtue and ritual propriety, not from discipline and punishment (政と刑)."[44] Students learn to be virtuous, responsible, and trustworthy not via coercion, but because the teacher models it with the way they engage learning and learners.

The most important virtue here is authoritative conduct (*jin* 仁). It is also translated as "benevolence," but the danger with this translation is that it suggests a transcendent absolute (*bene*). But *jin* is rather a response from I to Thou—literally the character has "person" on the left and "two" on the right 人+二=仁. This response begins with the caring of the teacher for their students. As we saw from the quote with Yan Hui, Confucius was very fond of his students and aware of their weaknesses and their strengths. Ames and Rosemont write,

> Confucius occasionally speaks in generalizations, but much more often gives a specific answer to a specific question asked by one of the

disciples.... Confucius based his specific response to the question on the specific perspective—lived, learned, experienced—from which he thought the disciple asked of it.[45]

Confucius knew his students, was concerned about them as individuals, and thus adjusted the teaching toward the particularities of each and how they are understanding things, rather than a focus merely on the abstract ideas that are taught. As a result of this relational benevolence, Watsuji similarly points out how Confucius's disciples—Yan Hui, Zilu, Zigong, Zengzi, and others—all form important figures in the *Analects*, rather than it being monolithically about the master.[46]

This care for the student and their lived experience is essential for teaching subject matter in a way that feels real and relevant. If I do not care about students, I cannot bridge the world of the subject to their world. Furthermore, this care for the student is essential in helping the student form their virtues. For example, Jin-*kun* would never have opened to learning responsibility and cooperation simply because responsibility and cooperation are the "essence of *ningen*." Rather, I think he was willing to change because he felt my caring, because he recognized my effort to validate his struggles with feeling isolated and measured, and I was genuinely willing to make space for him to find new habits in responding to learning and community. This is the essence of governance via virtue: the virtues of the teacher *call out* to the student and makes space for their virtues. (Corollary to that, if the student is virtuous but the teacher is not, the result is tragic. We cannot presume that teachers are virtuous, and if a student is trusting and open to a teacher who does not care about students, we risk disappointment, trauma, and even abuse.) Confucian education is often seen as one that demands virtue from its students, but Watsuji suggests that it demands virtue *in relation*—thus from both teachers and students and never one-sidedly.

Let us return to *Confucius*. This connection from the virtue of the learner to the virtue of the teacher results in an overall view of human development in moral life:

The Master said: "From fifteen, my heart-and-mind was set upon learning; from thirty I took my stance; from forty I was no longer doubtful; from fifty I realized the propensities of *tian* (*tianming* 天命 [mandate of heaven]); from sixty my ear was attuned; from seventy I could give my heart-and-mind free rein without overstepping the boundaries."[47]

This is actually the life story of Confucius. But in his interpretation, Watsuji highlights how the figure of Confucius was not sacralized but humanized, and this development of Confucius was then seen as a more dynamic, stage-based view of life and overall development.[48] True enough, Confucius is often cited even in Japanese theories of psychological development.[49] These show that receptive virtues like responsibility and willingness to learn gradually develop into more active virtues of authoritative conduct, gradually progressing in a transformative freedom of "giving one's heart-and-mind free rein."

Perhaps reading about the virtues of the teacher, some of you educators and parents might be feeling very pressured. But rather than ethical duties, perhaps we can turn to how this path unfolds in an actual life. For me, I really struggled with the model of relational learning above. When I was in university, I was a lot like Jin-*kun*, rather uncooperative and condescending toward the ideas of others. Philosophy classes rarely required groupwork, so I was able to get away with being a bit of an ass. When I did my doctorate in Japan, I also found that most professors taught in a very detached, academic way, further entrenching this solitary approach to philosophy. Thus, when I learned about collaborative learning at Kyushu University, I resisted this idea, considering it irrelevant to philosophy. I was quite happy to teach relational philosophy in a very unrelational, teacher-centric way.

What changed my mind was not abstract ideas but actual experiences of the function of learning communities. As my experience with collaborative learning grew, I saw just how much classmates can enrich each other's experiences, coming up with vivid examples that moved others. I slowly introduced these practices to my graduate class, and I found that students could challenge each other, get energized by each other, I saw that validation from their classmates could be so powerful in a way quite different from me validating them. And this led me to slowly form the graduate class into a *team*, where we learn things experientially together, where we share our attempts to integrate and apply it with each other, and thus form a mutually-supportive learning community. In this process, I was not just teaching my team; they were teaching me the virtues of being a team leader.

I understand that given how society is right now and the difficulty of virtue-in-relation, some may remain skeptical. But perhaps it is best to see Confucian education as something to try experimentally rather than as an a priori moral requirement.

The Virtues of *Ningen*

In Watsuji's theory of virtue, virtues of learning and teaching do not exist in isolation but in inter-dependence. This is captured in the virtue of "ritual propriety." In the *Analects*, it is written:

> Master You said: "Achieving harmony (*he* 和) is the most valuable function of observing ritual propriety (*li* 禮). In the ways of the Former Kings, this achievement of harmony made them elegant, and was a guiding standard in all things large and small. But when things are not going well, to realize harmony just for its own sake without regulating the situation through observing ritual propriety will not work."[50]

Ritual propriety is about knowing one's role, one's place in relation to other people. It reminds the juniors of their filial responsibility, and the seniors and teachers of their authoritative conduct. Both teachers and students contribute to maintaining social harmony within the academy, allowing everyone to walk the way together.

However, this points to an important logic of virtue that I have already hinted at. According to Shuttleworth and Tani Tōru, Watsuji sees virtues as part of the call-response structure of trust and truthfulness.[51] In *Ethics I*, after pointing out how all ethical phenomena have an individual and a communal side and demonstrating the back-and-forth between individualizing and committing to community, Watsuji points out that each ethical act must then carry this individual and social side. Rather than ethical acts being individual actions directly responding to some abstract goodness (like the categorical imperative), individual actions are *truthfulness* in response to *trust*: "[M]akoto as an attitude assumed in response to trust consists in the realization of socio-ethical unity via the path of negation and hence reveals the authentic feature of *ningen sonzai*."[52]

Trust is the call from the student to the teacher and to senior classmates, asking for their care and support and opportunities in their journey of learning (filial responsibility). Teachers and senior classmates respond to this in truthfulness by teaching students and helping them clarify their ideas (authoritative conduct/benevolence). Without the trust of the student (virtues of the cared-for), the teachers and seniors can try to teach, but this act of caring is never completed. Thus, virtue is not something that occurs individually but within these interlocking networks of relational virtue. As teachers, we are not trying to coerce students to be virtuous individuals, but cultivating virtue-in-relation.

Nel Noddings' caring education expresses a similar view of virtues. She saw certain "virtues" of the one-cared-for (virtues of the learner) that interlock with the virtues of the one-caring (the teacher). And like Watsuji, she saw these virtues and this caring relationship as beginning from home—the caring between mother and child. Schooling picks up from this family context and expands caring into a democratic society and the international sphere.[53]

However, stressing harmony can lead to a static view of the interlocking of roles. In *Ethics I*, Watsuji explains that truthfulness in response to trust is not merely about doing exactly what you are expected to do (all totality, no individuality) or doing what you want to do regardless of all expectation (all individuality, no totality). Rather, it involves responding to trust with personal discernment. "[B]eing true to one's promises: not only makes a fact and a word as well as a word and a deed congruent with each other in individual cases but also assumes the authority to deliberately make them incongruent, if and when the occasion necessitates it."[54]

In *Ethics II*, Watsuji develops this idea particularly in relation to *filial piety*—the key virtue from which filial responsibility is derived.

> Ever since, we have been taught about *the relationship from the child to the parent*, and not from the parent to the child. Here, a child is expected to behave with "filial piety" (*kō* 孝).... [However,] the original meaning of filial piety must be understood as refering to the mutual relation of parents and children.[55]

Watsuji proceeds to argue that children should not be seen as subordinate to their parents. Rather, the parents care for the child, aiming for the flourishing of the child (truthfulness), and the child receives that care (trust). But not only does the child trust in the parents, parents also have to trust in the child to develop, allowing the child to respond in truthfulness by taking care of oneself. And as the child begins to grow in judgment, this means having to respect the child's judgment and not merely impose the will of the parents on the child. Watsuji writes, "In certain circumstances, even the child's rebellion against one's parents can be because of truthfulness (*makoto o tsukusu*) toward them."[56]

Watsuji is thus suggesting to educators the need to consider virtue both as inter-dependent (group virtue) while making space for individual discernment. For example, responsibility sometimes means obeying one's seniors, and other times means giving honest criticisms of how your professor is running the class. (I had a student tell me that, while I teach about self-compassion and letting go of criticism, I have a way of being very critical and judgmental of my students as well! Ouch, but point taken.) Similarly, authoritative conduct sometimes means teaching wholeheartedly, but other times means withholding one's comments to empower students to work things out on their own.

*

Thus, what we see in Watsuji's *Confucius* is a more complete philosophy of education. Not only is education seen from the lens of the non-dualisms of individuality/totality and subject/object in the practical nexus, but we see the whole process of development of people as they participate in the sharing of culture. Instead of a world of students competing for qualifications, he sees a process of genuinely opening to relational learning, an interlocking of virtues of learning and virtues of teaching, and how these come together to form a harmonious but dynamic vision of learning. This is none other than the ethics of emptiness at work, the emptying of individual ego in order to open to others via the shared medium of what is learned.

It might seem like a rosy picture, and I have yet to see an entire university function as a Confucian academy. But in my own team and our shared struggles, I have found that this can be a real idea, and we can work toward it in small ways. We can care passionately about what we teach and communicate this passion to our students by genuinely connecting with them. We can set up our classes to allow students to connect to each other and be a significant part of each other's learning. And we can grow together with our students into the virtues that sustain this life of learning as *ningen*.

Post-Script: Positioning Confucian Education

Perhaps some might find the socializing focus above so strange compared to our usual focus in philosophy of education in the English-speaking world. For example, Nel Noddings' *Philosophy of Education*, one of the few textbooks introducing the whole history of philosophy of education, discusses the following philosophers: Socrates/Plato, Aristotle, Rousseau, Pestalozzi, Herbart, Froebel, Dewey, Analytic Philosophy, Continental Philosophy. With the exception of some mentions of Plato and Aristotle's communitarian focus, the book is largely focused on individual needs, reasoning, criticality, and care.[57] Although Deweyan Democracy somewhat sublates both the individual and the community, the book does show the tendency of philosophy of education in English to be focused more on the individual.

Mori Akira gives us another way of positioning Watsuji and his Confucian vision of education. In *The Practicality and Inwardness of Education* (*Kyōiku no jissensei to naimensei*, 1955), Mori writes, "Let us define education as human becoming, in relation to others.... The task of educational philosophical anthropology (*kyōiku ningengaku* 教育人間学) is to clarify the process of human becoming in relation to others according to the structure of human existence."[58] Like Watsuji, he was taking philosophical anthropology as an entry-point into education.

However, he saw education as having at least four different emphases: Education as natural growth (like Dewey and Rousseau), education as cultural transmission, education as social formation, and education as personal awakening. We see these four as tensional directions in the figure below. This is quite similar to Gert Biesta's more recent definition of the three functions of education—qualification (transmission), socialization (formation), and subjectification (awakening).[59] These give us a more balanced view of the functions of education, and we see that Watsuji's focus on cultural transmission and social formation was not odd, but rather constitutes a very important half of education.

In *The Philosophical Quest for Educational Ideals* (1948), Mori introduced concrete examples of each focus above, with natural growth explained via Rousseau and Dewey and personal awakening via Karl Jaspers's existentialism. He had several representatives for formation/transmission—the idealism of Kant and Herbart, the materialism of Marx—but closest to Watsuji's Confucianism is his treatment of Dilthey's *Lebensphilosophie*.

The philosophy of life is an approach by Wilhelm Dilthey (1833–1911), historian, early pioneer of qualitative psychology, and hermeneuticist. Mori explains that life (*Leben*) is the historical spirit behind every culture. It is a "spiritual nexus" (a nexus of shared ideas) which is then expressed as "objective spirit," or what we now call material culture, as found in scholarship, art, religion, and morality. We live within this cultural world but are not aware of it, and the task of

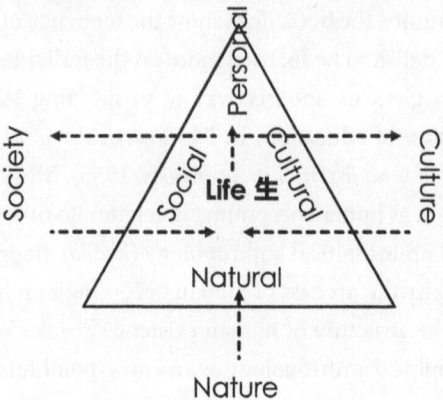

Figure 1.1 The tensional view of the human being.[60]

Lebensphilosophie is to make us self-aware in how we live out this spiritual life. Education is the process of bringing these cultural nuggets back to life again, allowing us to understand by re-subjectifying this objective expression of spirit, and experience the spirit behind a piece of literature, or a scientific discovery, or a philosophical idea. And the role of the teacher in this is to mediate this understanding, with a "pedagogic love" that is mindful of how each student is reanimating the objective expressions of culture.

Inaga Shigemi suggests that Watsuji was heavily influenced by Dilthey's *The Formation of the Historical World in the Human Sciences*,[61] and indeed Watsuji's idea of a practical nexus (wherein individuals and groups connect subjectively and objectively) is derived from Dilthey. Furthermore, Watsuji directly cites Dilthey for his method of ethics as hermeneutics, and writes,

> *Ningen sonzai*, in its everydayness, constantly manifests itself in the practical connections of life, expression, and understanding; and yet it does not become aware of this as expression. Hence, the effort to realize it as expression is a philosophical activity that assumes the form of a hermeneutic method.[62]

Watsuji's ethics is about hermeneutically realizing, understanding, and re-animating the objective expressions of *ningen sonzai*. In the same way, through Mori we see that Watsuji's Confucian education can be read as a way of realizing this Diltheyan hermeneutics in education.

As such, Watsuji's view is not some oddity but represents a major function of education in helping people find their place in society. It also connects to major sociological views of education (Emile Durkheim, G.H. Mead) and relational approaches to learning theory (Lev Vygotsky, Lave and Wenger's limited peripheral participation).

2

Relation without an Other

As we have seen in the previous chapter, social formation and transmission are essential to education. But at the same time, we cannot be naïve about the dangers of education that are primarily focused on creating the continuity of a cultural community. Let us first examine some concerns in Watsuji's *Confucius*.

Confucian Conservativism

When we read Watsuji's virtues, something gave me pause, and perhaps it might worry you as well: "Obedience," "not defying authority," "not initiating rebellion," "deference," "give your whole person in service of your ruler"—while these virtues can indeed support overcoming egoism to consider the larger whole, a person of these virtues seems uncritical and in danger of being exploited. Of course, Watsuji's ideas of two-way virtues, trust- truth, and individual discernment allow some resistance to exploitation of this submission. But is there enough here to allow for the criticality that Watsuji himself was asking for in *Ethics III*, of a leader who is able to *form history*?

Ordinarily, criticality is seen as an appeal to an order higher than the existing society—reason, *logos*, God—in order to resist certain problems in society and initiate change. Not only does Watsuji's *Confucius* not take up the problem of criticizing society, he deliberately highlights the *denial* of this "higher ground."

In the *Analects*:

> Zilu asked how to serve the spirits and the gods. The Master replied, "Not yet being able to serve other people, how would you be able to

serve the spirits?" Zilu said, "May I ask about death?" The Master replied, "Not yet understanding life, how could you understand death?"[1]

For the other teachers of humankind—Buddha, Jesus, Socrates—their deaths were clearly pivotal moments for their resulting philosophies, showing key aspects of their teaching like letting go, resurrection, and justice. Their deaths pointed to an order that clearly transcends the shared life of society. But Confucius was different. Watsuji writes, "*Confucius's transmission does not include the death of Confucius.*"[2] Confucius was decidedly this-worldly, refusing discussion of the afterlife. Watsuji continues:

> What matters is the way (*michi* 道), not whether or not the individual's will be saved when one dies at night, or if one will attain eternal life. If the way is understood and realized, that is enough. Furthermore, that way is the way of human relations (*jinrin no michi* 人倫の道), not the way of God or enlightenment. If only one walks the way of human relations, that is, realizing authoritative conduct, and doing your utmost and putting oneself in the other's place (*chūjo* 忠恕, loyalty and consideration), for Confucius there is nothing to fear or be anxious about.... In this way, the most striking characteristic of Confucius's teaching is that *he acknowledged the absolute significance of the path of human relations.*[3]

"Human relations" (*jinrin*) is the same word Watsuji uses for ethical (*jinrinteki*) organizations. They translate the Hegelian term "*Sittlichkeit*," and refer to ethical life as it is embodied in actual relationships in the family, school, society, and state. For Watsuji and Confucius, there is no transcendence outside of this socio-ethical life. But that also means the denial of transcendent ground—reason, God, awakening—by means of which one can criticize the existing socio-ethical order.

In addition, Watsuji directly lauds Confucius's conservativism. Watsuji says that despite Confucius's uniqueness as a teacher of humankind, he positioned himself as a return to and restoration of (*fukko* 復古) previous tradition. He writes, "Confucius, despite representing Zhou culture and having tendencies toward restorationism, is still a primordial thinker."[4]

Watsuji's insight is that even the form of the analects suggests traditionalism. Unlike Socrates's well-developed arguments, Buddha's philosophical sermons, and Jesus's relatable parables, analects are terse and narrate everyday interactions with little context. Watsuji writes, "If you think about it, analects/maxims are the result of countless people doing the same thing throughout a long span of time."[5] Confucius and his *Analects* could be terse because they were nothing new—they were merely crystallizing the culture of Zhou and a way of life that was familiar to readers and would continue to be familiar to those in this line of civilization.

On top of that, I also worry about self-criticism, something that began to draw my attention the more I counseled Japanese students:[6]

> Master Zeng said: "Daily I examine my person on three counts. In my undertakings on behalf of other people, have I failed to do my utmost (*zhong* 忠)? In my interactions with colleagues and friends, have I failed to make good on my word (*xin* 信)? In what has been passed on to me, have I failed to carry it into practice?"

One can see three features when analyzing this analect. First, there is the relentless self-examination that for Watsuji is essential to anybody in a school or in any moral community. Second, this self-examination is not vis-à-vis impersonal reason but is strictly relational—how one connects to colleagues, friends, and teachers. Third, this analect focuses on self-examination as *negative* (*fu* 不). One does not ask, "Did I do my utmost, act trustworthily, and live out my values?" Such a positive approach would be more focused on the joy of a life of friendship and learning. But instead, one asks, "Have I *failed* to do my best, *failed* to be trustworthy, *failed* to live up to what I have learned?" As another analect says, "To fail to cultivate excellence... these things I worry over."[7] Worry as virtue!

In psychology, this is problematic. A positive approach is guided by joy and a sense of fulfillment, which tends to connect to curious behavior like trying new things. A negative approach is guided by wariness—its predominant affect is fear, which tends to restrict one's behavior to ruts (narrowing of behavioral repertoire).[8] If the goal is to take one's place within a pre-existing harmony, the affect is not joy in finding new ways forward but the fear of deviating from the path. Essential to learning ritual propriety is none other than anxious self-criticism—a problem I have found in my psychology research to lie at the heart of the narrative identity of many Japanese students.[9]

Watsuji's *Confucius* comes at the price of a lack of social critique, where what little criticality exists is turned inward. In *Ethics III*, Watsuji demanded an education wherein people have the power to think for themselves and resist conventionalism, suggesting an education of a leader who has the capacity to lead a nation even when its culture falls into an impasse. However, Watsuji's Confucian education seems like it would form anxious, self-critical students with no ground for social critique, who seem much more likely to merely reproduce existing social orders.

Historically speaking, Watsuji's Confucian view of education did end up supporting a very conservative social order. In 1937, Japan's Ministry of Education published *Cardinal Principles of Japan's National Polity*.[10] This was a wartime propaganda piece on education supporting and articulating the well-known (and for some infamous) *Imperial Rescript on Education*. Watsuji was among the compilation committee of this book. And many of his ideas—the relational view of ethics, the importance of selflessness, the virtues of social life, the absolutization of social ethics—found their way into this book. In "Educational Ideals in Pre and Post-War Japan," I argue that this cannot be a simplistic condemnation of Watsuji's ideas, because on close inspection, many of his ethical ideas are as valid for Deweyan democracy as they are for imperialism.[11] However, the fact remains that these ideas of Watsuji were actually deployed in Japanese society, and often for very conservative ends.

Given the dangers above, what Mori writes of Dilthey holds true for Watsuji as well: In an education for transmitting tradition and socializing people into the spiritual nexus of a culture, the very idea of ethical critique becomes reduced to past tradition, making it impossible to criticize society when tradition itself has become dysfunctional for a people—as when it leads Japan to a "communal suicide" in the Second World War.[12] As such, many in Japan refuse to have anything to do with Watsuji. I have had established Japanese scholars approach me privately to warn me: "Anton, Watsuji is right-wing, imperialist garbage. Are you sure you want to work on this?" And perhaps some of you readers are also thinking that it is better to just throw out Watsuji along with all the totalitarian discourses that cling to his ideas.

But what do we do with all the positive insights from the previous chapter? Even in more progressive societies, teachers and parents worry when students become too entitled, psychologists recognize perspective-taking to others as a developmental task, learning theorists see promise in post-individual views of learning and cognition, and ethicists can see philosophic value in ideas like interlocking networks of virtue. Do we expunge these and turn merely to ideas like criticality, autonomy, and freedom?

If you value the positive insights from the previous chapter, an alternative approach is to clarify precisely where Watsuji went wrong—where he overstepped, what he lacked—so that we can critically reconstruct a more workable theory of relational ethics. In this chapter, I will broaden the dialogue to include other thinkers—Nel Noddings, Emmanuel Levinas, G.H. Mead—in order to clarify precisely that.

Loss of the Other

Following Watsuji's idea of drawing ethical insights from "everyday expressions," let us turn to a concrete example of what happens when ethical life is reduced to the social order. I remember I had a student who I was quite close to—let us call her Junko-*san* for this example. She was always eager to learn and we had worked on a few academic side-projects together. We became rather close, sometimes sharing our similar personal struggles. But one day, after failing to submit a paper for class, she suddenly stopped coming to class or replying to emails. When I met her, I asked her what was up, and she said, "I don't want to go class anymore." I was stunned. "But why?" And she replied, "Because you hate me." "What?" "You hate me. I'm no good. I couldn't even submit the paper. You're disappointed in me and you hate me." "Is there something I said?" "No, but surely you hate me." "Junko-*san*, you know I'm right here. Look at me. Do I look like I hate you?" I remember feeling so sad and frustrated, like I was standing right in front of her with concern and understanding, but all she could see was this fictive hate.

What is happening here? She was a serious student, mindful of knowing her place. Hardly egoistic, she cared about me, she cared about my feelings, and she was trying to live up to her "filial and fraternal responsibility" to me. And in turn, I was trying to respond to her with my own caring and kindness ("authoritative conduct/benevolence"). But something was terribly amiss.

Nel Noddings, looking carefully at experiences of caring for students, points out a similar experience but from the flip side:

> Suppose, for example, that I am a teacher who loves mathematics. I encounter a student who is doing poorly, and I decide to have a talk with him. He tells me that he hates mathematics. *Aha*, I think. *Here is the problem. I must help this poor boy to love mathematics, and then he will do better at it.* What am I doing when I proceed in this way? I am not trying to grasp the reality of the other as a possibility for myself. I have not even asked: *How would it feel to hate mathematics?* Instead, I project my own reality onto my student and say, *You will be just fine if only you learn to love mathematics.*[13]

I think this happens to a lot of teachers, both in Japan and elsewhere—despite caring for students, we seem to project and presume what is good for a student, without necessarily taking their perspectives. Care ethicist Michael Slote also discusses a similar case with parents in what he calls "surrogate success syndrome," where parents project their visions of success on their children, out of caring for them, but overriding the actuality of what is meaningful to each child.[14]

What we see in Junko-*san*'s case and those of the teachers and parents above is what Noddings calls the limit of empathy:

> The *Oxford Universal Dictionary* defines empathy as "The power of projecting one's personality into, and so fully understanding, the object of contemplation." ... The notion of "feeling with" that I have outlined does not involve projection but reception. I have called it "engrossment." I do not "put myself in the other's shoes" ... by analyzing his reality as objective data ... I receive the other, and I see and feel with the other.[15]

Examining advances in the psychology of empathy, Slote points out that this is not a critique of all types of empathy but a rejection of *projective* empathy in favor of what Martin Hoffman calls "*mediated associative* empathy," which "... involves having the feelings of another (involuntarily) aroused in ourselves ..."[16] Thus, what care ethics is suggesting as genuine caring means going beyond projective empathy toward associative empathy or engrossment. In the latter, caring avoids merely presuming what students or teachers want, but rather openly senses via direct experience what the other might be needing. What we have here is not a *thinking* process but a *noticing* process, observing, seeing, feeling, what the other needs, whether it agrees with our conceptualizations or not.

What both Junko-*san* and Noddings' sample math teacher fell into is projective empathy that blocks genuine care. For caring to happen, it is not enough to be oriented to the other. Both one-caring and cared-for need to have a receptivity to the other, allowing the other person, in their uniqueness (and often incomprehensibility) to stand before the other.

In contemporary philosophy, this idea of openness to the other is best articulated in Emmanuel Levinas's idea of the alterity of the other.[17] To truly respond to the other means to notice the other, to feel with them, and to feel a deep ethical call to respond to what they need. Levinas called this "responding to the face of the other."

In his phenomenology of the face, he talks about the experience of looking at someone's face, being drawn into their experiences and their pain, and feeling this ethical demand not to reduce the other to the totality of the same. "Reduction of the other to the same" happens when we project on the other, reducing them to our mental comprehension, without allowing our prejudices to be challenged by the rich experience of what they present to us. For Levinas, this reduction is tantamount to murder, effacing the visage of the other, killing the reality of the other with our mere conceptions of them.

Noddings similarly draws on phenomenology as she talks about observing the other person in the caring relationship, seeing what they might really need, suspending our presuppositions of what they are "supposed to need." And this is something that happens for both the carer but also for the cared-for who must see the carer in order to truly receive their care.

Something in Watsuji seems to struggle with this phenomenological attentiveness to the other. However, this is not a simple matter of cultural difference (as in "Westerners have a sense of individuality, but Asians are conformist"). In the *Analects*, "Master Zeng said, 'The way of the Master is doing one's utmost (*zhong* 忠) and putting oneself in the other's place (*shu* 恕), nothing more.'"[18] The virtue of *shu*, also translated as "consideration" is directly connected to empathy, a "likeness" (如) in heart-mind (心), and can be connected to our previous chapter's discussion on how Confucius adapted his teachings to the particularities of each of his students. And this allows one's response to the other to not merely be a repetition of social expectation: "The Master said: 'Reviewing the old as a means of realizing the new—such a person can be considered a teacher.'"[19]

The *Analects* has openings for a genuine sense of otherness and social creativity. But Watsuji's reading of Confucius tended to miss this and fall into projective empathy. Not only does he look at students virtues as passive and role-bound, this even shows in his attitude toward Confucius himself. Watsuji writes,

The teachers of humankind are forms of "ideal persons" (*risōjin* 理想人) constructed by the ideals of countless people over a long period of time. If the teachers of humankind are so, their true biography must be something that grasps the *path of crystallization* (*kesshō no keiro* 結晶の経路). That is an understanding of the development of the history of culture, not one of an individual life.[20]

Even Confucius gets reduced to a mere cultural artifact, a role. Why? This is not merely a matter of understanding Watsuji historically. When I showed a draft of this chapter to our team, many suggested that the problem of projective empathy is not just Watsuji's but of many students and teachers in Japan, and perhaps around the world. And so perhaps understanding Watsuji might help us understand anyone who falls into projective empathy.

Social Self and Roles

In the previous chapter, I quoted the following from Watsuji's *Ethics I*:

> We can now confirm an obvious everyday fact, that we always act within a certain capacity and that this capacity is prescribed by something whole, further that this whole is the relationship we construct by means of possessing a certain capacity. Simply speaking, we exist in our daily life in the being in betweenness.[21]

For Watsuji, *ningen* being relational means that we never exist merely as isolated individuals, as unadulterated "authenticity," but instead always having certain capacities (*shikaku* 資格) or roles, through which we connect with others, share in particular mediated relationships, and respond to certain expected virtues.

This is a very valuable understanding even in contemporary sociology. G.H. Mead (1863–1931) is a pragmatist and a founder of one of the main approaches in sociology—symbolic interactionism. Steve Odin has compared his insights to Watsuji.[22] In *Mind, Self, and Society*, Mead suggests that human beings, having evolved as a cooperative species, develop through a process of imitating others, internalizing their roles, generalizing the system of roles (generalized other), and thus building their own social identity. Individuals do not exist as monadic agents but within roles. This is what he calls "me" as distinguished from "I."

> The "I" is the response of the organism to the attitudes of the others; the "me" is the organized set of attitudes of others which one himself assumes. The attitudes of the others constitute the organized "me," and then one reacts toward that as an "I." . . . it is due to the individual's ability to take the attitudes of these others in so far as they can be organized that he gets self-consciousness. The taking of all those organized sets of attitudes gives him his "me"; that is the self he is aware of.[23]

Independently of one of the founders of microsociology, Watsuji acutely articulated the idea of a self with a capacity (me, social self) that responds to other roles (other social selves) that are organized as a whole (generalized other). From this point of view, as a teacher, I am not just Anton standing in front of Junko. Instead, I am Anton-*sensei*, I have a role vis-à-vis her, and there are other *sensei* (teachers), with whom this educational relationship is shared. And she is Junko-*san*, my student, among other students. Thus, there are certain expectations that accrue between us.

This kind of thinking creates a lot of social stability and coherence. But what about the Anton and Junko behind the *sensei* and the *-san*? As Mead would put it, what about the "I" behind the "me?" To answer this and understand precisely where Watsuji (and other people who fall into projective empathy) go awry, I turn to places where Watsuji is more likely to highlight the personal self behind social relations.

Masks and Faces

First, let us examine Watsuji's intensely phenomenological work on art in "Mask and Persona" (1935).[24] In this work, Watsuji tries to understand the face—the same metaphor Levinas used to show the alterity, the irreducible uniqueness of the other person. He argues that the face is integral to human relationships: we remember their faces when we write to people, when we remember people, their faces are necessarily a part of this process.

In art, the importance of the face results in various art forms like portraits or busts that seek to capture the essence of a person via the person's face. Watsuji focuses on one artform, the mask, which abstracts from all the other unessential features and leaving only that which is the core of recognizability, the facial surface. He compares Greek and Japanese *Gigaku* and Noh masks, writing,

> From my own humble viewpoint, it seems that among the wooden masks of Greece... they simply show the "part" of king or queen alone, and do not attempt the thorough typification of a specific look (expression 表情) that can be seen in *Gigaku* masks.... Japanese sculptors, rather than focusing on physical beauty, focused on the "person" in the physical and thus "the mystery of the facial surface"...[25]

Watsuji then goes on to a very close examination of the experience of the mask—how masks are meant to be worn and move, how the movement and shadow play across the mask creates boundless variety, different types of masks and how they show the muscular activity of the face, how the gender of the mask can alter the gender of the wearer... His focus is on the raw phenomenon of the face, its boundless richness beyond any conceptual categories. And like Noddings and Levinas, phenomenology leads him to realize the deep significance of the face:

> [T]he facial surface has a core significance for the existence of a person (*hito no sonzai* 人の存在). It is not simply one part of the physical body, but it is none other than the seat of the subjective (*shutaiteki naru mono no za* 主体的なるものの座) that subdues the physical body for itself, that is, the seat of personality (*jinkaku* 人格).[26]

The person in *ningen sonzai* is a person with an infinitely expressive face. Like I told Junko, with vulnerability in my eyes, "Look at me." Perhaps it is the same thing the mathematics student in Noddings' example wanted to say, "Look at my face and tell me that mathematics matters more than I do." The face calls teacher and student beyond projective empathy.

But then Watsuji says,

> What we have thought about so far cannot but naturally remind one of its associations with "persona." This word first meant the mask used in a drama.... The various roles in human life activity are personas. I, you, and he are the first, second, and third personas, and the various positions, statuses, and titles in society are personas.... However, persons each have their own roles and duties in society. Behaving according to one's own persona is how one gets done what must be done.... This being so, the persona must mean "personality" as the subject of acts and the subject of rights. Thus, "mask" has become "personality."[27]

I was stunned when I first read this. What had been a close phenomenology of the irreducible face quickly turned into a hermeneutics of *pre-given* social roles, with its accompanying duties, responsibilities, and rights. It is as if the student or the teacher, reaching out with the vulnerability of their personality, were suddenly reduced to persona of *-sensei* or *-san*. It is almost as if there is nobody behind these masks, no I behind the me. Why does this happen?

The Voice of the Other

Let us turn to another example of language, the remonstrations of other, like a teacher asking a student to take his perspective, or a student trying to explain why he really does not like mathematics. If someone looks past my face, I can resist the "violence of totalization" using my voice (what Levinas calls "the saying" in contrast with "the said").[28]

As mentioned in the previous chapter, language is a major part of Watsuji's approach. Methodologically, he constantly refers to etymologies in order to understand the structure of human existence. In terms of content, when he discusses his central organization, cultural community, he writes, "Within all cultural products, the closest at hand and universal is *language* (*gengo* 言語)."[29] Perhaps his view of language might provide a way past his view of masks.

To explain language, Watsuji examines the I-Thou (*ware-nanji* 我汝) relationship, a major theme in the Kyoto School which we need some back story for. In the Introduction, I mentioned Nishida Kitarō's "On Education." Here, Nishida suggested that education was about forming not abstract students but a "concrete personality," a concrete "Thou." If we follow this lead to Nishida's "I and Thou" (which Watsuji himself cites in *Ethics as the Study of Ningen Sonzai*) one finds that the Thou is both continuous to and discontinuous from the I. On one hand, both I and Thou share the fact that they are determined by the same environment (*kankyōteki gentei* 環境的限定), both physical and symbolic, and are thus continuous. On the other hand, I and Thou are not merely determined, but as self-determining, individuals reverse-determine the environment as well, and thus are discontinuous from each other.[30] In other words, while acknowledging shared history and culture, Nishida also pointed to the irreducibility of the other to what is shared, thus acknowledging the alterity of the Thou. And while we encounter the other objectively via language, the other is not a mere object to be reduced to that but a point of self-determination.

Let us return to Watsuji on language. Like Nishida (and using Nishida's terminology), Watsuji argues that language and thus thinking are not merely within the individual but are fundamentally relational. And similarly, he sees the I and Thou as "mutually determining," in that there is some form of continuity between the I and the Thou. However, while Nishida argued for a continuity of *discontinuity* (*hirenzoku no renzoku* 非連続の連続), a rupture between the rationality of the self and the other, Watsuji writes:

> Mutual determination is none other than *mutual understanding*. When the I timidly looks at the Thou, that way of looking is determined by the other, and in that way the overpowering (*iatsu* 威圧) character of the Thou is genuinely understood.... Of course, understanding can be lacking in various way, however as many artworks have taken up, such a deficiency is the root of tragedy. This shows us that mutual understanding is essential feature of relationships.[31]

Watsuji sees continuity and mutual understanding between the I and the Thou as primary. From the point of view of interacting (cooperating) agents, like farmers plowing a rice field, when we do things together, we already "get" each other, communicating with a glance or a simple gesture.[32]

It is within mutual understanding that he situates language: "Linguistic activity is the expression of this mutual understanding. Therefore, there is already a 'matter' (*koto*) that is mutually understood, and that 'matter' is separated and unified in linguistic activity."[33] Instead of defining language from the need to create understanding, he sees language as an expression of existing understanding. Hence rather than debate or explication, he uses subtle communication as examples—when someone fills in the blanks for you, when one leaves things unsaid, etc. This is very common in Japan. Instead of saying, "Your submission was terrible," it is sufficient to say, "Your submission was, well . . . (*Ano teishutsu wa ne* . . .)" That could be enough, or the student could fill it in for the teacher, ". . . indeed it was no good (. . . *yappari dame deshita ka*)." Watsuji saw thinking as the internalization of these dialogues, and thus fundamentally relational. For example, Junko-*san* might automatically imagine the dialogue above, even if I have yet to say anything.

Watsuji saw this as directly connected to education: "When an infant is added into the family, the first effort for raising this infant as a member of the family is to teach the child words."[34] Rather than seeing language as a tool the individual will need to assert their individual needs and rationality, Watsuji sees language education as helping people articulate the practical understanding that already exists between people. And thus socialized, one learns to say what is expected. This is in clear contrast with Nishida's "On Education," where educating the "concrete historical Thou" is about forming the capacity to create the *unexpected*.

Some will be quick to completely dismiss this view of language as nostalgic and exotically Japanese. But again, Watsuji can be interpreted as sociologically valid, at least partially. Mead suggests that language begins not with individual thinking but with social action. As a tool to this social action, gestures, "that part of the social act which serves as a stimulus to other forms involved in the same social act"[35] arise, resulting in language. Rather than seeing language as expressing thought: "The internalization in our experience of the external conversations of gestures which we carry on with other individuals in the social process is the essence of thinking . . ."[36] This view of language is hardly exotic but forms the core of understanding social action in symbolic interactionism today, allowing us to highlight the joint behavior and shared presuppositions beyond discursive language, resisting solipsistic views of cognition.

However, despite Watsuji's theoretical acuity, this theory of language strengthens the risk of projective empathy. Instead of genuinely listening to each other, the teacher and the student simply exist in this "mutual understanding," with the harmony of their words being the result of already existing understandings they have of each other. "You're my teacher so you must be disappointed in me." "You're my student so you must need to learn mathematics." Language seems to be a matter of talking past each other.

After my initial encounter with Junko-*san*, I sat with her in private. I reassured her that I did not hate her at all. I told her of the good times we shared, and I said I was sad not having her around, and worried how she was doing. "Don't say I hate you Junko, come on. You know me. You know I'm not like that." Here, language functions not as an explication of a pre-existing understanding, but as a resistance to a configuration of roles, of critical teacher and conforming student. For Watsuji, this is a tragedy, a failure of mutual understanding. Difficult, yes, but tragic?

Hermeneutics vs. Phenomenology

Let us look at one final aspect of Watsuji's thought. The tendency to privilege social coherence—pre-given roles, mutual understanding—goes down all the way to the methodology at the heart of Watsuji's work. In *Ethics as the Study of Human Existence* (1935), while struggling with Heidegger's *Being and Time*, he writes:

This phenomenological reduction is carried out under the presumption that the natural attitude already proposes transcendent being and thus takes a contemplative standpoint as its kernel. Therefore, it does not consider the unconscious, practical, and actional aspects in the natural attitude.... However, for hermeneutics, everyday life itself, as the practical and actional connection within the natural standpoint, is already the dynamic unfolding of expression and understanding in relationality.[37]

For Watsuji, what comes first is our attempt to cooperate in our milieu. We already have a practical understanding within that cooperation, to which thinking and language are secondary. If we were to take a phenomenological approach of gazing contemplatively upon this situation, we shift our stance from the "cooperating we" to the "contemplating I," missing the starting point of our everyday existence. This is why hermeneutics in Watsuji's sense avoided this contemplative experiential phenomenology and instead focused on expressing what is already apparent within our cooperative experience:

Thus, the hermeneutic method as the method of ethics, consists in grasping the dynamic structure of *ningen*'s *sonzai* through its most basic everyday expressions. *Ningen*'s *sonzai*, in its everydayness, constantly manifests itself in the practical connections of life, expression, and understanding; and yet it does not become aware of this as expression. Hence, the effort to realize it as expression is a philosophical activity that assumes the form of a hermeneutic method.[38]

This counterintuitive way of looking at people really helped me (partially) understand how my students approach life (albeit dysfunctionally): Imagine Junko-*san*. She is in the corridor, and she sees me. She is thinking, "This is my *sensei*, and I missed my homework. Oh no!" And I flash a look of concern. But she is looking at this not as an inalienable face but as a social mask, "The *sensei*'s face looks concerned ... that I am not doing well, that I am a disappointment." And her words are not an expression of some private self, but a socially patterned interaction between a disappointed teacher and a contrite student. "I don't want to go to class anymore. Because you hate me." "What?" "You hate me. I'm no good. I couldn't even submit the paper. You're disappointed in me and you hate me."

This is none other than a hermeneutics of a teacher–student drama in Japan, one I lived through, wherein I and Thou exist in a purported mutual understanding that precedes faces and language. Watsuji's hermeneutics allows me to understand what goes on in this drama, as seen from this "natural standpoint" of inter-acting selves. What we see here is the interplay of different "me" (social selves, *shikaku*) within a social act. On a side note, this hermeneutics is very similar to what Erving Goffman, deeply influenced by G.H. Mead, called dramaturgy—now a valuable method in microsociology.[39]

Discussing this with my students, an international student seconded my intuition that Japan seems to have a relatively high demand to be aware of the nuanced role expectations within society. A Japanese student also pointed out that this is complicated by Japanese "*honne/tatemae*" behavior, where people tend to deal with each other using established masks (*tatemae* 建前) and it is hard to be sure that what is broadcast as authentic feeling (*honne* 本音) is not in fact another strategically employed mask. So Watsuji is indeed helpful for understanding this world of *tatemae* and role expectations.

But at the same time, what about the "I," the perplexed teacher, the struggling student, behind the "me?" What happens when the "me" do not fit in their presumptions of the social act? Sakai Naoki, a contemporary Japanese philosopher, was deeply critical of Watsuji's purportedly social approach to ethics. He writes, "What is absent in Watsuji's anthropology is the very concern for sociality.... Normally, we do not ascribe sociality to a person who can only operate within prearranged social relations..."[40]

What we see above was that Watsuji, despite his sociologically insightful understanding of roles, cooperation, language, shared cognition, and hermeneutics, tended to miss the sense of an other, the part of the person that is irreducible to social roles. And what we see from his attempts is that it is the *lure of social order*, the *fear of deviating from social expectations*, that makes him miss this irreducible other. His attempt to empty individual ego has resulted the opposite extreme of reifying the social order. While critics like Sakai come down hard on Watsuji for this, I cannot help but feel sympathy for Watsuji, because in his struggle, I see the face of Junko-*san* and of other students and teachers who feel tethered to their roles. This is a human struggle, not just a philosophical one.

Critique from Mori and Mead

In the face of this human struggle, my question is: How we can move forward to help those who struggle with maintaining a sense of alterity without falling into the opposite extreme of closed individualism or solipsism? As we have seen in previous chapters, both Mori Akira and G.H. Mead had much in common with Watsuji—deeply in agreement with the dual-structure of individuality and sociality, showing how recent social science theories can back up Watsuji's theory of culture and the importance of education within it. However, on the point of this loss of the individual, they had some serious criticisms that can point the way more constructively.

First, while seeing the self as fundamentally connected to society, Mori did not see the self as *reducible* to society. This is captured in Mori's idea of the existential self:

> The human being (*ningen* 人間) is a possible subjective *Existenz* (*jitsuzon* 実存) beyond substantial objective actuality (*genzon* 現存). Therefore, the human being is not a thing that is there at a particular time but is a process (*dōtei* 道程). The human being exists not just as a determinate actuality but within factual behavior as an actual self, always bearing potential due to the freedom that is the foundation of always being able to decide (*ketsudan* 決断) by oneself what one is. . . . The human being always goes beyond the stipulations of social groups that are an endlessly renewed identity and faces the subjectivity of

constantly proceeding toward unknowable ends. Which is why the human being is, in one's deepest essence, radically split (*hikisakareteiru* 引き裂かれている). No matter how the human being thinks of themselves, while thinking, they confront (*tairitsu* 対立) themselves with themselves, confront others with themselves, and look from within all the oppositions of things.[41]

This processual *Existenz* that responds to itself and its own social roles is very similar to what Mead referred to as the "I" that reacts to the "me." Mead similarly wrote, "I want to call attention particularly to the fact that this response of the 'I' is something that is more or less uncertain."[42] It is possible to be radically relational, like Watsuji and Mead, without ignoring the uncertainty and indeterminacy of the "I."

Second, Mori saw an inescapable defect of society and institutions that can be seen in the process of socialization. There are two types of socialization, primary and secondary. Primary socialization is the socialization students receive in close face-to-face relationships such as at home. At home, one exists not as a generic "student" or "citizen" but as Anton and Junko, unique individuals, singularities. This is the space of the I-Thou relationship, where we respond to others in unique ways, fulfilling their needs directly. (Mead also saw this as the phase of development where a child does not yet have a sense of the "general other," and is still in early processes of imitating others with no sense of "me".)

Secondary socialization is the socialization students receive in order to enter *impersonal* relationships like in a bureaucracy, where you have a particular title and office, and where your behavior is stipulated not by your personal inclinations but by the demands of your office. It is continuous with primary socialization in that institutions also function to fulfill needs, but at a much larger scale—for example as a job gives a person a salary in exchange for certain services that fulfill the needs of others. School is in the middle of primary and secondary socialization, trying to link the sociality of the family to the more impersonal orders of society. (Mead saw this as the stage of forming a generalized other by moving from mere role-play to games with organized roles, and eventually to more impersonal institutions.)[43]

But for Mori, despite the continuity, there is an unavoidable *discontinuity* between primary and secondary socialization. In institutions, because needs are being fulfilled in a wide scale, they no longer see individuals as unique, but instead as generic functionaries. And the needs that are supposedly being fulfilled will at some point cease to correspond to actual needs of a person—for example when a teacher is given overtime pay but not necessarily the recognition and support for work they are forced to take on themselves. Thus, secondary socialization results in *alienation*.[44]

Watsuji misses this alienation. But why? One might think, with Watsuji's rather simple views of local communities, economies, cultures, and states, that the problem is that his conceptions of institutions and secondary socialization were naïve. But looking at the critique of Watsuji above, it seems that his weakness was in *primary* socialization—he saw even personal relationships like married couples or families as having rather stable role configurations, where one acts within one's role (ex. child to parent) and thus within the virtues expected of that role (filial piety). What he missed that both Mori and Mead catch is this whole process of forming that social self, and the presence of much more unstructured and indeterminate processes beneath it that do not necessarily link smoothly to the order of impersonal institutions.

This brings us to a third point. Because society and all its impersonal institutions are a larger scale attempt to fulfill needs, they often miss the particularities of individual situations as well as the changes in the surrounding situation. This means that society needs to be regularly adjusted, not just at cataclysmic points in history, but on a regular basis to adjust for changing context and rising alienation. For Mori, *Existenz* had the crucial role of standing up for the particular needs of the self and changing society. Mead writes:

> Over against the "me" is the "I." ... he is one who reacts to this community and in his reaction to it ... changes it. ... if the response to it is a response which is of the nature of the conversation of gestures, if

it creates a situation which is in some sense novel, if one puts up his side of the case, asserts himself over against others and insists that they take a different attitude toward himself, then there is something important occurring that is not previously present in experience.[45]

While the self is influenced by society, the self also influences society. This is an essential feature in Nishida's I-Thou as well, how the individual and environment are in *mutual* rather than one-way determination.[46]

Without reactively criticizing Watsuji wholesale, Mori and Mead show us specifically what he lacked. While Watsuji's view of relationality and social self is valuable, it must not come at the expense of the existential I, its tension with impersonal institutions, and the ability of the I to bring change to its relational nexus.

I find this is the same struggle with some students and teachers like Junko. The fear of straying from social coherence makes it difficult to see the person behind the mask. The regulation of relationships by roles feels unnegotiable. And society as a whole feels massive, opaque, and unchangeable. As I was talking with Junko, she shared with me how important it was to her to be a good student, and that she often worried about what teachers thought of her, falling into bouts of self-criticism where she could barely get out of bed. "I know what that's like, wanting to be a good student. But I wonder, how does it actually work for you? Does wanting to be a good student and seeing your teachers as measuring you help you when you try to learn these things you love?" And after hearing her various struggles with measuring up, I said, "I care about you Junko, that you really grow, that you learn these things you can be so enthusiastic about. I wonder if there's something I can change in the way I'm your teacher, so that I don't keep triggering this urge to measure up . . ."

My response was not a simple return to individualism, where I focus on the private needs of a teacher and a student, and language is a way to get the other to fulfill our needs. I still see that people are in relation and that our roles shape our encounters. But at the same time, I am reaching beyond the masks with my own vulnerability and care. I am also calling attention to the roles and institutions like education so that they can be seen critically in light of their effects on people. (We will see more on this process of I-Thou education in the next chapter.)

One small caveat. As a teacher, I am in a position to reach out beyond the role relationship when it becomes dysfunctional. But are students able to call out to the teacher as Thou, when the teacher reduces them to their role? I think this is a much more complicated power dynamic that I hope teachers can think about.

Watsuji's Struggle

Above, we have seen that despite Watsuji's very human limitations, it is valuable to understand him and to maintain his core relational insights. Furthermore, Watsuji himself was aware of these limitations, as we see in his post-war writing, thus suggesting that we can criticize Watsuji in a *constructive* way.

In *Ethics III* (1949), Watsuji was both trying to complete his systematic ethics (by adding a theory of history and milieu to extend the ideas of temporality and spatiality to groups) but at the same time reflect on things that the defeat in the war forced him to consider. First, he seemed painfully aware that while the dual-negative structure of *ningen sonzai* was originally intended as including *both* individuality and totality in tension, the actual development of this idea in *Ethics II* was primarily focused on groups, wherein the individual was merely a functionary of the whole and there was little room for the individual to change it. Thus, emptying the individual merely reified groups.

Consequently, in his discussion of history, he bolstered this idea of the individual as free: "One who takes the standpoint of individual liberation should be able to selflessly serve, and one who takes the standpoint of devoted service should be able to resolutely negate totality. Otherwise, freedom falls into simple bestial *self-indulgence* or *servility*."[47] Here he stresses that while he is against a self-indulgent vision of the free individual, the individual must have the power to *empty totality*, to negate how the teacher-role is being played or how education is, not from mere individual arbitrariness, but from a conscientious critique of society.

Second, this implied that society was not just something already existing and to simply be maintained. With the changes in context and history, the status quo could be dysfunctional. Thus, he began to talk about becoming self-aware of one's culture not to reproduce it but also to *correct* it and "realize its limitations."[48] He talked about all aspects of Japanese society from the family to economics to politics to architecture!

In relation to education, he took up filial piety (a key in *Confucius*) as a major point of debate: filial piety can end up closing the family from other relations, the relationship with one's family of origin can impede the independent formation of a new family via marriage, filial piety can turn into domination and loyalty instead of love, etc.[49] Furthermore, he criticized the tendency of Japanese research to be focused primarily on usefulness with no deep love for the foundational pursuit for truth. This leads to the following: "Universities are not communities for pursuing truth but develop into vocational schools.... What these phenomena result in is a *distorted interest* of the nation in studies (*gakumon*) that is *purely utilitarian*."[50] Instead of this mix of utilitarian learning that copies western technique but fails to reflect on Japanese ways of thinking, he suggests a more critical education. Let me repeat a quote from the previous chapter,

> Academe is not *memorizing* pre-existing knowledge or given formulae but cultivating *the power to think for oneself*. If this simple idea were to spread throughout the nation, that would reform education as a whole and restore the dignity of the everyday life and political activity of the nation. Citizens who have the power to think and decide for themselves will not fall into conventionalism or thought control.[51]

Third, a society needing change and the free individual come together for Watsuji's new theory of social change. Rather than seeing change as coming entirely from individual ideas (individualism) or as impossible (conservative collectivism), he saw change as coming from a dual-negation occurring within the individual:

> When an individual resolutely rebels against something that up to that point had held currency, and through strife and sacrifice finally manages to change the consciousness of totality, that individual had become clearly conscious of something that had already been vaguely felt in collective consciousness, and ahead of the masses had tried to form things toward how they ought to be, thus leading collective consciousness to self-awareness.[52]

This is again very similar to Mead, where a leader is not one with brilliant ideas, but one who is able to empty oneself in order to embrace the wider perspective of the whole (the first negation). But given the wider perspective, one does not merely immerse oneself in the status quo of the institution but expresses insufficiencies and dysfunctions that are, while already felt by the group, not yet articulated (second negation). These realizations that coalesce within the individual are then brought back to the community in a movement with "strife and sacrifice," showing Watsuji's regained awareness of the tension of the individual and the whole.

Thus, Watsuji himself tried to have a vision of a creative and free "I," that is able to realize the deficiencies of the social configuration ("me" and the generalized other), and is able to try to transform the group. This argument in *Ethics III* brings Watsuji back to Nishida's "On Education" and "I and Thou," for a much more creative and critical vision of education as forming those who will in turn agentically form society and history.

However, Watsuji was really stretched thin. While the relational part of his education was elaborated in *Confucius*, the critical creative part of *Ethics III* remains terse, abstract, and unmoored in the experience of education. If we are to rethink Watsuji, we need to look where in Watsuji we find these ideas of emptying society via creative individuals richly articulated (rather than forced in this scramble of post-war Japan).

3

Buddhism and Awakening to Self

In the previous chapters, I began with vignettes of various struggling students having difficulties with egoism, relating with others, losing themselves... I worry this will give the impression that educators only need philosophical reflection when something is clearly going wrong.

Allow me to begin from another angle. I had a student who I shall call Taro-*kun* for this exercise. Taro-*kun* was, from the beginning, one of my most academically gifted students. He was very quick to understand difficult lessons and eager to take on new challenges. He wanted to learn about how people wrestle with a sense of meaninglessness and how to help these people within the context of education. But he was deeply mistrustful of education and various theories of counseling. After much struggle, he ended up focusing on Acceptance and Commitment Training (ACT, a non-clinical counseling that is rooted in the philosophy of contextualism and has much in common with the Kyoto School's ideas of the emptiness of self and Buddhism's practices of "mindfulness").[1] But behind this academic interest, he had his own difficulties with the meaning of life and trauma in relationships. In this chapter, I will look back on our story, asking, "What does this student need to learn? And what kind of teacher does this call me to be?"

As we have seen in the previous chapter, Watsuji has a repeating tendency to privilege social coherence via roles and in so doing, lose the person behind those roles. While he tried to come up with a critical and creative view of the individual in *Ethics III*, he did so with a hurried hand. This kind of impersonal approach served me little when thinking about how to respond to Taro-*kun*, and perhaps you felt the same frustration as well, when considering your own experience with trying to form students. Where might we find hints for a more thorough engagement with this richer sense of the individual person and personal encounter in Watsuji?

Early in his career, Watsuji was an existentialist, writing his first books on Kierkegaard and Nietzsche. Watsuji "turned" from western individualism back to his eastern roots. But before he would tumble into more collectivist and sometimes totalitarian tendencies, he would deeply engage a tradition that is both profoundly influential in Japanese culture but less collectivist than Confucianism—Buddhism.

Watsuji was instrumental in bringing Buddhism out of the confines of Buddhology and into philosophy in general. He wrote *Pilgrimage to the Ancient Temples in Nara* (2012 [1919]), which is still read by travelers to Nara today.[2] He wrote *Research on the History of Japanese Spirit* (1926), that included *Purifying Zen* (*Shamon Dōgen*, 2011). This book is credited with "single-handedly rescuing Dōgen from obscurity," directly inspiring Tanabe Hajime to write about Dōgen.[3] He also wrote his dissertation on *The Practical Philosophy of Primitive Buddhism* (1927), examining Buddhism with inspiration from phenomenology and German thought, influencing Takeuchi Yoshinori's Buddhist philosophy. Dōgen scholar Steven Heine even suggests that Watsuji was the forerunner of all the Kyoto School research on Dōgen, including Nishitani Keiji, Karaki Junzō, and Abe Masao.[4]

It was through two decades of work on Buddhism that Watsuji built a foundation of ethics on emptiness. In *Ethics as the Study of Ningen*, he would express this foundation for the first time:

> The study of *ningen sonzai* must be grasped as the foundation of all the ideal matters in human existence, and, at the same time, the foundation of all natural being.... Existence of this sort is truly existence (*sonzai*) through the movement of becoming totality through being individual. Therefore, the foundation from which this movement arises is absolute emptiness.[5]

This is developed in *Ethics I*. Emptiness (*kū* 空) means not taking individuality as substance, and at the same time not taking totality as substance. Thus, these are seen in a mutually negating fashion, the back-and-forth movement of empty*ing*. Thus, when a person lets go of egoism in order to genuinely connect to community, that is an awakening to emptiness. In the same way, when a person negates the status quo of society in order to renew society, that too is awakening to emptiness.

In *Ethics II*, Watsuji expands his vision of emptiness to cast it as the absolute behind particular forms of culture—the formless form behind art, the ineffable behind language, the religious absolute behind religious beliefs. When an artist comes up with a new and moving expression, they are able to do so because they empty themselves of existing expressions and awaken to the absolute, and thus express that absolute in a creative way. In *Ethics III*, Watsuji connects this process of creation, of awakening to the emptiness behind history, to social change and the ability to lead a nation beyond crisis. This is the core insight that I tried to share in *Watsuji's Global Ethics of Emptiness*.

It seems a promising idea to link education to the idea of awakening to emptiness. But in *Ethics*, Watsuji was always short on specifics on the process of *learning* to awaken. This is where *Purifying Zen* can be so interesting. In this book, he shared his own attempt as a layman to explore the life of Dōgen (1200–1253), founder of the Sōtō school of Zen in Japan. He shows the process by which Dōgen tried to awaken to emptiness, but also how Dōgen tried to help others awaken as a Zen master, drawing from his more narrative writings in the *Shōbōgenzō Zuimonki* and Dōgen's philosophical masterpiece, the famously difficult *Shōbōgenzō* (written from 1231–1253). In other words, this book can be read as a philosophy of *education for awakening*.

This reading is corroborated in *Confucius*. Allow me to repeat a quotation:

[F]irst, the joy of learning, second, the joy of the community of friendship bound by learning, and third, the results one can achieve in this community.... Not only are these ideals shared by the Platonic Academy, Buddha's *sangha*, and Jesus Christ's church, they continue to be serviceable today. If the spirit of learning expressed in these three are lost, there can be no living learning.[6]

One of his models for "living learning" is Buddha's *sangha*, which was the focus of his work in the 1920s, and in *Purifying Zen* we see key ideas of Watsuji that are in tension with his Confucianism—criticality, the pedagogic encounter, awakening to self, and creativity.

Negating Totality

In Buddhism, the path to awakening begins with questioning, with a growing doubt about the presuppositions of everyday life. For Siddhārtha Gautama Buddha, it was seeing the ravages of old age, sickness, and death. This led to his first insight, the first noble truth of suffering—that everything is marked by existential suffering. However, Dōgen had entered the monastery at an early age, and the teachings of Buddhism were not new to him. But looking at the *Zuimonki*, we find that questions began to arise in his mind in a different way.

Eisai (also known as Yōsai, 1141–1215) was the founder of the Rinzai sect and one of Dōgen's first teachers. Dōgen recounted how despite the limited supplies of the monastery in this time of social unrest, Eisai gave away copper sticks that were meant for a statue of Yakushi and donations for the monastic community in order to feed the hungry. Watsuji writes,

> Eisai's conduct had made a deep and lasting impression in Dōgen's mind.... In a time when the pursuit of superficial prosperity such as rank and power were the normal practice of monks, one monk endured all the persecution and oppression and was absorbed in the quest for truth and the practice of compassion...[7]

According to Watsuji, Dōgen's path began with discontentment with the shallowness of monastic culture during his time, that became clear in contrast to his teacher. Watsuji writes,

> [T]he religious authority of Nara and Mount Hiei, which had controlled the public for centuries, was freeing itself of the old political regime at the same time that it refused to submit to the new regime, and was now

displaying the might of its own independent economic and military influence.... The monks and priests threw away religious ecstasy, threw away truth, and pursued nothing but worldly gains. The public unrest born of this social revolution, and the audible cry for religious faith coming from within this turmoil, were of no concern to the monks.[8]

However, the shallowness that vexed Dōgen is not merely blatant egoism but includes a superficial view of the "good" in secular morality. After Eisai passed, Dōgen studied under his student, Myōzen (1184–1225). When Myōzen was about to visit China to learn about Buddhism, one of his teachers, Myōyū, was awaiting death. He asked Myōzen to defer his trip until after his passing. But Myōzen said,

> [B]ecause staying here would deter me from my aim of enlightenment, [my master] may receive bad karma.... If the merit in this [pilgrimage] is good, then I will be fulfilling my obligation to my teacher.... To waste precious time for the sake of one person is not in accordance with the Buddha's will. Therefore I cannot change my resolve regarding our upcoming pilgrimage.[9]

As we have seen in *Confucius*, filial piety is a central virtue, wherein one takes care of one's teacher out of gratitude to having been taught. However, Myōzen showed Dōgen that even secular morality can become narrow, with virtues like filial piety obstructing spiritual life, and thus needing to be recast.[10]

In Watsuji's interpretation, the beginning of Dōgen's spiritual path was a questioning of the *social order* during his time—both the egotism of the monks but also the secular morality that bound them. Dōgen became acutely aware of the worldliness of the world, its pursuit of desires, its pursuit of social order, without a genuine anchor in truth. Watsuji writes,

> At the heart of Dōgen's teachings is the manifestation of eternal values. Therefore, the destruction of all worldly values must be the starting point of his project. Dōgen expressed this destruction of worldly values through the traditional Buddhist expression "You should contemplate

impermanence." He says, "The impermanence of the world is not a problem to think about, but rather a fact before our eyes. In the morning we are born and in the evening we die. The people you saw yesterday are not the people of today. We ourselves may contract a terrible illness this evening or be killed by a burglar in the night. If this precious life is the only value we possess, then our existence is truly without value."[11]

Worldly values, from desire for material objects to desire for social order, are all forms of attaching to something that is fundamentally impermanent and unreliable. Dōgen pushed us to see the unreliability of these things and seek eternal values—the truth of emptiness. His journey to emptiness thus began as a *negation of totality*, guided by his teachers.

I understand that Zen masters may seem far removed from our contemporary secular life. But let us attempt an experiment, seeing what *Purifying Zen* might connect to in our experiences of education. As educators, have you not seen students who have this deep sense of a negation of totality, a questioning of how things are? While many students seem content to merely go through the motions, to submit to the social order and its expectations, some students come to us with burning questions. Every year, I see this in at least one or two students.

This was what I found in Taro-*kun*. I began by teaching him the basics—education, ACT, its place in school counseling theory... While he learned these ideas very quickly, he expressed deep doubts. "Isn't education just a form of brainwashing?" "Is counseling really compassionate acceptance of suffering or just an attempt to erase it?" "Do counselors really get to the core of existential suffering?" He worried that counseling was no more than a band-aid to a problem that education and society were actively causing.[12] He had many questions filled with real anguish, and sometimes I felt like I was being put to the test. It was this criticality, this deep questioning in him, that made me feel that I was called to more than simply dispense information as a professor. He needed more than bits and pieces of information that he could digest himself—he needed a guide as he rethought the very idea of mental health, the very idea of caring, and the very idea of education itself.

Encounter

A central point of *Purifying Zen* is that when what is to be learned is not mere information but an *entire worldview*, an entire mode of being-in-the-world, we need a different kind of teaching. I understand this may seem intimidating to teachers, but if we want to convey a way of being, education needs to be transmitted not by fragmentary ideas but via a role model. Role models teach not merely by what they say or the exercises they give or how they respond but how all of these consistently *come together*. This is how people begin to walk the way, as we saw with Dōgen and his teachers. Watsuji writes, "[T]hat which moves people and urges them toward enlightenment is the strength of the personality that embodies the truth. This same personality will move others and push them on toward enlightenment in the same way."[13]

As one deepens one's journey of questioning worldly values and letting them go, one continues to be guided by such role models. Watsuji writes,

> This involves direct moral education from one person's personality to another's. Just as Dōgen's own self-cultivation was guided in large part by a strong personality, the method of self-cultivation he teaches also relies on the strength of this personality. The innermost meaning of the practice of the patriarchs is not transmitted by fixed general concepts; it is transmitted as the strength of a living personality.[14]

In Buddhism, this is found in the idea of "face-to-face transmission." Watsuji explores these points via Dōgen's *Shōbōgenzō*:

> In order to emphasize this transition, Dōgen explained the face-to-face transmission between buddhas (*Shōbōgenzō* "Menju" [面授]). It is only possible to capture and appreciate the truth by seeing a person who understands and embodies the truth directly before your eyes, and by

being seen by such a person.... I think his words "When you see a master, you see yourself" point to this lesson. This is where the most correct meaning of the word "master" exists.[15]

This kind of a teacher does not merely transmit information. Rather, this is a person who sees how different ideas come to form a *Gestalt*, grasps the implications of such a worldview for life, and actually lives out these ideas. In Zen koans, one sees many stories of students encountering teachers, "testing them," and seeing if they indeed have the understanding necessary to be guides along the way. This may seem too esoteric, but actually for ACT instructors, there is a rigorous process of training, personal practice, supervision, and sometimes certification, because ACT instructors have to function as role models to model various psychological flexibility skills.[16]

However, when one finds a teacher who can be a good role model, what is next? Watsuji writes, "'Practice' is the abandonment of all old views, all our current analyses, and all of our desires, in order to follow the words and deeds of the patriarchs. In other words, practice is the surrendering of all worldly values in order to become an imitator of the pure patriarchs."[17] Here we have a part of Zen that western Buddhism is squeamish about. For Dōgen, practice requires *blind obedience*. Dōgen says,

> There are people in the world who say, "My teacher's words don't suit me." This line of thinking is mistaken. If the *reasoning of the sutras* that appears in your teacher's words doesn't suit you, you are just common and foolish. If the *teacher's own words* don't suit you, why did you choose that person as a teacher in the first place? Further, if you are using your own opinions to criticize your teacher, then you are caught up in an endless distraction. Once you have a teacher, you must throw away all your own views and defer to him regardless of whether or not he suits you.[18]

Sounds terrifying, like a recipe for abuse. But why would Dōgen say this? For example, Taro tended to struggle with the idea in ACT of "acceptance," which suggests that psychological flexibility and mental health require the willingness to go through negative emotions and make space for them instead of trying to avoid them or control them.[19] He believed it was more thoroughgoing a transformation to *get rid* of negative feelings like attachment. However, how does his personal take on it function? While his idea has validity in other approaches, in ACT, the idea of "acceptance" is not just one byte of information—it is connected to the view of the mind in Relational Frame Theory, where we see that while we can "add" thoughts (relational frames), we cannot "delete" frames. And the very process of checking "has my negative emotion gone away?" actually reinstates the networks of these negative emotions.[20] It also connects to the view of mind and behavior in contextualism (that evolved from pragmatism, which we will see more of next chapter), where instead of a "mentalist" view that thinks that changes in the mind (controlling anger) will change behavior, it is actually changes in the behavioral context that allow long term changes to the mind.[21]

While I would not call it "blind obedience," I needed him to *trust* me as he learned the basics of ACT, learned Relational Frame Theory, learned the philosophy of contextualism, and *how it all comes together*. It takes time to teach all the parts and get them to come together. So this requires a negation, a momentary suspension of his existing modes of thought and the worldview it was in, to genuinely encounter a new way of seeing the world. (In my context, this suspension is much more time-bound than Zen—when I see that Taro-*kun* is able to understand one main network of ideas in a real way, I generally encourage him to question it.) Thus, there is a tricky relationship between "critical thinking" and learning a worldview, and we have to be careful that critical thinking comes *after* one has had sufficient exposure to a worldview (to criticize it intelligently) and not before that.

Practicing Negation

Going back to *Purifying Zen*, we see that while there is a cognitive aspect to realizing the truth that requires one to let go of one's biases, there is more to the path. Realization "does not arise from taking the standpoint of a realist ontology. It arises through raising epistemology via the higher standpoint of *practice*, and doing epistemology via the power of practice."[22] For Zen, this is the embodied practice of *zazen* (seated meditation), which in Dōgen was a practice of just-sitting, letting go of thoughts, and immersing oneself in the total experience of sitting-here-now.[23]

Zen practice brings us beyond words: "When one's own expression of the truth develops and becomes self-cultivation and strenuous *zazen*, it becomes the development of the highest and most stable seat, in which one does not speak . . ."[24] Again, Watsuji highlights the relational nature of sitting: "From the very beginning he advocated *single-minded zazen* as the core of Buddhist practice. This is because *zazen* was the means of self-cultivation for the patriarchs themselves, as well as their way of direct transmission."[25]

In learning ACT, as is true for all forms of "mindfulness in education," practice is an essential element. One can know, intellectually, that one is supposed to accept negative emotions. But when one is counseling a student, and that student begins to wallow in guilt and self-criticism and one gets uncomfortable just watching, the counselor can often shift the subject—performatively reinforcing avoidance instead of acceptance. Thus, ACT practitioners need to be able to go beyond a merely intellectual understanding of acceptance and practice acceptance themselves before (and while) counseling others.

There are various mindfulness exercises in ACT. To build acceptance, for example, one deliberately recalls a time when one felt difficult emotions like disappointment, sadness, or guilt. One then notices the different bodily sensations that come up (the knot in the throat, the tension in the abdomen). Without trying to change these emotions, one simply breathes with those sensations, loosening up *around* the tightness, and making space to *feel what is already there*. This helps people behave more flexibly despite the presence of negative emotions, rather than narrowing one's behavior in an escape to flee difficult feelings.

However, practices are difficult and can be misunderstood. For example, our team wrote a phenomenological paper that explores these challenges,[26] and one danger we saw is people using acceptance exercises in an effort to make the emotion *disappear* rather than accept it. How do we prevent this? Students meditate under supervision, discussing their practice with a guide who understands acceptance exercises. Just as a math teacher needs to know how students are cognitively understanding (or misunderstanding) a lesson, the guide needs to recognize the experience of ACT processes and experiential blocks that prevent embodied understanding. This recognition is made possible by the personal practice of the guide, as is required of all mindfulness teachers.[27]

Supervision, however, results in a very different teacher–student relationship. In this process of shared practice, I needed to listen to Taro's experiences of exercises, difficult childhood memories that get triggered by practices, and empathetically put myself in his place. This empathy awakened similar struggles I experienced when I was learning ACT, and I sometimes shared these with him to normalize his experience. That means that we both got to know each other in rather personal ways. Through this understanding, we were able to adjust and reframe exercises to help him learn acceptance in an experiential way.

This may seem strange for those used to a more scholastic presentation of academic material but this process is common in *practical* fields—from mindful education, to learning participant observation in anthropology, to learning a martial art. When an idea, embedded in a network of ideas, is connected to a network of *practices*, a student needs a certain amount of trust in a teacher to let go of existing thoughts and practices and learn via modeling. But to make good on this trust, the teacher needs to be that role model, to have a holistic understanding of the content, and an experiential understanding of the student undergoing formation that resonates with the teacher's personal experience.

Awakening to Self

For Dōgen, genuine transformative learning requires *negation* of self. But Watsuji says this in an almost despotic turn of phrase: "Clearly there is no concern at all for individuality here. Whether or not one imitates, whether or not one follows, grasping the eternal truth is the only important thing."[28] Analyzing the "*Raihai-tokuzui*" (礼拝得髄, Prostrating to the Marrow of Attainment) fascicle, Watsuji points out that this negation was not just for the self but for the entire social order: "Dōgen inflicts his crushing blow against all forms of discrimination happening in the world."[29] The value of the dharma makes social status, monastic status, and gender all irrelevant. It is by negating the "ego" on all levels that we make space for the realization of truth.

What is this truth that we awaken to? Watsuji struggled to articulate this part of Dōgen's insight. But he gets glimpses of it in discussing the "*Busshō*" (仏性, Buddha-Nature) fascicle, one of the fascicles of the *Shōbōgenzō* that has the most philosophical research.[30] Buddha-nature is our ability to become Buddha, to awaken to the eternal truth. However, Dōgen suggests that rather than people "having" Buddha-nature, "The totality of existence is buddha-nature.... This authentic, ineffable suchness permeates all living beings within and without; that is to say, it is all existences of buddha-nature."[31] Furthermore, rather than seeing awakening something that may happen in the future if the time comes, "Watsuji writes, 'Time' is total-existence. There is no point in time that is not time. 'If the time comes' means time has already come..."[32]

Watsuji, despite being a layman and coming before Dōgen specialists like Nishitani Keiji and Abe Masao, had already untangled a key aspect of Buddhist philosophy. What one awakens to in *zazen* is the truth that buddha-nature, the very truth we went out looking for, has been there all along, in the very being of beings, in the very happening of time. Watsuji writes, "Here, the difference between phenomenon and substance is totally smashed away. There is no difference at all between worldly meaning... and a higher meaning or primary meaning."[33] As Dōgen writes in the "*Genjōkōan*" (現成公按, The Realized Universe) fascicle, "To learn the Buddha Way is to learn ourselves. To learn ourselves is to forget ourselves. To forget ourselves is to be experienced by the myriad *dharmas*."[34] (Watsuji unfortunately did not go as far as

Abe, who deliberately uses the unity of Buddha-nature and emptiness to affirm reality as it is and expresses a fourth unity, directly between Buddha-nature and impermanence—which would have more clearly answered Watsuji's doubts.[35])

When one is confirmed by all things, all expressions of the eternal truth, all that was negated comes alive in a new light. Rather than substantial things to be clung to, things can be seen "as the self-expression of emptiness."

This means, however, a reinstatement of the individual self. Watsuji continues:

> Clearly there is no concern at all for individuality here.... This does not mean the disposal of individuality but rather the exultation of it.... Realization of the truth has its own distinctive personality. Only in the moment of realization does that individuality shine out as unique in all the universe.[36]

Watsuji explains this further, writing,

> Those who doubt their masters and do not devote themselves to the truth cannot realize the truth in the same way. But in the case of those who cast aside doubt and confusion and realize the Buddha's essence, that which allows one to attain realization in the end is nothing other than one's self. It is the utter sincere faith that emerges from the bottom of one's personality.[37]

In these two quotations, we see that one's surrender to one's master allows one to let go of ego, of selfishness. But this does not mean becoming a shell, an empty receptacle for one's master. Instead, it uncovers a selfless self, a unique and creative self that can engage reality in a different way.

The creativity of this engagement is most apparent in Dōgen's "*Busshō*" fascicle. I have introduced the essence of this fascicle, but now we turn to its method. To come up with his interpretation of all beings = buddha-nature, Dōgen was reinterpreting a line from the *Mahāparinirvāna-sūtra* that is usually read as "all living beings possess buddha-nature through and through."[38]

There is an interesting tension that shows here. Watsuji writes, "Dōgen, who was pious toward the founder of his religion, constructed his theory ... commenting on ... commentaries on buddha-nature."[39] In line with his obedience to his teacher and the patriarchs, Dōgen was deeply respectful of scripture. "But for Dōgen the question was not how these words are explained *by the Mahāparinirvāṇa-sūtra*. He treats these words of the Buddha independently of the sutras and goes digging down within them to find value."[40] Deep respect does not mean a loss of individuality but its creative negation, resulting in his view of buddha-nature as one with being, time, and emptiness. "Though his interpenetration of the sutra was his own, the fact that Dōgen understood the *Mahāparinirvāṇa-sūtra* and at the same time defied it indicates how well he understood Mahāyāna philosophy."[41]

The theory behind this is explained in the "Kattō" (葛藤, The Complicated) fascicle. In this text, Dōgen takes up the story of Bodhidharma calling his disciples and checking their understanding of Buddhism.

> The disciple Daofu replied, "Not attaching to letters and not detaching from them, I do what I should for the way."
>
> Bodhidharma said, "You have attained my skin."
>
> The nun Zongchi replied, "It is like seeing Akṣobhya Buddha's land just once and not seeing it again."
>
> Bodhidharma said, "You have attained my flesh."
>
> Daoyu replied, "The four great elements are originally empty and the five skandhas do not exist, so as I see it there is nothing to be attained."
>
> Bodhidharma said, "You have attained my bones."
>
> Finally Huike bowed three times and stood where he was. Bodhidharma said, "You have attained my marrow." As expected, Bodhidharma made Huike the second patriarch and transmitted the way to him.[42]

This is usually interpreted in a "measurement-centric" way—that skin, flesh, bones and marrow reflect different levels of depth of understanding. But Watsuji highlights Dōgen's different approach: Each disciple grasps the teaching differently, but these differences are *all* expressions of the truth. Dōgen says, "*The master's body-mind is the master with skin, flesh, bones, and marrow. It is not that the marrow is close and the skin is distant.*"[43] The differences between these views ought to be valued in themselves.

> [E]xpressing the truth can appear in thousands or even tens of thousands of different forms. However, if the expression of the truth appears in various forms, where should we recognize the ultimate Buddha-Dharma when we encounter contradicting and conflicting words? Dōgen replies that the Buddha-Dharma manifests itself just where all the differing views become mixed up in one another. The word he uses to express this thought is "entanglements." ... Dōgen insisted that this entanglement is the very thing to transmit the Buddha-Dharma truthfully.[44]

Or to put it simply, "each attains their own enlightenment."[45] And it is this respect for the singularity of each person that allows Dōgen to creatively transform even scripture.

*

Watsuji's Buddhist view of education, an education for awakening to emptiness, can be seen above. One begins on this journey to self-awakening by a deep doubt, a question that allows one to shake past the shackles of social convention and empty totality. However, walking this journey and letting go of oneself is not done alone but by trusting the guidance of a teacher. Through the personality of the teacher, one is able to learn a whole way of seeing and being-in-the-world. But after this process of negation of self, the social order, one's ways of thinking and doing, one awakens to the eternal truth and finds that it has been there all along—in the very impermanence of the being of beings and the happening of time, in an emptiness that is neither being nor nothing. In this emptiness, the self, its expressions, and its thoughts are reinstated as expressions of emptiness, allowing for each to have their own awakening, their own creative expression of this truth.

I tried to show through my relationship with Taro-*kun* that this philosophy of education is not reserved for spirituality alone. As is true for all practical fields, so long as we are not teaching fragmentary ideas but worldviews and practices, education needs to be mediated by someone who embodies these worldviews and practices. But when worldviews and practices begin to implicate all of life, we draw much closer to the content of *Purifying Zen*.

However, what we see here in both the student and the teacher is very different from what we saw in *Confucius* and *Ethics II*. Instead of highlighting the social self ("me" as student or as teacher) and the secondary socialization of roles, capacities, and masks, all of which are subordinated to a given social order, Watsuji is highlighting a dimension irreducible to the social order. What awakens for Dōgen and Watsuji is what G.H. Mead would refer to as "I"—that can step back from various social and institutional roles, criticize that order, and transform it creatively. In Mori Akira's philosophy, this is an "existential self"—not a determinate thing or role but a *process* of responding to reality, a locus of decision (*ketsudan* 決断) and self-reflection. Furthermore, this *Existenz* awakens by encountering another *Existenz*—not merely by being one role in a society of masks. Thus, Watsuji's theory is not reducible to "*nakayoshi*"—superficial harmony—like critics like Sakai Naoki say, but it has areas where it is able to emphasize this *personal* encounter, a face-to-face transmission (*menju*) where I and Thou stand *unmasked* before each other.

Watsuji's Journey with Dōgen

Watsuji has been criticized for having a superficial understanding of religion, and because of that, *Purifying Zen* has not been widely researched. However, in this section I want to step back and examine Watsuji as he was writing on Dōgen.

During Watsuji's time, Dōgen was mostly forgotten outside the Sōtō school of Zen. But for Watsuji, the spirit of Zen was lost within that sect as well:

[T]hese days to enter a Zen school is actually to distance oneself from Dōgen. This is because the sect that takes Dōgen as its founder is no longer solely concerned with the establishment of the kingdom of truth, but concentrates on building massive halls and pagodas and on the pursuit of the position of abbot.[46]

We find here a Watsuji not harmonizing with a social order but criticizing it in order to retrieve something he found fundamentally meaningful. "Because of this, Dōgen will become not Dōgen of one sect but Dōgen of the human race, not Dōgen the founder of a sect but our Dōgen. The reason I use such arrogant words is because I think that up until now Dōgen has been killed within the sect."[47]

Furthermore, Watsuji was not merely trying to write *about* Dōgen:

According to [Dōgen's] instructions, the ways to learn directly are to consult good teachers and to do strenuous *zazen*. What we read of him now is either his own writing or the writings of his students. In these [writings of Dōgen], his strong personality appears vividly between the lines. In other words, we are able to meet him there.[48]

Watsuji was trying to encounter Dōgen's *personality*. While he was limited to the writings of the master, he did not read Dōgen as a scholar or historian would but as one personally embarking on this path, within which Dōgen is his *master*.

Furthermore, his attempt to encounter his master has resonances with Watsuji's personal life. Watsuji's reminiscences on his middle school days have recently been made available in English (and soon his whole autobiography will be published as well) and what one finds is that it is peppered with reminiscences of his teachers—both ones he loved and ones he did not[49]—in a degree of detail that far exceeds my own capacity to remember my own.

Watsuji was deeply influenced by his principal, Inazō Nitobe, and his university professor, Raphael von Koeber. But the greatest influence on Watsuji is the novelist Natsume Sōseki (1867–1916). In several essays, Watsuji shares the story of his relationship with his *Sensei*. At first, Watsuji admired Sōseki from a distance, when the latter was a teacher of other classes in Tokyo First Higher School (Ichikō). He started reading Sōseki's literary works, and eventually wrote him in 1913. In this period, Watsuji's relationship was with a persona—*Sensei*—with a projective empathy bordering on adolescent infatuation. But their relationship would deepen beyond this mask when Watsuji joined the Thursday Club—an intellectual salon of sorts that met in Sōseki's house. Sometimes seniors even challenged and criticized Sōseki, and we see Watsuji watching, seeing how his *Sensei* would take it (quite well, it seems).

Towards the end of the essay, Watsuji writes about meeting Sōseki's son in Germany, hearing about the family conflict that his *Sensei* had, struggling with the son's hatred for his father. How could Sōseki the *Sensei* and Sōseki the father/husband be so different?[50] Here, we see Watsuji going beyond mere projective empathy, beyond mere masks and given social roles, to a living personality struggling with reality.

What he would learn from this living personality is telling:

> When I realized this [the family problems of Sōseki], I felt inclined to reflect meaningfully again on the breakdown of marital life as depicted in *Grass on the Wayside*. Neither the protagonist nor the wife in that novel are bad people. However, they are both selfish and do not honestly try to understand and care for each other.[51]

In his obituary for Sōseki, Watsuji writes:

> One cannot understand *Sensei*'s personality without thinking about his passion for justice and his effort to drive out selfishness from love. Sensei could not forgive individuals for loving themselves even though self-love is naturally the strongest form of love. Sensei was constantly vigilant against such selfishness within himself. As a keen observer of human psychology, he expressed to us how this selfishness constituted a grave dark side of human nature.[52]

What Watsuji learned from Sōseki the person was selflessness. Graham Mayeda suggests Sōseki influenced Watsuji's views of seeing the interpenetration of the experience of self and group, the tension within relations, the concreteness of relational ethics, and the importance of transcendence,[53] and likely resulted in Watsuji's turn from western existentialism to eastern ethics.

But there is an interesting overlap with Dōgen:

> Dōgen says body-mind must be abandoned for the sake of the Dharma [the truth of Buddhism]. This abandonment of body-mind has extremely important meaning for "loving thy neighbor as thyself." The greatest force obstructing love is selfishness, which takes root in what Dōgen calls body-mind; this can be nothing other than attachment to self. When one throws away all desires to preserve one's body-mind, empties the self, and lets oneself enjoy coming into contact with others, then love freely flows with the force of one's whole personality.[54]

In *Purifying Zen*, Watsuji attempts to directly encounter the personality of Dōgen, and, from that personality, uncover the value of selflessness and love, just as he had with Sōseki.

Furthermore, the question of "eternal truth" was not merely Dōgen's. In the preface, Watsuji writes,

> [W]hy do humanity's religions not exhibit a single form, but rather appear in various "particularized forms"? And second, why do these particularized forms have "history"? Religious truth is the root of all of these particularized forms, of all their discriminations and all their values. This cannot be apprehended by the "worldly wisdom" that deals in classification. It can only be felt through direct experience... I often get closest to it in moments of prayer to "the unknowable being." ... It is my life and the life of the universe.... It is the eternal now, which can be grasped in this moment.... I believe in the idea of *logos*. I believe in the idea that the life of the universe is constantly creating.[55]

Watsuji himself was seeking the eternal truth.

When one reads Watsuji's discussion of "Dōgen's 'Truth,'" he really struggles. "Though I try to explain these ideas clearly, I could never get beyond even the outer boundaries of this 'truth.'"[56] He is not just being modest—his following discussions are a mess. But as I pieced together his explanation of the four fascicles, what I found was interesting: In "*Raihai-tokuzui*," he shows the equality of people in their ability to attain the dharma, with their value coming from the dharma itself. But at the same time, he argues that dharma does not exist as a separate entity from people. In "*Busshō*," we saw the unity of buddha-nature with all beings in time. In "*Dōtoku*" (道得, Expressing the Truth), expressions of the way are seen as meaningful only in union with face-to-face transmission. And true language is seen as the self-expression of *logos*. Finally, in "*Kattō*," people's grasp of the truth via their own complications is one with the universal truth. The *ideé* is expressed and dialectically develops with each complication.

To put it simply, what he is grasping at is none other than the unity of the universal (dharma, truth, buddha-nature) and the particular (individuals, expressions, impermanent beings)—not in a merely intellectual level, but a personal sense. ("I believe in the idea of *logos* . . .") Watsuji himself was unclear on this point, but my own interpretation of it is as follows: if we negate particulars and do not see them as substantial, we learn to let go of them and our attachment to them. This results in seeing the eternal truth. But this eternal truth, emptiness, does not exist except in its self-expression via particulars. Thus, each particular is able to come to light, not as things to be clung to, but as expressions of emptiness.

Structurally, this has much in common with Nishida's view in "I-Thou": "At the bottom of the self-determination of our individual self, we arrive at absolute nothingness."[57] It is also similar to Nishitani Keiji's "standpoint of emptiness," wherein all reality is seen as empty and at the same time as a rich expression of nothingness: ". . . not that the self is empty, but that emptiness is the self; not that things are empty, but that emptiness is things."[58] Watsuji's insight would connect to deeply religious insights in the next several decades. And not only that, he himself would develop these insights for the next twenty years or more, developing the idea of emptiness as the negation of individuality and totality, as the formless form behind all cultural expressions, as the *logos* behind each moment of history. *Purifying Zen* was the path of Watsuji's own education for awakening—of negating totality, of encountering his teachers and the force of their personalities, and his awakening to a genuine sense of the unity of the one and the many.

The Bounds of the Teacher–Student Relationship

I imagine that for many of my readers, one great doubt in your mind right now is whether this kind of education is possible. Students awakening, really? Nishida scholar Takaya Shōko suggests that in educational applications of the Kyoto School of Philosophy, it is always necessary to consider what awakening means in an educational context, and if educators can or should have anything to do with it.[59] Perhaps some readers feel uncomfortable with the degree of closeness between me and Taro. Do we really have to know that much about our students, their trauma, their intellectual and emotional habits? And also, the idea of a demand for mastery over the whole *Gestalt* of ideas and practices may seem all too heavy.

Mori Akira's philosophy of education allows us to clarify much of this. In *The Philosophical Quest for Educational Ideals*, Mori gives three types of teachers.[60] Scholastic teachers are those focused on simply conveying the requisite information and skills, thus allowing for a focus on qualification. In this kind of education, critical thinking can be very helpful, because it helps students make sure that they fully understand the information, and that the information they are getting is from the right sources. However, while scholastic teaching has its uses, it also has its limitations. Does a scholastic teacher really help you *dwell* in a practical nexus?

The *master* is different in that the master embodies the truth. Mori got his image of the master from Wilhelm Dilthey. The master is one who understands the nexus of ideas (what Dilthey called the "spiritual nexus"). I remember my English professor in university—rather than just being able to memorize standard interpretations of Shakespeare's sonnets, she lived and breathed Shakespeare, she could feel it in her bones. And when she spoke of Shakespeare, she was not just giving information but drawing us into a world, to participate in a particular way of inhabiting, of dwelling. She had "pedagogic love," seeing the student as more than just a customer in a school enterprise, but a human being, with their own experiences, struggling to grow.

While many of us might agree that the idea of the scholastic teacher is limited—How would you feel if someone said you were merely a peddler of information?—the problem for many is that the idea of the "master" seems impossible. Any field, like ACT, is so complicated. There are so many elements like practices, efficacy studies, theoretical underpinnings, laboratory experiments, philosophical underpinnings ... Can one really master them all and know the entire *Gestalt* of ACT? Furthermore, can one know all the practices and do them enough to fully embody "psychological flexibility" and be a mindful teacher? It seems impossible! And the same is true for pretty much any field, where the quantity of research has burgeoned beyond count.

However, Mori Akira suggests that perhaps it is not simply a matter of having too much research but a fundamental shift to the postmodern condition. In the medieval world Watsuji depicts—a world of masters and disciples—the world still seemed bound by meta-narratives of faith and religion, a sense of certainty about the meaning of life. However, do we still have that certainty today? Mori suggests that while there may be pockets of religiosity in different forms scattered throughout society, the mythic sense of meaning is no longer shared throughout society. As such, communal social life has become more and more secularized and anthropocentric.[61]

And yet despite this anthropocentrism, we have no consensus as to the meaning of the human being. In *Introduction to Philosophy of Education: The Limit Situation of Philosophy of Education* (1948), Mori discusses the fracture of transcendence (where we seek meaning). Many seek meaning only in material conditions, wealth, and health (outward transcendence). Others seek the authenticity of human existence in rationality or God (upward transcendence), and others who seek it in relatively particular cultural-historical life (downward transcendence). And there are those who refuse transcendence altogether.[62]

What does this mean for education? While education has always presupposed the formation of a "true human being,"[63] we no longer know what that is. Jaspers, the existential philosopher who was

Mori's main dialogue partner, writes about "boundary situations" in *Philosophy II*:

> Situations like the following: that I am always in situations, that I cannot live without struggling and suffering; that I cannot avoid guilt; that I must die—these are what I call boundary situations. They *never change*, except in appearance. There is *no way to survey them* in existence, no way to see anything behind them. They are like a wall we run into, a wall on which we founder. We cannot modify them; all that we can do is to make them lucid, but without explaining or deducing them from something else. They go with existence itself.[64]

To this, Mori provides an interesting perspective to existentialism—in addition to thrownness, suffering, guilt, and death, *education itself* is a boundary situation. As human beings, we need education to *become human* (*ningen seisei*), a point famously argued by Immanuel Kant. But at the same time, we cannot have a final answer to what it means to be human.[65] This places educators in a paradox between pedagogic enthusiasm and despair:

> In this way, while we feel that as human beings, becoming a teacher of humanity is slothful pride and a failure to know one's place, we also are moved and try to affirm its necessity in reality and in principle. . . . At times, one feels moved by the sacred mission to be the teacher of humankind, showing the human pathos of pedagogic enthusiasm. Other times, one feels the impossibility of a human being educating a human being and one is petrified before this sacred mission, instead hoping to walk the path of self-education while heavily criticizing oneself. Educate the other, or educate the self? . . . Here, one becomes self-aware (*jikaku*) of the "limit situation toward philosophy of education" in the direction of subjective reflection.[66]

Perhaps some found my being something like a master to Taro-*kun* a kind of hubris, as if I have the right to teach someone how to see the world and act. Within the bounds of a specific practice like ACT, maybe it is possible to be a master. But as this broadens into questions of what it means to live life, can I really reduce Taro's experience of life to mine? Mori would say no.

But this postmodern situation—the confusions of education, the fragmentation of the meaning of life—can result in people withdrawing into the scholastic model of teaching. In the effort to avoid hubris, teachers can end up avoiding *imposition*: "I'm not saying this is the truth—this is what the book says." "You don't have to believe me, this is just what I think." But from Mori's point of view, this may inadvertently result in avoiding *engagement* with the struggle of people in trying to help them find their ways in life, and when necessary calling them out when their existing habits keep them from encountering a new world they are trying to learn.

Thus, what Mori calls us to is a third model beyond the scholastic teacher and the master—the Socratic teacher, the midwife, the gadfly. He gets this from Jaspers' *The Idea of the University* (1959):

> In Socratic education, the teacher and his student ought to stand on the same level. Both are meant to be free. No hard and fast educational system exists here, rather endless questioning and ultimate ignorance in the face of the absolute. Personal responsibility is carried to its utmost and is nowhere alleviated. Education is a "midwifery," in which the student is helped to give birth to his abilities and powers.[67]

While Jaspers was hesitant to see this as occurring in actual education, Mori sought to make this more central in the field of educational science and our practice as teachers in schools. In this, he spoke of education as journeying together:

> Our ancestors already spoke of education as teachers and students "journeying together" (*dōgyō* 同行, lit. to go + the same,) and practiced this kind of education. The teacher who is thought to be relatively superior to the student does not lead. Before the absolute, all relative distinctions are erased. Here we have the confession of the experiential belief that such a teacher and student both walk and are made to walk the path of rising and liberation by the absolute.[68]

The image Mori chooses here is rich. *Dōgyō* is a Buddhist term, referring to how all those on the Shikoku pilgrimage are walking with Kūkai. One might also translate it as a "shared pilgrimage." In this shared pilgrimage,

I see the student's process of becoming human, a path with dilemmas before which I find myself equally lost. And while I cannot lead them on this path, I can journey with them as they seek what it means to live a meaningful life.

While existentialism (especially in Jean-Paul Sartre and Nietzsche) is often seen as individualist and solitary, Mori and Jaspers show that there is a more relational (*aidagarateki* 間柄的) path to *Existenz*. When teacher and student, I and Thou, connect not on the level of "me" but on the level of "I/*Existenz*," we have a different kind of communion, an existential communion. In this relationship, "'the self and the other self create each other in turn,' and while doing so, 'come to terms with themselves (*jiko o tsukamu* 自己をつかむ)."[69] In this encounter, I and Thou are engaged in "loving struggle," where people do not merely statically accept each other, but dynamically challenge each other and support each other as they discover themselves. This is a recurring theme in the Kyoto School. Mori refers to his mentor, Tanabe Hajime, suggesting that while those more advanced along the religious path help others, before the absolute, they remain mindful of their inherent equality.[70]

Watsuji also had a similar, less hierarchical view of awakening that he discusses in the process of linked-verse poetry. In "Japanese Literary Arts and Buddhist Philosophy" (1935), Watsuji explored various aesthetic expressions of Buddhism. One art form he highlights is *renga*, where an artist composes one verse and others respond. When one artist composes a verse, the other must empty themselves and genuinely connect with that verse so that "each verse is linked to the one before in taste and feeling."[71] This shared process becomes a deep sense of mutual connection: "[G]roup creation will be possible only when the linking of one verse to another becomes, at the same time, a bond between one person and another."[72]

Watsuji directly links this art form to the dual-negative structure of his ethics:

However, the communion between person and person does not mean their becoming merely one. It is only through the fact that people are unique individuals that a cooperation between "person and person" can be realized.... A *renga* can be created organically only through the practical realization of dialectical unity of the individual and the whole by the composers.... It is by means of attaining emptiness, which each remains individual to the last, or in other words, by means of movements based on emptiness by persons who have attained their own fulfillment, that the company will be complete and interest for creativity will be roused. Viewed in this light, the composition of *renga* itself is extremely similar to the practice of Zen.[73]

*

I have been many kinds of teachers to Taro-*kun*, not as a matter of ambition, but as a response to the kind of teacher he needed me to be. I have been a scholastic teacher, giving him information on ACT and the field around it. When his questions grew deeper and he tried to learn a whole worldview, I tried to be a more holistic guide, seeing his worldview and where he struggled to learn things like emotional acceptance. And I guided him too with the practices that allowed him an experiential understanding, demanding the same pedagogic tact that Dilthey requires from one who would guide the experience of another.

But I remember one time, he asked me, "Why is it that the more I see the truth of how people suffer, the more people withdraw from me? It's like I'm living in a world where people say we need the truth, but nobody really wants it, and they shun those who actually seek it." I looked away and I remembered how, when I realize the core struggles that keep my clients locked in suffering, I often find it impossible to share these insights because it triggers people's defenses or makes them fall into despair. I told him, "Well someday maybe you'll tell me."

In that moment, there was no teacher, no student, no master, no disciple—just two people asking difficult questions. Some days, I still dispense information, I still form experience. But recently, more and more of his struggles are like this. And so we journey, together, fellow pilgrims along the way, trying to find our way together back to ourselves. And sometimes, it is he who is the teacher, and not I.

Allow me to end with a few practical takeaways from this example. If we take "master" and "midwife" as abstract ideals and clear stages, we might feel overwhelmed and self-critical by our incapacity to meet these ideals and how far our institutions are from supporting them. However, if we apply these more flexibly and opportunistically (a mindset I clarify in the next chapter), one might find that there are small openings in our everyday life that allow for these ideas to grow roots.

First, one must realize that these ideals of teaching are not fixed but a response from one person to another. It would be dangerous to insist on being a master or a midwife to someone who was unwilling or not ready for it. Rather than applying these ideals top-down in basic teacher training, all I am hoping for is to nudge people toward increased *awareness*. With the awareness that education is a shared process of becoming human, one notices times when one is called to give more than just information. There will be times when one is called to be a "partial master"—where one embodies a certain aspect of the path, but still in a holistic way. (For example, I have a high personal mastery of ACT principles as applied to educational counseling, but not for clinical cases like schizophrenia or psychopathy!) And where mastery ceases to function, one might be called to be more of a midwife. Second, these ideas apply not just to teacher–student but can apply even between students, between teachers, between parents … Third, rather than merely criticizing institutions for their failings, we might look at different institutions to see what we can learn from them to improve. For example, teachers have a practicum system that perhaps applied philosophy has a lot to learn from. Therapists have a system of supervising how to understand personality (case conceptualization) that might be partially integrated in further learning for teachers. In doing this, we might find that despite the despair of postmodernity, there are still people we can befriend who are out there taking responsibility for human becoming.

Part Two

Mori Akira

4

The Practical-Pragmatic Nexus

In the first half of this book that focused on Watsuji Tetsurō, we have seen two contrasting images of education. On one hand, we have a more Confucian vision of education as *finding one's place*, that is focused on going beyond selflessness in orienting oneself to others and to one's community, a relationship that is stabilized by various social roles, forms, and virtues. On the other hand, we have a more Buddhist vision of education as *awakening to oneself*, which transcends selflessness in directly encountering the personality of another, awakening, and learning to transform the very fabric of society. These two views are not polar opposites—there is a demand for obedience and self-negation in Buddhism and a demand for personal discernment in Confucianism as well. But like the two sides of yin and yang, although there is a spot of the opposite in each side, they have clearly different emphases (see Figure 4.1).

Many researchers like Sakai Naoki and Bernard Bernier have criticized Watsuji for the more traditionalist side, ignoring the fact that the more radical side does exist within Watsuji's work.[1] When reading

Figure 4.1 Yin and Yang.[2]

Watsuji's writing in the 1930s and 1940s, there is a tendency to overlook his Buddhist work from the 1920s, despite the Buddhist terminology and imagery he continues to use.[3] Other researchers, myself included,[4] have criticized Watsuji for vacillating inconsistently between this more conservative and this more progressive side. But thinking as a human being, really, which is better, education as learning one's place, or education as awakening to oneself? Can you imagine a student who *always* engages their groups transformatively, critically rethinking *everything* the group presupposes? That is counter-productive filibustering. Or can you imagine a student who *always* finds their place and never deviates from it? That would result in total stagnation. There is something distorted about these images, something inhuman (*hi-ningen-teki*) about it, and it is thoroughly dysfunctional. There are times that call for learning one's place, sitting down, shutting up, and learning the rhythm of the world around you (something I personally needed when I first arrived in Japan, constantly being the annoying foreigner). But there are times that call for empowerment, finding one's voice, and learning how to engage society critically (as I find I am doing more now, as tenured faculty).

It is a *good* thing that Watsuji has both of these images of education, without resolving either of them to each other. Seen together, the Confucian vision of "learning one's place" and the Buddhist vision of "awakening to oneself" form Watsuji's education for emptiness, where the flexible back-and-forth and mutual emptying between individual and relational existence allows us to be genuinely *ningen* (see Figure 4.2).

Figure 4.2 The mutual negation of *ningen*.

However, there are two problems that remain. First, if we look at his *Confucius* or his *Shamon Dōgen*, when he talks about totality, the individual seems almost completely effaced by the lure of roles and social coherence. And when he talks about the individual in Buddhism, it seems like individual awakening is enough, without really considering the transformation of roles and institutions. If one looks at the yin-yang diagram, it is crucial that the white side have a little circle, a "window" to the black side, and vice-versa. Watsuji tended to lose sight of these windows almost as if he could not hold on to his own insight of a *tensional* dual-structure.

I think we need to make Watsuji's "windows" on each side of finding one's place and awakening to oneself clearer. This means that in contradistinction to common readings of Watsuji's ethics, we need to *actively* read his Buddhist ideas into his later more Confucian ideas.[5] This means that we should think about the I ("personality") behind the roles (*shikaku*, "masks") when considering learning one's place, resisting the tendency of social coherence to eliminate alterity. At the same time, when thinking about awakening to oneself, we must avoid closing that up into a merely individual quest or a closed monastic community. Instead, we need to highlight how individual awakening transforms roles, institutions, and society via widening circles, linking *Purifying Zen* to the insights in *Ethics III*.

This brings us to the second problem: What are the criteria for a healthy movement of double-negation? When is it time for yin to shift over to yang and vice-versa? For example, when the individual has a novel philosophical insight (a window from totality to individuality), we need to differentiate between what is genuinely creative (and thus worth negating the status quo over) and what is simply bizarre. Conversely, when the group demands a certain compromise from the individual, we need to differentiate between healthy compromise and needless coercion.

This chapter bridges from Part I to Part II. I will begin by examining ways in which Watsuji tried to answer the question above by considering the *objective* side of *ningen sonzai*. Then, I shift my focus to Mori Akira, the focal point of Part II. Through Mori's view of pragmatism, I show the limits of Watsuji's understanding of "objectivity." Then, I show what a pragmatic approach would look like in the case of individual learning and in that of social change.

Cooperating in a Shared Milieu

The dual-negative structure of individuality and totality is not just about a dialectical view of meaning in human existence but is connected to the demands of living together in a material world. In other words, Watsuji combines the non-dualism of individuality and totality with the non-dualism of subject and object. In Watsuji's most widely-read and oft-translated book, *Climate and Culture* (*Fūdo: Ningengakuteki Kōsatsu*, 1935), he wrote,

> It was in the early summer of 1927 when I was reading Heidegger's *Being and Time* in Berlin that I first came to reflect on the problem of climate/milieu.... I found it hard to see why, when time had thus been made to play a part in the structure of subjective existence, at the same juncture space was not also postulated as part of the basic structure of existence.... I perceived herein lay the limitations of Heidegger's work...[6]

Influenced by his trip to Europe and his observations on the different climates and how they seem to shape culture, Watsuji was intent on expanding philosophical anthropology beyond time to consider space and our environment, which go beyond subjectivity to objective material conditions. And so he focused on the idea of "*fūdo*" (風土, wind + earth, the original title of the book in Japanese). Geoffrey Bownas translated this word as "climate," but as Berque suggests, it is better translated as "milieu."[7] Watsuji explains the word as follows:

> I use our word *fūdo*, which means literally, "wind and earth", as a general term for the natural environment of a given land, its climate, its weather, the geological and productive nature of the soil, its topographic

and scenic features. . . . It is not without reason that I wish to treat this natural environment of man not as "nature" but as "climate [or milieu]" in the above sense.[8]

Watsuji distinguishes milieu from "natural environment" because he wanted to capture milieu as something both objective (like nature) and subjective (as something lived in a meaningful way).

This is most clear in his well-known "phenomenology of the cold." On one hand, the cold is a subjective experience. The cold can affect one's mood, how we see people ("a cold personality"). Furthermore, this is a shared experience, as we talk about the weather in set ways, "*Kyō wa samui desu ne!*" (A cold day, isn't it?) But at the same time, it is not merely something to be subjectively contemplated, but to be objectively *responded to*. "In these experiences [of the cold] we do not look towards the 'subject'. We stiffen, or put on warm clothes, or draw near the brazier when we feel cold."[9] And collectively, our style of clothing (puffy quilted jackets) and our architecture (the steeply slanted roofs in Hokkaido) show our active response to the cold. Thus, the phenomena of the cold show the dual-structure not only of individuality-totality but subject-object.[10]

Despite the uniqueness of these ideas, this book had a mixed reception in academic circles, and would need to be further developed. In *Ethics as the Study of Ningen*, Watsuji would pick up the key idea of *Climate and Culture* and develop it with greater rigor, resulting in the idea of the "practical act nexus" (*jissenteki kōiteki renkan* 実践的行為的連関)—the mesh we live in as we live cooperatively in communities.

As mentioned in Chapter 1, the practical nexus was originally based on Wilhelm Dilthey's hermeneutic philosophy. Dilthey's *psychical* nexus suggests that people are united by sharing the *Geist* of a culture such that meanings and signification are held in common to create a subjective sense of oneness.[11] In Watsuji's *practical* nexus, he adds the objective side: People cooperate as embodied beings in a shared space, forming interconnections that are both objective (shared behavior) and subjective (shared meaning).

Watsuji developed this idea through the history of thought. Dilthey's view resonates with Georg Hegel's dialectics of individuality and totality. But they both tended to be idealist. Watsuji tried to balance this out by turning to philosophical materialism:

> Grasping the human as an acting subject (*shutai* 主体), as sensitive activity, and placing that within the social nexus, is none other than grasping the human (*hito* 人) as *ningen*.... Considering [Feuerbach's] theses six and eight, such a person is none other than *ningen* as the practical act nexus. In such a way, Marx refused materialism that sees the human being as a *natural object* and stressed instead subjective existence of *ningen* as activity and practice (*katsudō jissen* 活動実践).[12]

Through Feuerbach, Watsuji pushed philosophy to consider not only reality as it is thought but material reality as it is directly sensed. But viewing material reality passively like a detached scientist is not enough to capture the lived experience of life. Through Marx, Watsuji argued that we use our senses to *act* upon matter like engaged engineers rather than mere observers. One deals with objectivity, for example, not merely by feeling the cold but by dressing up in warm clothes or building houses in a certain way.

With this, he sought a method for looking at human reality in an individual/total and subjective/objective way. Watsuji attempted to construct a method for looking at the human being both from an individual and a group unit of analysis, and looking at both empirical and subjective aspects:

> Thus, the hermeneutic method as the method of ethics, consists in grasping the dynamic structure of *ningen*'s *sonzai* through its most basic everyday expressions. *Ningen*'s *sonzai*, in its everydayness, constantly manifests itself in the practical connections of life, expression, and understanding; and yet it does not become aware of this as expression. Hence, the effort to realize it as expression is a philosophical activity that assumes the form of a hermeneutic method.[13]

In this hermeneutics, rather than remaining merely in the world of ideas, one looks at everyday expressions like roads and transportation or postal systems and communication. And one tries to grasp, from these objective realities, their subjective meaning for both individuals and groups. The goal is to be able to grasp the "practical understanding" (*wake*) that is implicit in the expression. (For more on Watsuji's hermeneutics, see Maraldo.)[14]

Watsuji thus meant to balance materiality with ideas, the objective with the subjective. Watsuji shared this overall project with other members of the Kyoto School like Nishida, who also attempted to see both the subjective side of the historical world and the objective side of the material world in the dialectics of mutual formation of the individual and environment in "I and Thou."[15]

Educationally, these ideas suggest that being relational (as in Confucian education) and individual (as stressed in Buddhist education) is not simply about ideals but about the demands of living life in a shared environment. In other words, as Jin-*kun*'s teacher, I know he needs more "finding his place" because he needed to cooperate better with his teammates. In the same way, I know Junko-*san* and Taro-*kun* need more "education for awakening" because they were learning to express themselves and stand up for themselves in their communities.

The Praxis of Social Change

What does it mean to fully consider someone's relational context, both subjectively and objectively? In Chapter 2, we examined some connections between Watsuji and G.H. Mead. This comes from Steve Odin's *The Social Self in Zen and American Pragmatism*, which suggests that both Watsuji and Mead had a radically relational view of the self, both rooted in the worldview of contextualism, where the acting self is always continuous with its relational context and the environment around it.[16] But while Watsuji is contextualist and tried to consider the praxis of objective life, is he a *pragmatist*?

The difference becomes clear when we return to Watsuji's discussion of social change in *Ethics III*, which we briefly discussed in the end of

Chapter 2. After Japan's defeat in the Second World War, Watsuji wrote of the need to transform Japan. He reiterated that each nation had its own uniqueness that allowed it to contribute to and cooperate creatively with other nations and the international community as a whole. However, that uniqueness also gave each nation limitations. The process of overcoming these limitations is "not a simple task like the training of an individual, but an extremely large historical task of complex multi-faceted revolution of national culture via complex ethical organization."[17]

For Watsuji, in order to initiate social change, "the proper cognition of their nation's particularity needs to be realized among the mass of citizens... Furthermore, from within this cognition, the strong demand to overcome the limits contained within this national individuality must arise."[18] A very big impetus for this is the encounter with other cultures. Watsuji suggests that as we encounter cultures, some with greater scientific development, others with greater artistic development, we realize the limitations of our culture and have the opportunity to learn from other cultures.

When the nation is able to realize its limitations, "[E]ventually this will call forth a genius who can create culture anew."[19] This leader takes the perspective of the group and intuits shared values, enabling that individual to lead the group to its realization. However, Watsuji saw this process of social change as often resulting in conflict, even the suppression and martyrdom of those who would try to lead.[20]

What are these values and directions intuited by leaders? Watsuji writes,

> Nations with backward civilizations must become self-aware of the backwardness reflected in the particularities of [their] morals, and *must revolutionize their morality* through the effort of attaining civilization. A nation that has climatic particularities within its social structure should reflect if their particularities are a plus or a minus for the realization of the way of ethical life (*jinrin no michi* 人倫の道), and *should strive to overcome those limitations.*[21]

For example, he discusses how true scholarship needs the pursuit of truth and not worldly gain, and that Japan needs to improve academic culture throughout the nation. Unfortunately, Meiji culture had a utilitarian interest in academic matters, and thus only focused on usefulness rather than "pursuit of truth."[22] It was in light of this problem that he proposed an education for more critical thinking for oneself, that we have taken up in Chapters 1–3.

However, what struck me was that while Watsuji explores many ideals like "pursuit of truth," "rational thinking," and "filial piety," and he has many musts and shoulds about Japan, he does not seem to point out any objective consequences of failing to meet these ideals, nor any material changes that will arise from achieving them. Furthermore, other than articulating his own ideals, which clearly differed from others with more utilitarian views of scholarship, he did not seem to have any criteria that he could point to, outside of the coherence of his own vision, in order to convince or build consensus with those with differing views. This suggests that while Watsuji argued for the non-duality of subjectivity and objectivity, when faced with actual problems, his discussion tended to simply impose subjective ideals on objective reality, without really responding to practical contexts and consequences.

Pragmatic Learning

How else might one consider objective material reality? From here on in this book, I will shift the focus to Mori Akira. As we saw in the Introduction, Mori Akira began his writing career with *The Philosophical Quest for Educational Ideals* (1948), a book where he began his lifelong dialogue with existentialism. Existentialism has much in common with Watsuji and the Kyoto School in that it is a kind of "philosophy of awakening" (*jikakushugi* 自覚主義). Like Watsuji's work on Dōgen, Mori highlighted the awakening to existential self. And like Watsuji's work on Confucius, he tried to consider self-awareness in relation to relationships and socio-political life. This part of his work had a primarily idealistic focus.

However, after that book, Mori began working in earnest on the pragmatism of John Dewey (1859–1952), with occasional reference to other pragmatists like William James (who Nishida drew the idea of pure experience from) and G.H. Mead. At first, he had intended to critique pragmatism. But instead, he realized that it was his own understanding of Dewey that was superficial, due to tendencies in Japan to focus on the application of Dewey in education without fully understanding the empirical and pragmatic worldview where that application was conceptualized. And to the contrary, it was the idealistic tendencies of the Kyoto School that needed to be critically reconsidered.[23]

Mori wrote two books on pragmatism, *John Dewey* (1951) and *Empiricism and Educational Principles* (1951). In the latter, he explains the origin of the term pragmatism:

> Kant made a distinction between the concepts of "*praktisch*" and "*pragmatisch*," and considering ideals like moral law, God, soul, etc., arise in the realm of the *a priori*, he asserted that *praktisch* referred only to this a priori realm. In contrast, *pragmatisch* refers to the quality in the realm of behavior according to experience.[24]

Here we finally answer the question of why Watsuji has no clear criteria for when to do which side of the double-negation. When we look at Watsuji's view of social change, we see that his practical act nexus is *praktisch*—it looks at ideas and compares reality to ideals, with "practice" being an action upon reality from a priori theories. However, *pragmatisch*—pragmatism like Dewey's and Mead's—suggests that thinking is a posteriori, a direct extension of one's experience of material reality that serves to improve one's intercourse with reality. Here, there is no dualism between the subjective and the objective. From this point of view, in contrast to Odin, I argue that Watsuji is practical and relational, like Mead, but he is *not* pragmatic, and so he cannot really tell you when to move the cycle of double-negation in a certain direction.

First, let us examine what pragmatic learning might mean for the individual. In *The Practicality and Inwardness of Education* (1955) and *Philosophical Anthropology of Education*, Mori criticized problems surrounding learning in Japan with points similar to Watsuji's. But Mori sketches out a different *process* of learning to deal with those problems:

1. Perception, 2. symbols, these connect to 3. the actions of the perceptual motor system, and this develops into 4. meaningful action, which divides into two types: 5. problem-solving learning and 6. symbolic learning, and together, [5 and 6] give rise to self-awareness (*jikaku no kakusei*).[25]

The first five steps come from Dewey's pragmatism, which sees thinking as part of action and evolutionary adaptation to one's environment rather than mere idealization. In *How We Think*, Dewey points out that thinking starts from the perception of some difficulty, a real problem. With the use of observation (1) one notices real challenges one faces and employs symbols (2, thinking) to clarify the nature of the problem.[26] When Watsuji looked at problems in education, he began entirely from subjective discomfort: "How is this education fulfilling its essence as a pursuit of truth?" In contrast, Mori did not look merely at a deviation from ideals but practical consequences like how totalitarian tendencies in education tend to make students unlikely to participate actively as citizens in their self-governance, or how capitalism tended to create a palpable sense of alienation and meaninglessness in students competing for entrance examinations.[27] These are not merely subjective discontentment but empirically verifiable by youth voter turnout or youth suicide statistics.

Having clarified the nature of the problem, one then tries out possible solutions (3), in a tandem of perception, symbolic thinking, and action.[28] This process of intelligent trial-and-error result in meaningful action (4). For example, Mori tried out different ways of relating to his students to help them be more agentic and have a greater sense of meaning in their education, and learning from his successes and failures, came up with models for education that we will see in Chapter 6. Watsuji's ideals never even reached this level of possible "actionables," trial-and-error, and monitored consequences.

Meaningful action is key to pragmatism. Here, we have learning that is not merely about what "makes sense" but about *selection via consequences*—the heart of Darwin's evolutionary theory that subsequently shaped pragmatism.[29] Evolution is not merely about genetics but any process where you have variation (ex. varying lengths of giraffe necks), selection (longer-necked giraffes get more food), and retention (better-fed giraffes reproduce more). Learning is an evolutionary process in that one has different attempts, both enacted and simulated (variation), and these meet with differing levels of success (selection), and successful behaviors are learned (retention).

However, pragmatism must not be reduced to a shallow process of trial-and-error, and must connect to problem-solving learning (5). This learning points to the intelligence of meaningful action. For example, as Mori tried different ways of teaching his students, he emptied the tendency to mere routine (merely repeating things that seem to work) and moved beyond surface phenomena to conceptualize *why* it worked (a linking of induction to deduction). The succeeding chapters will show an overall theory of what gives meaning to education—things like connection to personal experience, identity formation, identity change, and so on—which comes from Mori's pragmatic engagements.

These first five steps are Mori's contribution to the Kyoto School from pragmatism—with a view of ideals and philosophy built not top-down from abstractions but bottom-up from our day-to-day engagements and problem-solving. In other words, Mori's way of "the non-duality of subject and object" is not merely the application of subjective ideals in objective behavior, but ideals themselves arising from acting upon the environment and seeing its results.[30]

These clarify what Watsuji tended to lack: despite his view of objectivity, the subject's ideals were not really attuned to the consequences of the objective world. This was not a matter of ignorance on Watsuji's part, but of active refusal. In "America's National Character" (1943), Watsuji describes American thinking using Francis Bacon's philosophy of invention, detailing the process of the scientific method from induction to theorizing and then deduction. However, he saw these as leading to mere "mechanical civilization" of calculation and domination of nature.[31]

As a result of refusing this experimental approach, Watsuji's "practical nexus of act" stiffens into idealism, making it impossible to say under what conditions one should assert relationality (Confucian education) and when it is time to shift to a more individual focus (Buddhist education). Like Chapter 2, these seem to come from Watsuji's excessive focus on social coherence, which tends to be idealistic at the expense of a pragmatic balance of subjectivity and objectivity.

However, while I am tempted to criticize Watsuji wholesale, I cannot help but remember my students and their challenges. The reason why Jin-*kun* tended to hold on to a competitive view of education was because it *made sense* to him, how he saw himself, and what he had been taught about school. Junko-*san* reduced our relationship to superficial roles because that was coherent in her experience of education. The same coherence is behind Taro-*kun*'s tendency to repress certain emotions as "wrong." All human beings tend to get caught up in ideals that make sense to them, even when the pragmatic context has changed, and our inner rules no longer work. Pragmatism calls us to be cognitively flexible, to look to see if our stress on relationality is still working or if we are now called to turn to the opposite side of *ningen* to be more individual, or vice-versa. But this flexibility is *difficult*.

Self-Awareness on a Pragmatic Base

Despite the limitations of idealism and the philosophy of awakening, Mori did not simply abandon these. In *Practicality and Inwardness*, he writes, "I am to unify naturalism and the philosophy of awakening and praxis."[32]

Thus, in addition to the first five *pragmatische* steps for learning, he continued to more *praktische* processes beginning with "6. Symbolic learning."

> When children are carrying-out behaviors, we must not neglect to guide them to occasionally stop and think, "Am I really right?" "Did I really do the right thing?" In other words, *stop and think*. In these times, we need to transmit [communicate] to students ideas like that's right, that's good, "cooperating is a good thing," "this attitude means taking

things seriously." ... This kind of consciousness will be the ground of the "conscience" I will later discuss.... And this guidance is actually the beginning of education for awakening.[33]

This is not about imposing social ideals on students. Rather, Mori suggests that we need to not only learn helpful behaviors, but also become aware of the principles and the values that guide these behaviors. These products of individual inquiry then need to be connected to *social* inquiry by being situated in social discourses on right and wrong.[34] Thus, learning does not stop at the individual level but continues to the community and its discourses.

As we have seen in the quote on pragmatic learning, problem-solving learning (5) and symbolic learning (6) give rise to self-awareness (*jikaku no kakusei* 自覚の覚醒).[35] While the sixth step is more idealist, thinking is still pointed outward to behavior in the world, to which thinking provides the support of cognitive and social coherence.[36] But in the seventh step, Mori fully returns to his roots in the philosophy of awakening:

> The self-awareness of *ningen* does not occur without an other and community. But at the same time, if our thinking and our attitude is merely pointed outward, full self-awareness (*honkaku no jikaku*) will not occur. Thinking and attitude ... are "reflected" inward, and "reflection" occurs. When one clearly realizes "self," for the first time full self-awareness (S2) awakens.

Self-awareness occurs when thinking and sense-making is pointed inward. It has two parts—S1 and S2. S1 forms a base, a conceptual understanding of one's identity and one's different roles. Mori connects this to Mead's "me" in *Philosophical Anthropology of Education*.[37] However, on top of S1 is another type of self-awareness, S2:

> This "self-awareness (S2) within self-awareness (S1)" is the true self-awareness. Dewey's self-awareness is no more than the first self-awareness.... Self-awareness (S2) is an activity of the subject that becomes self-aware of this self-awareness. It is a double self-awareness.... It is this three-dimensional self-aware subject that truly has "individuality" and is an existential person.[38]

S2 is not the content of identity but the activity, the *movement* of relating to oneself, as Kierkegaard and Jaspers suggest. Beyond social self, in this interior space of self-relation, one asks the question of how to take up one's own existence as one's own. This grounds identity, thoughts, and behaviors with an existential *gravitas*.[39]

This weight is best explained by a detour to the idea of conscience:

> My criticism toward [Dewey's] view of self-awareness applies to his theory of conscience. In particular, according to his theory of conscience, when [for example] Japanese reflect on their mistakes and sins, their reflection often includes a consciousness of "I feel sorry before society" (*seken ni sumanai* 世間にすまない), "it is inexcusable to the world." However, I do not think such consciousness is really "conscientious." Rather, I think it is the loss of "conscience." As Kant correctly suggests, conscience needs to include as its essential moment the self-reflective personal self-awareness (*jinkakuteki jikaku*) wherein *the self judges itself*. . . . I want to consider the subjectivity, personality, and existentiality of conscience as above, but at the same time, emphasize the empirical, social, and intellectual aspects of conscience.[40]

Dewey's pragmatic view of conscience had to do with reflection on the basis of a problem-solving social agent. However, it lacked Kant's sense of a self, standing before itself, judging if it could indeed stand up for this maxim as universal law. This involves a moment of existential decision and a sense of the duty of *ningen*.

The seven steps of pragmatic-practical learning—realizing a problem, articulating the problem, trying solutions, learning meaningful action from consequences, spreading this to other problems, clarifying principles, and self-awareness—are recapped in a specifically moral form in Mori's theory of moral decision. Allow me an extensive quote of his phenomenology of the experience of moral crisis:

> In a problematic situation of crisis, wherein easy decisions are impossible, where one is pressed to decide on the basis of norms like right and wrong or good and evil, one must accurately cognize the situation, carefully predict the consequences of action, and have the resolve to take responsibility for one's action. One gives one's final

decision from a strict self-awareness of the *duty of ningen* (*ningen no honbun* 人間の本分).... In the end, it is the *authentic self*, strictly realizing the *duty of ningen*, that gives an unconditional imperative to itself. In that instant, "conscience" reaches its peak tension, and one feels like one's entire *Existenz* is at stake in the decision of one's conscience. There, neither society, others, the world, nor culture can support this person. Furthermore, when one faces the crisis (*krinein*) of *either-or*, it is as if one is facing the abyss of absolute nothingness (*zettaimu no shin'en* 絶対無の深淵).... One tries to confirm one's grasp of the situation and one's insight into the future. This is an intellectual effort to understand the empirical and relative conditions. Moreover, one further deepens one's self-awareness of the *duty of ningen*, heard as if the voice of the absolute, and moved by this self-awareness, makes a final decision and acts. For this person, this decision permits of nothing other, and is in this sense necessary, absolute, and unique. In the *moment* of this decision, one experiences a phenomenon that can only be described as the collision of the relative and the absolute collide where *eternity* appears in *time*.

Like Watsuji's practical act nexus, Mori includes both individual behavior and social conditions one contributes to. But unlike Watsuji where praxis is guided one-way by ideals, Mori's moral decision-making starts from and regularly returns to pragmatic observation of objective situations and consequences. However, Mori reconstructs the Kyoto School's philosophy of awakening *on top* of this pragmatism by progressing to the clarification of ideals and the existential self-reflection of the I, face-to-face with the maxims of the me. In the end of the quote above, we see Mori draw directly from Nishida's parlance, pointing out that this *Existenz*, in its decision, is none other than the moment of encounter with absolute nothingness, the eternal now. This is the irreducible self that shapes history, that the educator tries to form in "On Education." Thus, Mori tried to combine the practical and the pragmatic for his own vision of awakening that unifies subject-object in a more thorough way.

To put it in Watsuji's terminology, Mori was able to see the mutual emptying of subjectivity and objectivity even more clearly than Watsuji.

The brute material reality and the tendency toward mindless repetition are emptied in order to realize intelligent understanding. But this intelligence too is emptied in order to observe objective antecedents and flexibly respond to consequences. This is another dimension of *education for emptiness*—the non-duality and mutual negation of idealism and praxis (see Figure 4.3). (However as a historical note, while Tanabe actually connected experimentalism to the idea of nothingness,[41] Mori did not use the terminology of emptiness and nothingness despite using the idea of awakening.[42])

*

What might these mean for us in the classroom? In my team, I often encourage my students to clarify their personal values as they engage their research. For example, a student researching on counseling might realize their deep desire to help others. Another who is working on the philosophy of society might realize their yearning to empower others. However, our first intuitions of our values do not always lead in a workable direction. We saw in Chapter 3 how Taro-*kun* deeply valued fully eliminating emotions like anger and attachment, and this drove a lot of his initial research and practice. But this ended up leading to experiential avoidance, a tendency to repress emotions he found objectionable.

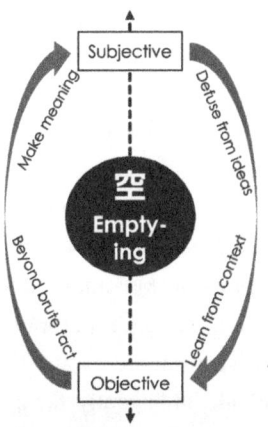

Figure 4.3 Non-duality of subject-object.

As we were learning Acceptance and Commitment Training/Therapy (which is derived from pragmatism), we tried a different approach to his values. Instead of starting with what he believed in the most, we began with concrete experiences. "In your personal experiences of education, where are you actually feeling a sense of meaning, fulfillment, and deep satisfaction?" When we explored this question, what we found were not moments of supreme mastery over his emotions but times of inner reconciliation where he learned to see the angry parts of himself and recognize where they come from, and sit with this anger without being controlled by it.

This pragmatic learning was further developed in the direction of practical ideals—clarifying his own values like "acceptance" and "acknowledging my inner child." And when this sense of being a friend to himself *clicked*, we could both sense a deep existential movement, as if he was learning to encounter himself fully in a very different way. The journey of his values does not end there. As he continues to live by these values and identities, he will probably also come across their limits, and thus allowing the practical-pragmatic process of learning to continue.

Social Change

However, learning and problem-solving is not merely an individual matter, but also a social one. How do individual realizations extend to society wherein it can make an actual difference?

In Watsuji, after the individual leader realizes the limitations of their culture, they work to create change within their culture. However, Watsuji says nothing about how the leader communicates their realization to others. In *Democracy and Education*, Dewey writes. "Society not only continues to exist *by* transmission, *by* communication, but it may fairly be said to exist *in* transmission, *in* communication. There is more than a verbal tie between the words common, community, and communication."[43]

We need the individual, intelligently facing their own particular context, to become aware of social problems. But after this individual realization, an essential part is how this problem is shared with the rest of those involved. Mori talks about how this is done on a smaller scale, as in student council meetings, where students share problems, clarify the nature of problems together, and look for solutions. Of course, there is also time to think about problems and solutions oneself—something Mori insists we take time away from the group for. But these realizations always need to be communicated to the group, because they need to be equally involved in the solution.

As we saw in Chapter 2, Watsuji's theory of language focused on subtle expressions and unspoken words, lacking the process of *deliberation* in order that *differing* points of view may be shared. If you try to lead a group without being able to communicate the direction you are trying to lead it in, it is very likely that your leadership will be felt as an imposition, leading to "martyrdom and strife."

Furthermore, Watsuji did not have anything to appeal to in circumstances where ideals were at odds (as in the case of utilitarian education vs. scholarship as pursuit of truth). This came from his tendency to see culture primarily in terms of ideals like "expressing the absolute" without considering material consequences. In contrast, Mori's *Philosophical Anthropology of Education* drew from different social scientists to clarify three aspects of culture: technological/material culture, ideal/abstract culture, and social/governance culture. He saw these as corresponding to needs fulfillment functions (substructure), personal formation functions (superstructure), and social governance functions (social structure).[44] This model is still in use in contemporary anthropology, where it is called the "barrel model" of culture.[45] This radically alters Watsuji's vision by considering material *function*, allowing for selection by consequences.

For example, in the case of Watsuji, one cannot justify his call for more critical education other than by appealing to subjective factors like saying that it manifests the ideal of pursuit of wisdom and the dual-negative structure of *ningen* better. But education connects to instrumental and integrative needs, suggesting that we can use the experiences of students and teachers as a means of verification. For example, we see needs clearly in Jin-*kun*'s difficulty with cooperating with his peers in Chapter 1 (social structure needs) and in Junko-*san* and Taro-*kun*'s struggles with a sense of meaning (superstructure needs). These create a justification for changes in the educative relationship. Mori saw these needs more broadly through sociological analyses of student cooperation, political participation, or mental health. Thus on both micro and macro levels, a clear sense of needs and consequences allows building consensus, where empirical facts act as an arbiter preventing ideals from merely talking past one another.

This connects to an academic problem surrounding Watsuji. There is an entire body of literature—Robert Bellah, Bernard Bernier, Sakai Naoki—asserting that Watsuji was fundamentally totalitarian.[46] Even Odin, after connecting Watsuji to pragmatism and democracy, says that inevitably Watsuji falls into a collectivism with no individual difference. However, was the problem really about the balance of individuality and totality? I suggest Watsuji's problem was an excess of *social coherence*, to the point of *pragmatic insensitivity*, not totalitarianism. On one hand, social coherence can be totalitarian in a case where it reinforces the status quo. On the other hand, it can lead paradoxically to an overly-strong individual merely imposing ideals on others, without communicating it or building consensus, not unlike Plato's philosopher king. Watsuji had both problems! So rather than a problem of individualism vs. totalitarianism, I think the key to making Watsuji more democratic is by following Mori and loosening up the attachment to social coherence via the flexibility to context suggested by pragmatism.

Let us bring this question of social change back to a level that is closer to our experience. Jin-*kun*, Junko-*san*, and Taro-*kun* are part of the Kyushu University Clinical Pedagogy team, which I have led for almost a decade. The team has around ten members, doing research on different things from counseling to philosophy to qualitative research. Members are long-term, one of whom has been with me for seven years! We operate as a team, not just attending class together, but doing research around connected themes, doing counseling and meditation practices together, and sharing our personal journeys with each other.

Just as each member learns to balance individuality and relationality through a process of practical and pragmatic learning, the same holds true for the team as a whole.

One of the main foci of the team is counseling theory—Acceptance and Commitment Training/Therapy (ACT), Mindful Self-Compassion, Narrative Therapy, Schema Therapy. Many individual students shared that what they personally found meaningful in our team was the ability to learn about themselves, to share their experiences, and to slowly grow as human beings. This is something I personally value as well, and this value of "personal growth" become one of the core ideals of our team.

However, over the years, the atmosphere of the class slowly shifted to something resembling group therapy. And while there were good things about that, I noticed that many students were so focused on their own healing that they were not thinking about how to mature as researchers in the graduate school and how to dialogue with the academic community. In this situation, if I took a Watsujian stance, I might not have noticed these objective consequences at all, or I could have merely imposed an ideal of "pursuit of truth" on the students.

However, guided by ProSocial,[47] a group application of ACT that is similarly based in pragmatism, I decided to explore our experiences of meaningful education instead. We had an open discussion asking, "What have you experienced as a member of the team that feels personally meaningful to you? What have you experienced that feels *against* what is meaningful to you?" Students like Junko and Taro shared positive reminiscences of the team as a safe space, a place to connect with themselves and to grow. But we also talked about more painful experiences—presenting in the university and not being understood, difficulties in understanding deeply the parts of theories that are not immediately pertinent to one's own case, being unable to write with sufficient theoretical rigor and related literature, difficulties in the job hunt. These experiences were not simply about subjective meaning but practical consequences within the context of the university, the academic community, and capitalist society.

In sharing these subjective and objective considerations with each other, what we found was the need to clarify values in the team that connected not merely to personal growth but to a *connection* between academic and personal growth. This also led us to clarify more specific values, like what mindsets we would cultivate when facing things like writing papers or giving presentations.

Now, while there are still group therapy elements to our classes, we also have more academic endeavors: I held symposia with other members of my team in conferences for qualitative psychology (2023), ACT (2023), and comparative philosophy (2024). And one very clear outcome of this shift is *this book*—that tries to combine examples with what I hope is a sufficient dose of theory and scholarship. But what I want to emphasize is that these changes are a result of *practical-pragmatic group discernment* and not merely subjective ideals.

Post-script: Philosophy and Science

I hope I have conveyed above the philosophic importance for considering not only subjective ideals of *ningen* but objective considerations of our context and the consequences of our action. If we are to be concerned with the physical world, action, and material consequences, what does that imply for our relationship with *science*, empirical sciences that are focused on understanding individual, social, and material phenomena, not from the basis of mere ideals, but actual experiential observation?

One fact that is rarely mentioned in English research about Watsuji is his deep interest in scientific theories as he tried to consider these four tensional facets of *ningen sonzai*. Because experiences are objective and social, they enter the empirical world rather than remaining in the world of ideas. Thus, he did not confine himself to reading philosophers but drew extensively on the sociology of Emile Durkheim, Gabriel Tarde, and Georg Simmel, and the anthropology and economics of Bronislaw Malinowski, the history and geography of Giambattista Vico and Lucien Febvre, and so on.

However, he often found that empirical sciences failed to capture the whole of the practical act nexus. For example, he was critical of psychology's tendency to suppose "that it is the individual human being that thinks."[48] But also, "Sociology tries to avoid a confrontation with contradictory relationships in its attempt to think in separation from individuals, as though it were possible to deal with 'society' alone."[49] He was also concerned that empirical sciences tended to stop with the objective facts of *ningen* and not what it interpretatively means. In response to these deficiencies, his hermeneutic method tried to consider empirical things but by searching for their meaning for *ningen*.

In a sense, Watsuji was challenging philosophy and the Kyoto School to dialogue with the empirical sciences that examine the same things that philosophy theorizes about. How well have we taken up that challenge? In Japan, some have taken up the question of how to realize Watsuji's ideas of *ningen sonzai* in relation to the human sciences. For example, Yuasa Yasuo and Kimura Bin tried to connect Watsuji to psychology.[50] Inukai Yuichi has published *Watsuji Tetsurō's Sociology*, looking at how to recast *Ethics as a Study of Ningen* as a sociological theory.[51] In English, other than Odin's and Joel Krueger's work on Kimura,[52] few have taken up the question of the implications of Watsuji for the human sciences. (However, I am hopeful with the recent rise of research on connections between science and the Kyoto School.[53])

One of the most thorough engagements of the empirical sciences from the Kyoto School is by Mori Akira. According to Yano Satoji, Mori's most important contribution to the Kyoto School of Education was to develop philosophical anthropology by unifying all of the sciences of education from biology to psychology to sociology, anthropology, political science, and history.[54] In a sense, he was following in Watsuji's footsteps in trying to combine science with philosophical insight:

> In general, idealism tends to omit the emergent empirical consideration of morality. However... The reason for the recent rise of psychological, social psychological, and sociological research on moral consciousness is not merely the needs of educational methods but touches upon the very essence of morality. But in order to grasp the essence of morality,

we need to become self-aware (*jikaku*) of the meaning of that empirical research within our own subjective self-awareness.[55]

But he went beyond Watsuji in not merely considering scientific *theories* but actually looking at scientific data, running his own educational experiments, and getting data on his own classes as well! (We will see more in the next two chapters.)

However, in my various speaking engagements, I have noticed that many philosophy researchers, particularly those who research on critiques of modernity like the Kyoto School, postmodernism, or poststructuralism, are very wary of my engagement with science. They warn me that science is reductive, is too prone to be used for unethical purposes (too "operationalized"), and fails to grasp the depth of human existence.

I disagree with this anti-scientific stance. Like we saw in the cases of Jin-*kun*, Junko-*san*, Taro-*kun*, and our team as a whole, beautiful ideals like competence, relationality, self-mastery, and personal growth can run amuck in actual life, leading to a whole host of unintended consequences. Without science's focus on empirical consequences, how do we protect the natural world's ability to "talk back" against the din of our lofty ideals and the various "-isms" of the world?

However, is their problem really with science, or with a particular kind of science? A hint of this lies in Odin's book connecting Watsuji and pragmatism. In it, he refers to Stephen Pepper's four "world hypotheses" of science (philosophies of science)—formism, mechanism, organicism, and contextualism.[56] Most of what we think of as "science" is mechanism—a paradigm that sees parts connected deterministically to each other to form a greater "machine." In this worldview, scientists begin from the parts and deterministically connect them to form a whole. Their theory of truth is realism (reality is out there, regardless of subjectivity) and its epistemology is positivist-empiricist (scientific truths correspond to reality). Perhaps philosophers are wary of science and operationalism because this deterministic view eliminates human agency, freedom, and meaning

However, there is another kind of science called contextualism. "Contextualism takes as its root metaphor the ongoing act-in-context, or the behavior of a whole organism, considered within, and inseparable from, its historical and situational context."[57] Contextual science looks at a unique situation within which an agent is emplaced and how this particular agent freely tries to *respond* to this situation.

James, Dewey, Mead, and Mori are contextualists. They were deeply involved in the sciences of psychology and sociology, examining data and gathering it themselves. However, they did not merely look at individuals as data-points like mechanistic science does. They explored the experience of individuals, how individuals agentically find their way in life, and how these ways intertwine in groups. They were scientific, but with a different sense of objectivity and universalizability. Instead of seeing "objectivity" as complete isolation of the world from "contamination" by the subject, Dewey saw objectivity as our willingness to test our ideas via their practical consequences. Instead of "universalizability" being about being completely free from particular contextual limitations, Dewey saw the need to see how learning could be abstracted from one particular context so that it could be applied in *another particular context*—but not thoroughly decontextualized.[58]

Pragmatism, which is by its nature contextualist, provides us a view of science that still sees unique agents acting in a particular context. This view of science is still present today, for example in the individual sciences we have Contextual Behavioral Science (CBS, which includes ACT and ProSocial), narrative psychology, and phenomenological psychology. In sociology, we have social constructionism and symbolic interactionism.

In order to value human freedom and the richness of experience, I agree that we need to resist mechanistic determinism. But in order to avoid falling into dogmatic idealism and the individual and social consequences that arise from the inflexibility of mere coherence, we need to continue valuing contextual science and how it allows us to learn from consequences.

5

The Rhythm of Life

In the previous chapters of this book, we have seen how education is *complicated*. Students need to have a genuine sense of connection with others and community. But at the same time, they need to find a sense of their own authenticity and agency. Learners need to find and build coherence and sense in life. But they also need to make that coherence flexible and functional by pragmatically facing the objective world and its consequences. This education for emptiness has four *tensional* aspects: individuality, communality, subjectivity, and objectivity. And emptiness calls us not to adhere to any of these aspects but instead to allow their dynamic to-and-fro (see Figure 5.1).

How does it all come together, not just as a diagram, but how does it actually make sense? All these entanglements of education are a part of the ebb and flow of *life*. But life, what is life?

The Kyoto School's philosophy of awakening (*jikakushugi* 自覚主義) is an answer to that question. For example, Nishitani Keiji's *Religion and*

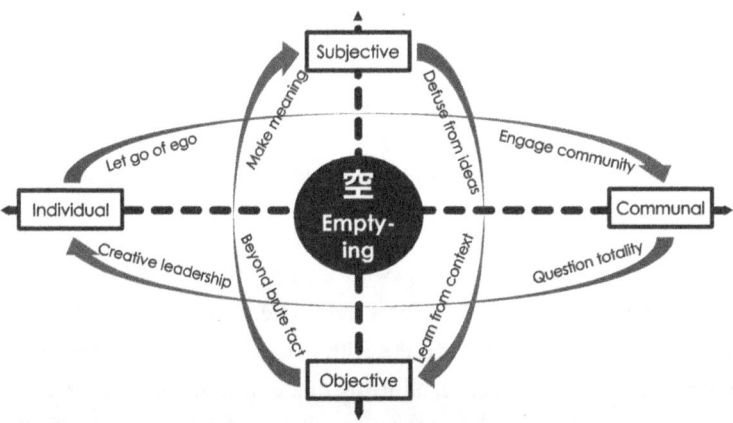

Figure 5.1 Two non-dualities in emptiness.

Nothingness[1] suggests that life starts with us thinking that everything is about us, and we reduce everything to our own definitions and purposes (the standpoint of consciousness/ego). However, when we realize that we cannot just reduce *ourselves* to our own definitions of ourselves, when crises in life like our own mortality strike us and, instead of running, we learn to become the question, we awaken (*jikaku*) to our nothingness (the standpoint of nihility). When this nothingness opens up, not as the opposite of meaning and being, but as the space where reality can be playfully re-engaged, not from one's own ego but in genuine encounter with things as they are, then we awaken (the standpoint of emptiness). Nishitani's view is similar to Watsuji's view in *Purifying Zen*.

Mori Akira's teacher, Tanabe Hajime's *Philosophy of Metanoetics*[2] answers this question in a different way. Life is where we think that we can save ourselves by ourselves and attain the meaning of life by our own wisdom and practice. But when life strikes us down and we realize that we are incapable of solving life's mysteries by our own power, we have metanoia (*zange* 懺悔). In this, we awaken to nothingness as absolute mediation, through which we can engage others who are on the way, as mediators for the saving power of grace.

We also saw through Watsuji and Confucius another answer to this question:

> The Master said: "From fifteen, my heart-and-mind was set upon learning; from thirty I took my stance; from forty I was no longer doubtful; from fifty I realized the propensities of *tian* (*tianming* 天命 [mandate of heaven]); from sixty my ear was attuned; from seventy I could give my heart-and-mind free rein without overstepping the boundaries."[3]

Here, we see life as beginning with a need to find one's place in a community. This happens via a receptive form of learning that progressively leads to mastery. But with mastery, the virtues of learning shift to become more active, allowing one to lead one's community in a transformative way. This is the same flow we find in *Ethics* with the double-negation of both egoism and collectivism to realize creative communal existence.

There is more recent research on *jikakushugi* in Kyoto University's department of education. Nishihira Tadashi's *The Philosophy of No-Mind* points out the process of learning to have mind (the mind of ego that controls the world), to extinguishing mind through various practices of negation (180-degree no-mind), and to the arising of everyday mind (no-mind 360-degrees) and the yonder shore that shows itself in the primordial freedom of everyday mind.[4] And Yano Satoji's *The Education for Awakening in the Kyoto School* (Japanese) presents the historical research on how this whole tradition of awakening *actually* influenced the educational system in Japan, from educational policies to moral education and even to pedagogical practices.[5]

In this chapter, we will focus on Mori and see his answer to the question, "What is life?" Unlike the Kyoto School of Philosophy, he would not go by way of religion or any cultural ideology. As we have seen in the previous chapter, his engagement with pragmatism would point him to science, particularly developmental psychology and sociology, which would radically transform his view of awakening. Through these, he would come up with a theory of self-awareness, of coming to terms with life, that is even closer to everyday experience, not only in its elements, but in its *rhythm*.

Education as Becoming Human

Mori approaches the question of life via his transformation of the philosophy of human existence (*ningen sonzai* 人間存在) into a philosophy of human becoming (*ningen seisei* 人間生成). Watsuji, Miki Kiyoshi, Kuki Shūzō, and Kōyama Iwao all wrote in a genre of "philosophical anthropology" (*ningengaku* 人間学), which refers to anthropology prior to its separation from philosophy as an independent social science. Mori applied this to education, allowing him to think about education in a much broader way. Education is not simply schooling, or learning information and skills, or maturation. Instead, education is *becoming human*: "Let us define education as human becoming, in relation to others.... The task of educational philosophical anthropology is to clarify the process of human becoming in relation to others according to the structure of human existence."[6]

Through applying *ningen sonzai* to education, he expanded human *being* to *becoming*.[7] I struggle to translate *ningen seisei*, literally human + becoming, because of its multiple implications. First, as we have seen with Watsuji, *ningen* is not simply the human being in an individual sense but includes both the individual (*nin*) and relational/group (*gen*) aspects of human existence, which are both needed in education.

Second, "becoming" (*seisei* 生成, to be born + to become) as compared to "existence" emphasizes the *processual* character of human be-ing, the dynamism of emptiness as it manifests in time. Mori clarifies his stance vis-à-vis Nicolai Hartmann:

> A glaring lack of Hartmann's ontology is that he was so focused on establishing the spatial hierarchy of matter, life, psyche, and spirit that he closed off the relation vis-à-vis becoming (*seiseiteki* 生成的), or to borrow a concept of contemporary biology, the genetic hierarchy (*hasseiteki dankaisei* 発生的段階性) of matter, life, psyche, and spirit.[8]

This could apply to Watsuji and the entire Kyoto School's philosophy of awakening—they miss that children are not born immediately able to realize emptiness and awaken. An infant does not speak or have a sense of self. An elementary student often absolutizes the demands of the collective, making thought and language inflexible, leading to the dominance of social self. In adolescence, many are so caught up with realizing themselves that they are unable to balance this with a sense of others. Yes, human existence (*sonzai*) has a dual-negative structure, but how can we become (*seisei*) human in a way that allows us to realize this dual-negative structure? While the Kyoto School tends to start with the adult, faced with challenges of egoism, self-enclosure, and self-power, Mori's philosophy of education tries to see the *process* of a child becoming an adult, showing hints of how we can deconstruct and overcome the egoism (standpoint of consciousness, self-power) that the Kyoto School presupposes.

Third, becoming has both normative and descriptive aspects. "Human becoming" (*ningen ga seisei suru*) is about the facts of how human beings change, something that needs to be studied empirically— via developmental psychology. Simultaneously, "becoming human" (*ningen ni seisei suru*) is about what kind of growth is worthy of the name "human," a question that has occupied ethics since Socrates. Becoming carries this tension of is and ought within itself.

Fourth, in both its facts and its ideals, this process is not smooth but punctuated by crises that mark the turns in the process of emptying and negation across the four aspects seen in Figure 5.1. Mori writes,

> The philosophy of becoming correctly considers the heteronomous individuality of the various layers of existence, but simultaneously must investigate the generative relationship between these layers. Needless to say, this is a difficult task. On one hand, one grasps the layers of existence in a discontinuous relationship, and simultaneously one tries to investigate the relation of generative continuity between them.... Becoming is not merely continuity, but discontinuous continuity (*hirenzokuteki renzoku* 非連続的連続).[9]

"Discontinuous continuity" is an idea shared by Tanabe Hajime and Nishida Kitarō. In Mori's view of becoming, people "develop," but development includes moments of *discontinuity* and crisis, making it impossible for development to be explained by virtue of one principle. For example, natural life (as an organism) is *continuous* in that it "develops" into historical life (conscious life) and into personal life (as self-awareness). But historical life cannot be explained purely through natural principles, nor personal life purely through historical principles, resulting in a continuity of discontinuity.[10]

Mori defined education simply as "human becoming/becoming human." As an educator, to me this means that I look at my students and I know that no matter what kind degreeocracy society we are in, here, *life is happening*. These people are finding their way on the path of *ningen*, trying to mature, but also trying to find their way as themselves, with all the detours and cul-de-sacs that entails.

Individual Development

One way of foregrounding a sense of life as a whole is to zoom out and look at the overall map of the journey. My students often ask (as I once did): "So I go to school, what then?" "I get a job, and then what happens?" "I start a family, okay. And then I retire?" "And then I die?"

Mori's answer to these questions is the philosophical idea of becoming. But this abstract idea needs to be grounded in the actualities of people and their material lives. As such, Mori turned to his own experience of the children he was teaching (he regularly taught in elementary, middle, and high schools, and of course university and graduate school, giving him direct involvement with almost every developmental stage of people). And he clarified these broad experiences via the developmental psychologist Erik Erikson (1902–1994).

Erikson developed one of the most influential models of the human life-cycle: "The Eight Ages of Man." However, Erikson did not arrive at these eight stages merely by speculation. Trained under Anna Freud, he specialized in psychoanalysis for children. He also was trained in the Maria Montessori School,[11] whose method of education highlights stages of development. He even examined the upbringing of other cultures, such as the Sioux tribe, cooperating with anthropologists. As such, he had direct experience of the actual changes children go through and the crises they face. Furthermore, he carried out narrative research on biographies of Martin Luther, Mahatma Gandhi, and even Adolf Hitler, allowing him to extend his understanding of children to adults and the aged.

Based on this empirical (but not positivist or mechanist) approach, Erikson sought to examine the "triple bookkeeping" between "(1) The group ... (2) The patient's organism ... (3) The patient's ego."[12] And he saw identity as developing not in a closed individual but in the complex interaction of these three processes.

Mori Akira had a love affair with this developmental theory. It forms the core of his theoretical discussion in *Practicality and Inwardness* and is his key to explaining how to understand children in *Moral Education We Hope For* (1958). He discusses it extensively in his *Philosophical Anthropology of Education* and continues to wrestle with it in his last book, *The Fundamental Principles of Human Formation*. Peculiarly, it turns up in his textbook for middle school students as well! We see in his work that he did not only study this theory, but he confirmed his observations via his own activities as a teacher and research by Japanese educational scientists. Let us see how this developmental theory shows the rhythm of life.

The first stage, Erikson calls "trust vs. mistrust." Mori renames it in *Moral Education We Hope For*, writing, "Children Want Warm Love."[13] Mori highlights how the newborn infant is thoroughly dependent on others for its survival, but at the same time has highly developed sensitive and emotional faculties. In this state, the key challenge is to build a sense of trust that the world is something that one can engage in. However, this is only possible if we receive warm love within our attachment relationships that help us develop an emotional equilibrium and a felt sense that the world is not a hostile place. Mori also cites Watsuji's idea of trust and recasts this ideal as a need that begins in infancy and continues throughout life.

The second stage is called "autonomy vs. shame and doubt," and Mori expresses the task of this stage as, "Children Try to Do Things Themselves."[14] Here, the toddler builds a sense of self via the will to do things. But as children try to do things that they do not have the skill for (like toddlers trying to climb stairs without holding anyone's hand), there are clear dangers that arise. Here, a "tug-of-war" happens between (a) the parent who tries to discipline the child or do things for the child and (b) the child who wants to do things for themselves. While Erikson was most worried about the excesses of discipline leading to a sense of shame, Mori felt that in Japan, the danger was spoiling the toddler by doing everything for them that resulted in a sense of dependence. Either way, it is necessary to let a child develop a sense of their own will, but within bounds of safety.

The third stage is "initiative vs. guilt," which Mori calls "Children Seek Opportunities to Grow." In this stage, the pre-school child is beginning to learn the symbols of the adult world at a rapid rate. We see this in their curiosity, "Why, mama, why?" Children also begin to copy adults in what is referred to in Japanese as *"gokko"* (imitation games), learning complex networks of symbols via roles. Furthermore, what was once raw will is now directed as a sense of initiative and having one's own purposes and plans. In this stage, Mori urged parents to value the curiosity of their children, to try to pay heed to their relentless questions, and to not over discipline. Or else, children would stagnate and lose their creativity, with a sense that there is no point to trying things on their own.

The fourth stage is "industry vs. inferiority," which Mori describes as "Children Hope to Be Full-Fledged Members (*ichininmae* 一人前)."[15] Interestingly, Mori is using Watsuji's virtue of local community from *Ethics II* showing that in this stage, it is not merely about family relations (where everyone knows the child personally), but a more *impersonal* stage of relations where the child is but one member of the community. This usually accompanies the entry into school, where the child is now subject to more impersonal rules as a student. Mori phenomenologically describes the experience of this stage with the story of a child nervously preparing to go to school and asking for tips from his big brother. Here, parents and teachers need to help the child expand the self to include the objective world of tools, ideas, and social order.

Mori points out how this is a massive shift, from the earlier stages that focused on the trust, autonomy, and initiative of *person*, one is beginning to experience the need to conform as an *impersonal role*. There are many dangers that lurk here: a child's repeated failures might lead to an internalized sense of inferiority. Children become excessively preoccupied with status hierarchies and competition, and there is a risk that they will lose their own sense of values for a purely competitive social view of right.

Fifth, we have Erikson's "identity vs. role confusion," which Mori referred to as "Youth Repeatedly Assert Themselves." With the bodily changes of adolescence, children become acutely aware of themselves, with the symbolic apparatus of ideas, norms, and roles suddenly being turned inward toward their own identity. This new sense of self is emerging, exacerbated by how adults can flux between treating the teen as a kid and as an adult. (We will see more on this next chapter.) Teens thus have this strong urge to understand themselves. In tension with the more compliant aspect of the previous stage, rebellion is a key part to how teens pragmatically understand this new sense of self. Despite being a moral education teacher, Mori was very much supportive of adolescent rebellion! Amidst these changes, Mori suggests that teens need educators who understand them. They also really need new kinds of friends who can connect with them in this deeper way.

Mori was primarily focused on school children when he developed his moral education, but he already hints at the further stages of Erikson as part of challenges that continue beyond adolescence but already need to be considered in youth. The sixth stage of Erikson is "intimacy vs. isolation," which is about going beyond the self-centered focus on identity to open to deeper connections with others. Mori refers to this via "Intimacy: Youth Seek Human Understanding," where youth need to engage their peers in much deeper ways. The seventh stage of Erikson is "generativity vs. stagnation," which is about a realization of one's finitude and a growing concern toward the next generation. Mori connects this even to the young as "Aspiration: Youth Pursue their Ideals," where youth learn to find personal values that they can stand up for *before others*. Finally, the eighth stage of Erikson is "ego integrity vs. despair," which Mori calls "Independence as a New Departure" where he touches on via the idea of "having a spine" (*sebonekan* 背骨感)— one's own grasp of morality and life—a path that takes a lifetime to realize. It is important that teachers be aware of these future stages because all three build on but sublate the inward movement of identity to turn outward as an overflow of generativity.

Developmental psychology is a requirement for educators for a reason: Educators need to know the overall trajectory of life, to know that their first-grade class is likely to be struggling with the transition to becoming members of a group of "classmates," or that their middle-schoolers are likely to be struggling with questions of identity and belonging that can clash with their academic concerns. While this understanding is an important requirement, some educators adhere too rigidly to the stages of development, insisting that "Oh you're X years old, you must be going through this Y phase."

This is a grave misunderstanding. In *Philosophical Anthropology of Education*, Mori warns:

> As Inhelder and others have suggested, stages of development, called variously depending on the researcher—*Entwicklungsstadium*, -phase, -*etappe*, -*stufen oder-sequence*—are divisions that are methodological aids (*hōhōteki hojo shudan* 方法的補助手段) and actual development does not proceed according to it.... All the qualitative types of thinking previously observed in a child are observed again (even after). This means, "The hierarchy of the forms of thought are not according to a random accumulation of new cognition, nor to only a logical system of implication (*logische Implikationssysteme*), but a unique developmental process (*eigentliche Entwicklungsprozesse*)."[16]

Instead, Mori is suggesting that while these stages are a guide, we need to look at the particularities of each individual student. Timing varies, like Jin-*kun* still struggling with questions of industry in university. Furthermore, stages are never fully overcome, so they could, like Junko-*san*, be dealing with identity questions and at the same time dealing with wounds from an earlier stage of not being allowed a sense of initiative.

For me, while these "stages" give me a *general* sense of the flow of life, more importantly, they make me sensitive to the *particular* challenges students might be struggling with. Nishihira calls this "education as generative care," where education is not merely imparting skills but answering to deep human struggles in the life-cycle.[17] There are those who struggle with a core sense of not being welcome in the world and others who struggle with a sense of their own agency. There are some who struggle with their sense of achievement and industry despite being quite excellent at it, and others who are struggling with who they are and what their place is in the world. And some are already facing shadows of later stages like intimacy, generativity, or even hope vs. despair. These developmental needs show us that life is hard, and hopefully we can offer a helping hand to each other.

The Structure of Personality

When we engage development philosophically, what does that tell us about the lived experience of life and how it hangs together? First, the path above presents us with a confusing tension of different forces. From infancy, we have this vital force of growth, but it soon has to contend with various intellectual needs for ideas and roles, but then we have the challenges of identity turning these forces inward, and then we have these forces turned out again . . .

Mori captures these tensions in the process of becoming human as a triangle (see Figure 5.2).

We have seen in Chapter 1 how this shows the four differing emphases of education: education as natural growth, education as

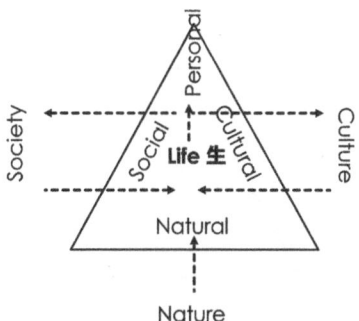

Figure 5.2 Tensions within.[18]

social formation, education as cultural transmission, and education as personal awakening. But more experientially, these are the various forces that push upon us in the complex interaction between organism, ego, and group.

Furthermore, the balance of these forces is not static (see Figure 5.3). In infancy (the leftmost triangle), the bottom arrow shows that natural life and growth predominate, and the influence of society and culture are weaker and one-way. But in childhood (second triangle), social formation (left) and cultural transmission (right) become more dominant and the direction of influence becomes more clearly two-way. Finally, in youth (third triangle), personal life (the top arrow) and its awakening begin to manifest.

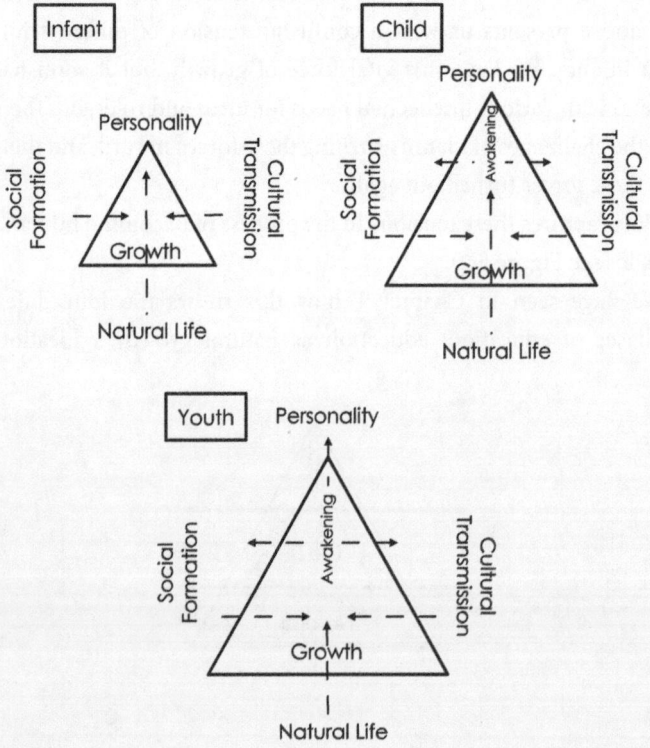

Figure 5.3 Shifting emphases[19]

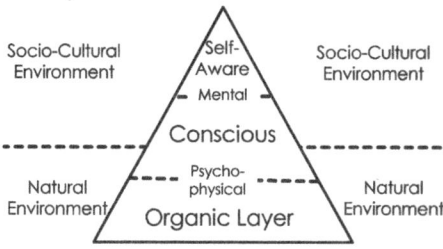

Figure 5.4 Layers of personality.[21]

Mori Akira develops these triangles into a three-layer view of personality that he derives from Erich Rothacker, a proponent of philosophical anthropology. Mori writes, Rothacker "broadly divides personality into the layer of the subconscious depths of personality, the conscious depths of personality, and the conscious personality, which can be renamed as (1) the organic layer (*seitai sō*, or life layer *seimei sō*) of personality, (2) the conscious layer (*ishiki sō*), and (3) the self-aware layer (*jikaku sō*)."[20] This is seen in Figure 5.4.

But what we have seen from the previous section is that the experience of this shifting of emphases between layers is one of *crisis*. In the first two stages, trust and autonomy, the primary focus is on natural growth, this vitality of the infant and toddler. Here, the focus is on the first layer (organic). This roughly coincides with Karl Jaspers' experiential world image (*erlebtes Weltbild*),[22] which is our direct experience of our environment. Mori tried to support growth in this layer via active forms of education like Rousseau's negative education that support spontaneous and curious behavior. But at the same time, education in this layer also needs discipline and realizing the consequences of their action, which Mori explains via Thorndike's behaviorism.[23]

However, with initiative and industry, the child shifts toward the importance of the symbolic, toward imagination, ideas, meanings, roles, plans, expectations, rules . . . This is part of the development of a second (conscious) layer:

> As the individual develops in a human manner, the satisfaction of desires becomes more indirect . . . Between the loss and restoration

of equilibrium, intelligence and customs are interposed ... With the indirectness of the satisfaction of desires, the individual starts to have more of an inside (*naimen* 内面).[24]

This "inside" is Jaspers' objectivized world image (*objektiviertes Weltbild*), which begins to play a central role in our lives (usually in school age or slightly earlier). Mori Akira draws on Ernst Cassirer, showing that our relation to the world is not merely direct but is mediated by symbols. The way a child perceives objects begins to be influenced by their names: "chair," "table," "honesty," "lying." We experience things and act on them, all the while naming them, making sense of them, and building them into a symbolic system.

However, the shift from the organic to the conscious layer is challenging for the elementary child. In Japan, this is referred to as the "elementary first grade problem" (*shō ichi puroburemu* 小1プロブレム). Children are so used to the directness of personal relations that the rules and rhythms of school can seem shockingly impersonal.[25] What we have here is a "discontinuity," a shift from directly relating with the environment to a richly internal (but also social) life of symbols and consciousness. But this discontinuity must be bridged with a sense of continuity. Mori thus tried to bridge symbolic learning and socialization with Dewey's meaningful action, in order to let the symbolic system have more of a sense of grounding in direct experience as well.[26]

After this outward use of symbols, with the stage of identity vs. role confusion, this symbolic apparatus is turned inward, forming the third layer. Mori divides it into two—"S1" and "S2," which we have seen in the previous chapter. S1 is one's identity, when one looks at the various roles one plays in different communities—son/daughter, student, friend, sibling, boy/girlfriend—and tries to build a self that pulls together these different roles.

However, with the development of S2 arises from the realization that one's meaning is not reducible to one's social identity. One realizes one's physical differences from others, one's conscious differences from others. One realizes that one is not only conscious of oneself but is also conscious of this consciousness itself—a subjective center of reflection that can dynamically relate to itself.²⁷ This layer is remarkably discontinuous with the others:

> Is this "growth"? No, it is not a growth that has continuity but deals with the discontinuous leaps and turns of man. Is it "formation"? No, rather than a forming that gives shape, is it not the explosive combustion of the soul? Then, is it "transmission?" No, it is not the reception of something but the spirit's inward "fulfillment" (*jūjitsu* 充実).²⁸

Again, this transition from the conformity of the conscious layer to the radical inwardness of the self-aware layer is one of crisis. The hard-won sense of outward belonging is now challenged in this need to turn inward to oneself. If one holds on too tightly to the conventional thinking and morality of the conscious layer, it prevents the self-aware layer from forming. This transition would be further challenged, when identity must become generative—that is, an outward contribution from a movement that was primarily inward!

Tension and Crisis

Most of philosophy separates these "layers" into completely distinct visions of the human being—as a biological organism, as a thinking being, as a social being, as a spiritual being. Mori's point is that the challenge of human becoming lies in the fact that we are all these at once. Thus, life has many different needs that are irreducible to each other. And the relationship between these tensional parts is dynamic, evolving throughout life.

This complex evolution entails *crisis*. When I teach this, many teachers ask me how to avoid their students falling into crisis. I think this is human; it is very stressful watching a student go through a life crisis. But can we avoid crises? Erikson writes: "The strength acquired at any stage is tested by the necessity to transcend it in such a way that the individual can take chances in the next stage with what was most vulnerably precious in the previous one."²⁹ Because stages have a discontinuity, the transition to the next stage requires a letting go of the previous, like Jin-kun struggling to let go of a mindset of competitive competence to be able to focus on what is personally meaningful for him.

However, behind this very human aversion to crises, perhaps there are tendencies that make it difficult to face this more tumultuous view of life. In Japan, teachers are regularly instructed for "prevention and early detection" (*yobō to sōki hakken* 予防と早期発見) of developmental crises, to ensure that students are able to smoothly (*mondai naku*) transition to the next stage. But Erikson warns us:

> In fact, some writers are so intent on making an *achievement scale* out of these stages that they blithely omit all the "negative" senses (basic mistrust, etc.) which are and remain the dynamic counterpart of the "positive" ones throughout life. The assumption that on each stage a goodness is achieved which is impervious to new inner conflicts and to changing conditions is, I believe, a projection on child development of that success ideology which can so dangerously pervade our private and public daydreams and can make us inept in a heightened struggle for a meaningful existence in a new, industrial era of history. The personality is engaged with the hazards of existence continuously...[30]

Rather than a simplistic addition of skills, identity development suggests a more existential sense of crisis and change. While it is human to avoid crisis, Mori and Erikson warn us of the controlling ego, both on the individual and social levels, and the search for stable success. The logic of ego is in conflict with the *koan* (公案, Zen riddle) presented by development via crisis.

When I look at my students as people, journeying through life, I see these needs, changes, tensions, and crises. Just as Nishihira referred to education as "generational care," this caring is one that responds to "generational crises."[31] While I may spend much of my time primarily transmitting information to the "cognitive apparatus" of a student, I know that crisis comes, where the progress of even the brightest students can grind to a halt as they face deep needs that they have not fulfilled or perhaps cannot fulfill. And as we saw with Taro-*kun*, these are the times that call me to be more than just a teacher on an intellectual level but to connect with them as a whole personality that is finding its way in life.[32]

Developing Relationships

Individuals develop on the path of life. However, as Erikson's idea of triple bookkeeping suggests, relationships develop too. He writes, "Each successive stage and crisis has a special relation to one of the basic elements of society, and this for the simple reason that the human life-cycle and man's institutions have evolved together."[33]

In *The Philosophical Anthropology of Education*, Mori presented the following chart of Erikson's stages (see Figure 5.5).

In this chart, Mori lists the personal needs (upper left) that develop from infancy to childhood and to early adulthood. The developmental realizations are listed in the middle (security, autonomy, initiative, ability, individuality, self-actualization). However, the bottom half is unique to Mori Akira. He pairs personal needs with social needs (lower left) and social developmental realizations (trust, belonging, togetherness, role, solidarity, mission) that correspond to individual developmental realizations.

In other words, for personality to grow, there must also be corresponding changes to the kind of relationships we have. Thus, Mori suggested that if education is to aid human becoming, the kind of educative relationship needs to change depending on development, as we saw in the change from education for growth to education for

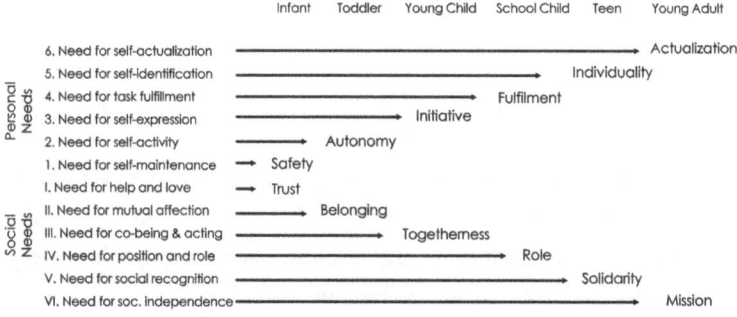

Figure 5.5 Stages of human development through personal needs and social needs.[34]

cultural transmission and socialization and to education for personal awakening. However, this also implicates surrounding relationships outside education. Even if schools and universities change, if families, local communities, companies, and the nation-state do not give room for certain aspects of self, we cannot expect education to succeed.

First, we have the organic layer of the growing child seeking to develop peace and autonomy. Supporting these is primarily the domain of education at home—parenting and other supports by the family. Through responding to the child's physical needs, giving the child affection, exploring the world together, the child is able to build a sense of trust and belonging.

This form of connection can extend beyond the family to the whole community. Drawing from sociology and anthropology, Mori explores "primitive foundational society" (*shigenteki kiso shakai* 始原的基礎社会), groups extending from the family to the tribe, of people who share territory and a certain way of life in living within that shared space.[35] These are communities formed from the interlinking of people's organic layers. In his *Philosophical Anthropology*, Mori shows how primitive community can develop into "substantial complex society," resulting from the formation of abstract culture, protoscience, and philosophy, idealist ways of maintaining the continuity of organic ways of life.[36] What we have here is a community of organic layers entrenched by ideals and myths.

However, there are dangers when this mode of relation becomes dominant in society. While connection primarily on the level of the organic layer can result in a sense of trust and belonging, they tend to be dominated by groupthink, and if it stays in that layer it can prevent the formation of the agency of the self. Mori writes, "[T]he 'individual' is extinguished, and the 'totality' dominates everything." This can result in harmful forms of patriotism like Imperial Japan's "extinguish the self, serve the public" (*messhi bōkō* 滅私奉公).[37] While we need these kinds of relationships in families or playgrounds, having the whole society stuck at this stage is pernicious to human becoming.

Second, there are communities that arise from the sharing of the conscious layer, building a sense of togetherness and role. Here, education shifts from natural growth to cultural transmission and social formation. Mori stressed how Deweyan education connects to democratic citizenship, allowing people to come together in an intelligent way through participation in group efforts:

> Participation is not primitive "sharing" (*bun'yū* 分有). In participating, the individual, as a more or less autonomous individual, becomes aware of the "role" he/she carries out within the totality. And by critique and cooperation with others . . . realizes shared ends together.[38]

However, it is difficult to have democratic Deweyan education if society is primarily locked in traditionalism and idealism. Instead, this kind of education requires a larger milieu of what Mori calls "National Integrated Society" (*kokuminteki sōgō shakai* 国民的総合社会), where the community is not driven merely by maintaining ideals that are divorced from experience, but driven by functional pursuit of empirical ends (like GDP growth).[39] Mori's critique of traditionalist society was also in service of creating a society wherein individual becoming and agency would become meaningful.

What about communities that nourish our sense of self-awareness? At home, in school, and among friends, when the youth have the space to explore their individuality and their stories, they are able to develop an awareness of their identity. And the connection on this level of identity results in groups of solidarity, a sense of kinship of those who share certain identities or ideals. Beyond schools, this connects to what Mori called "communities of nation, class, and humankind." You can have solidarity among citizens, among feminists, among the working class, and even a sense of unity with all humankind, as we find in some trans-national organizations and social movements.

But there remains a final level—self-realization and mission—that develop in the overlap between self-awareness S2. This is not merely a sense of solidarity based on identity but a sense of connection on the very dynamic of seeking ourselves and responding to ourselves—*Existenz*. For this *journeying together*, we have a highest stage of "personal/fraternal solidarity." Mori Akira writes:

In order to sincerely realize humanity and personality, national and class solidarity must include personal/fraternal solidarity. Even a group of like-minded companions become a truly ethical union only when in the end, they are a solidarity of personality and *fraternité*.[40]

Instead of a broad group where everyone is bound by shared values or ideals, Mori is suggesting that the highest form of solidarity is *personal*—a direct I-Thou relationship between two unique people, sharing via loving struggle in the later stages of development (intimacy, generativity, ego integrity). This often happens between best friends but can be shared by a group of more than two, provided there is an existential face-to-face relationship between members.

Together with individual development, communities develop as well. And it is through the bonds within these communities that individuals have the space to develop. But just as identity has crises, the development of communities is fraught with tension. The first tension is between feudal substantial society and modern national society—what Tönnies called "*Gemeinschaft und Gesellschaft.*" This tension is clear in the history of revolutions that changed ideal, mythically-bound groups into democratic nation-states. And for Mori, Japan remained in a half-feudalism, yet to transform into a real democracy that would allow the formation of agentic citizens.

The second tension is between institutionalized society and more personal groups that resist institutions. This occurs in the crisis of modernity itself. Modernity frees the individual for meaningful action and intelligent intercourse with the environment. But at the same time, as society as a whole becomes arranged in order to address needs, relationships are institutionalized. As mentioned in Chapter 2, "Institutions once formed begin to function independently from people's needs and often suppress the fundamental needs of people, coercing and pressuring them, and giving rise to Marx's self-alienation of *ningen*."[41] For example, only when informal learning relationships are institutionalized as schools can learning be spread to a whole nation. But at the same time, this means that what is to be learned tends to become standardized, people are treated not as unique beings but as mere functionaries (teachers and students), and people whose needs differ from others are forced into situations that they cannot find meaning in. In response to this, you have more personal groups (close friends) that can sometimes deliberately reject social institutions (like deviant groups or cults).

Therefore, society is not completed in some utopia where all layers of the human being are fully addressed. Rather, society bears within itself all of these types—primitive, substantial, functional, ideal, and personal connections—in an unending tension, pushed by the actual needs of individuals and their struggles.

As an educator, this suggests to me a certain depth and complexity when looking at our team. Rather than merely a graduate student laboratory, I understand this as a community of people who are finding their way in life; there will be many facets, tensions, and developments within this team.

At first, my students had a rather base level of togetherness simply from the fact that they are together, that they read the same things, that they get stressed in the same way when I do spot-quizzes, and so on. This is kind of a primitive, mechanical solidarity type of community. And this is an important part of community that I try to deliberately nourish through team events like drinking or watching fireworks together. I think this organic layer connection is essential for rapport. But at the same time, mere rapport can result in cliquishness, where some become content simply to have a sense of belonging, resulting in an excessively closed and hierarchical group.

As we saw in the previous chapter when the team sought its values for academic life, it was very important for us to build a clear sense of functional solidarity. We are not just a bunch of buddies, but a graduate school team, training for future researchers in the field of Clinical Pedagogy. This sense of shared academic objectives is important for the team. And each member finds their own roles—some specialized in the psychological side of our work, others specialized in the more sociological side, some focusing on sharing real-life examples ... Incidentally, we also have a rather longish manual detailing the rules and expectations of this team!

However, there is also a distinct coldness to this kind of a functional solidarity, which is why it is also important for us to regularly explore our *personal* values as members of the team and share them with the team. There are those who are personally hoping that they can help others. Some who value their personal healing. Some who value helping see people in a different way... And in these connections, they are able to resonate with each other in our shared values.

But the deepest connections from personality to personality simply cannot be manufactured. When a student struggles with their deepest issues, a sense of despair about the world, a dread that they will never be able to find their own voice, sometimes they will deeply connect with me. But sometimes I am not the right person for them to share their vulnerabilities, and I am not the companion they need right now. Situations like these are hard for me, but I know I really cannot and must not force the issue. I can only hope that someone else in the team or someone I can refer might be the one they need.

Criticizing the Philosophy of Awakening

Above, we have seen Mori's attempt to come to terms with life as it is lived individually and in communities. This allowed him to build his own philosophy of awakening amidst that of the Kyoto School of Philosophy.

However, there are different criticisms of this philosophy of awakening. First, we have the issue of developmentalism. Philosopher of education Paul Standish, while noting the value of the Kyoto School's insights, writes:

> But there are still, in the philosophy of education derived from the Kyoto School, certain assumptions of progression or development that are in tension with possibilities of transformation. Can a theory of becoming, especially under institutional pressure towards explicit formulation, avoid sliding into claims regarding stages of development? Can it avoid losing sight of the variety of human experience.[42]

Standish points out the example of Nishitani, the development of awakening follows a diagram from ego to the Great Doubt and to awakening to emptiness.

Second and corollary to this is the danger of a sense of "perfection," as if the process of human becoming can be completed. Saito Naoko and Akiyama Tomohiro discuss the Clinical Pedagogy of Kyoto University (which is the tradition I am part of), pointing out how the Kyoto School's philosophy of awakening tended to rely on an image of a "whole, perfected person" (an enlightened person), which could be employed toward totalitarian and idealist tendencies that lack a sense of criticality and flexibility. They conclude:

> In sum, there is a sense of being trapped in the self-justifying, circulatory and even narcissistic discourse in the defense of the whole person. There is a surreptitious preoccupation with perfectibility and completeness, combined with the idealization and the romanticization of the whole person. Despite the defense that the idea of the whole admits conflicts, tension and agonies, there is a drive toward inclusivity and comprehensiveness that unwittingly expels the deviant—an undeniable tendency towards the assimilation of difference into the whole despite the façade of respecting individuality and particularity.[43]

Saito and Standish were not arguing for nihilistic relativism. Rather, they were arguing for an image of trying to improve oneself without ever closing the ideal of what it means to be "whole." It as a "perfectionism without perfectibility" drawn from the pragmatism of Stanley Cavell and Ralph Waldo Emerson.[44]

Third, when I teach the Kyoto School's philosophy of awakening, some students and teachers find their ideas to be elitist. If one looks at Nishitani's *Religion and Nothingness* or Watsuji's *Purifying Zen*, awakening seems to be the realm of artistic geniuses and sages. Tanabe, who strongly criticized this "path of sages," can be misinterpreted as restricting "metanoia" for people who have experienced deep moral tragedy, like complicity in a world war. Education for awakening thus seems too distant, and "masters" capable of it too rare, for it to be feasible in contemporary life.

Given the criticisms above, we see the value of Mori's philosophy of awakening and life, and how it combines awakening with pragmatism and with Erikson's empirical view of development. It suggests a way to address these criticisms from *within* the tradition of the philosophy of awakening.

First, as we have seen above, although stages may point to general features of development, the actuality of human becoming is not reducible to stages. The particular individual has their own timing for each stage, and previous and future stages are constantly present at any given time. Kawakami has pointed out connections in this sense of indeterminacy with Tanabe Hajime's and Kuki Shūzō's idea of "contingency" (*gūzensei* 偶然性).

However, this is not merely an ideal point but comes from the empirical data—pragmatic study of the growth of children demonstrates this variability and multi-layering. Furthermore, this is coherent with a pragmatic and contextual approach. While there may be an overall structure to the organic, conscious, and self-aware layers, the organic layer is about a particular agent behaving within a particular objective environment. This is the very definition of contextualism and explicitly resists the generalizing tendencies of other scientific approaches.[45] Furthermore, the ideas of the conscious layer do not come from *logos* but from the pragmatic attempt to make sense of our particular behavior and its consequences. Finally, identity and existential self-awareness are not abstract but are the responses of the I to the various behaviors and rules expressed within the particularity of the organic and conscious layers. While Erikson's stages may seem fixed, they are merely guidelines for the particular struggles for persons given likely tensions and crises between animal, symbolic, and existential life.

Second, Mori's "self-awareness" never ends. In his first book, he suggested that instead of clinging to an absolute ideal (absolutism) or simply abandoning ideals for the muck of concrete life (relativism), we need to embrace a constant tension between facing the present challenges of one's life and making sense of it via ideas. This is a *search* that does not presume the presence or absence of its telos. Mori names this "questing self-awareness" (*tankyūteki jikaku* 探求的自覚)[46], an image of constantly being on the way. In his last book, he suggests that while self-awareness tries to come to terms with the fractures of the layers of personality and the tensions in society itself, this process never ends:

> In this way, the fact that human beings are beings that awaken to themselves means that human beings are existents that bear a schism between self and nature, between self and self, and bear a fundamental link. Human beings are beings that give birth to new schisms in the effort to unify those breaks (multiply schizoid existence), but both integration and splitting have a deep connection with the multiple development of human self-awareness. In this way, human beings are multiply self-aware (*tajū jikakuteki* 多重自覚的) existences, existences that have to build self-awareness over and over.[47]

Third, instead of focusing on a single major breakthrough in adult life, like a developmentalist interpretation of the Kyoto School would, Mori found the movement of self-emptying everywhere. With the idea of "multiple self-awareness," we understand why his diagrams show a hint of awakening in every stage of development even prior to the identity crisis of adolescence. Awakening is a process of trying to integrate schisms amidst crisis. That means when elementary first graders try to resolve organic with symbolic life, that is a form of self-awareness. When adolescents try to resolve symbolic and collective life with their own sense of identity and values, that is a realization of emptiness. Furthermore, developmental crises are not resolved once and for all but through a continuing pragmatic process of finding ways to reconcile one's deeper needs with the challenges of one's situation. This means that all education, in so far as it is a journeying of people as they face the key crises of life, is an education for self-awareness, an education for emptiness.

Because of the above, education for awakening becomes democratized and pluralized. One does not need to experience *satori* in order to go through education for awakening. Similarly, one does not need to be an enlightened master to guide others. Taro-*kun*, despite his youth, has already engaged and deeply struggled with crises, having his own glimmers of realization that combine intellect, emotion, and will (*chi jō i* 知情意). When I see Jin-*kun* and Junko-*san* confiding in him, I know that there is a little master, a little Socratic midwife already there. And when I see my students face their crises and genuinely grow, their light chips away the darkness of my own struggle with despair, and in that moment, they are my teachers.

Generative Self-Awareness

"What is a life?" has a correlate: "I'm going to die." The awareness of a life is an awareness that it is bounded, that it begins and that it ends, and somehow, we are tasked with the difficulty of figuring out the meaning of it all. And the other problem is that you never actually know when you are going to die!

Mori wrote his final book while struggling with illness—an illness that would abruptly end the book. Toward the end of his life, he finally got a deep religious experience along the lines of Tanabe's metanoia and Nishitani's Great Death.

> For two years, I could never figure out how to structure and develop a theory of human lifespan (*ningen shōgai ron* 人間生涯論), much less a theory of the stages of life.... A new idea came to me in November 14, 1976, deep in the night. The previous night, at ten o'clock, I had just received my second dose of sedatives, and I battled with sleepiness from one to five o'clock, ended up with a heart attack and called the doctor. It was in the midst of that silliness that I realized this idea. (November 15, 1976)[48]

In his near-death experience, a common site for profound religious awakening, Mori breaks through his philosophical deadlock. His realization had to do with the very nature of lifespan development itself

The Rhythm of Life

and crystallized as a metaphor of the "arched bridge of life" (*seimei tsuzumi hashi*) that addresses the very questions we raised above.

> Looking at the figure [Figure 5.6], it was written presupposing that one's lifespan is completed. However, any infant or child can pass away, nobody knows who will live their lifespan in full . . .
>
> I was looking for images, and I thought of a recent engineering method of an arched bridge (*taikobashi* 太鼓橋) going from this shore to the opposite shore (*mukō gishi* 向こう岸). Isn't human life also something that takes up creating "life" forward, forward, to the yonder shore?[49]

His resulting view of development as an "arched bridge" combined his learnings from five different thinkers: Like a bridge is headed somewhere, life has a drive toward maturity (Jan Martinus Langeveld). But at the same time, bridges do not all head north, but their direction depends on context. Similarly, human beings grow in their own way, as found in the concept of "more growth" (John Dewey). But life is not only forward and upward, but like a bridge, it descends and declines (developmental psychologist Charlotte Bühler).[50] And the shape of a particular bridge is unique, with some bridges that seem to go on forever, and others that are short, like a life cut short by death (from philosopher Heinrich Döpp-Vorwald).[51]

This is the existential side of our life bridge. We are on a bridge, aiming forward. However, from where we stand on the bridge, we are not sure where it lands. But we do know some day, it starts to head downhill, although we know not when. This is the path of awakening in

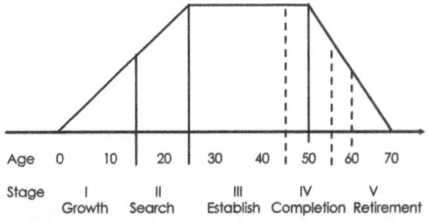

Figure 5.6 The rise and fall of life.

Watsuji's *Purifying Zen*, where Dōgen urges us to come to terms with the impermanence of life.

But there is another aspect of this bridge that he gets from Erikson: A bridge, a life "cycle" exists in itself, bounded by birth and death. But at the same time, a bridge takes off from the previous generation and ends in the next generation.[52] Erikson suggests then a "generational chain." "[I]t seems possible to further paraphrase the relationship of adult integrity and infantile trust by saying that healthy children will not fear life if their elders have integrity enough not to fear death."[53] (See Figure 5.7) Thus, while the existential side of this cycle is inescapable, *at the same time* there is a socially generative side, by which we reach out to the yonder shore, the next generation, and try to give a gift of something that makes some kind of sense in this perplexing life.[54]

Tanaka Tsunemi, who heard this theory dictated first hand, interprets the life bridge theory as follows:

> This book, *Fundamental Principles of Human Formation*, develops the idea of the making and crossing of the life bridge as the mutual quest for meaning of different generations. Educational mutuality gives a generational continuity that transcends individual death, and eventually weaves the generationally continuous public sphere. This is the conclusion of *Fundamental Principles of Human Formation*, and had Mori not died, the conclusion of Chapter 4 would surely have been a more detailed form of the theory of the life bridge.[55]

This view of generativity seen in Mori, Tanaka, and Nishihira has much in common with insights from Watsuji's Confucianism. Our self-awareness is never completed in ourselves. We grow from the caring

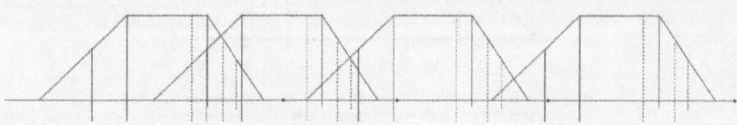

Figure 5.7 Multi-generational bridges.

and authoritative conduct (*jin* 仁) of the previous generation, and our struggle allows us to reach out and care for the next. In the call-response of trust and truth, generational bridges connect us despite (and because of) the finitude of life.

In this way, Mori brings together the different aspects of Watsuji's education for emptiness—the Confucian education of emptying ego to finding one's place through generational care, and the Buddhist education of emptying totality to awaken to the creativity of existential self. However, using pragmatism and contextual science, he combines these idealist insights with emptying brute materiality to realize ideals and emptying calcified ideas to flexibly respond to objective reality.

What is life? Life is a journey of tension and crisis. I walk on my bridge, continuously finding ways to reconcile the different contradictions of my fractured existence, walking toward that final contradiction that is my own death. But at the same time, I do not walk alone. I am guided by those who have come before me, guiding those who will remain after I am gone. This latter half is my *koan* now—I have not come to terms with this arched bridge of life.

6

Learning to Live

One of the most common complaints I get from students when I teach philosophy is that it is too abstract. There are a lot of great ideas in it that can make intuitive sense—the emptiness of human existence, this back-and-forth between individual and group, how culture is shaped by climate ... However, often a beautiful idea only has a glimmer of connection to the everyday lives we live. Like in *Ethics I*, one struggles to find examples of what "emptying totality to realize individuality" might be like. Also, ideas can be concrete but distant, like when Watsuji talks of the "mutually complementary" relationship between the husband in public roles and the wife at home—true a hundred years ago in Japan, but not for many today, especially in more liberal cultures.

Some people might defend philosophy and tell complaining students, "Hey, this is philosophy. If you want something concrete, read a cookbook." But Mori Akira suggests that while it makes perfect sense for *idealism* to be abstract—it is after all about arranging ideas in a way that is internally coherent—it is bizarre to have a philosophy of the "non-duality of subject and object" that does not connect to our lived experience.[1] No, not bizarre, it is a *performative contradiction*. The Kyoto School of Philosophy is founded on the philosophy of nothingness and is thus fundamentally not only about subjective meaning but objective materiality as well. If I reduce it into an abstraction, or if the objective reality it comes from is so historically removed from our reality, it turns into a mere subjective idealism. Furthermore, the central focus of the Kyoto School of Philosophy is awakening (*jikaku*). Nishida Kitarō argued that *jikaku* was a way of bringing back emotion and will (*jō i* 情意) to philosophy, which had ceased to be about the unity of intellect-emotion-will (*chi jō i* 知情意) and had been reduced to mere intellectualizing.[2] If the philosophy of nothingness does not connect to our present experience in an embodied way, it is merely the intellection and not the unity of experience.

It is Mori Akira who hammered this point home for me. On one hand, he had a complex philosophy of human becoming, which included four facets of education representing different sides of individuality (*nin*) and totality (*gen*), a total view of human existence (*ningen sonzai*) that includes both our practical-material existence and our symbolic-ideal existence and their continuity-of-discontinuity. In Watsuji's terminology, Mori had a sophisticated philosophy of emptiness that includes the mutual emptying of individuality and totality, as well as the mutual emptying of subjectivity and objectivity.

However, he constantly opened this philosophy to everyday experience. Tanaka Tsunemi suggests that the main approach for teaching philosophy of education to practitioners involved "enlightenment from above," (*keimō* 啓蒙) where the philosopher would expound abstract philosophical ideas, many beyond the reach of practitioners, and practitioners tried to adjust their practices to these ideas. However, Tanaka says that Mori deliberately resisted this approach, trying to communicate with practitioners in ways they could understand by using concrete examples, easier concepts, and even *desu masu* spoken speech in some of his books. His goal was to ensure practitioners understood him, could decide for themselves which ideas resonated with their experience, and could cooperate with him to *co-construct* ideas.[3] As we will see in this chapter, this is the same attitude he took even toward elementary and middle school students! It is Mori's method that pushed me to write this book in this way—with an effort to renew the connection of philosophy to everyday life.

The clearest example of "philosophizing together" rather than "enlightenment from above" comes from Mori's mid-career where he wrote on moral education. We have already seen key insights from *The Practicality and Inwardness of Education* (1955) in Chapter 4, where we saw Mori's philosophical points combining subjectivity and objectivity and detailing the four functions of education and the four layers of human existence. We have also seen the most important parts of *The Moral Education We Hope For* (1958) in Chapter 5, where he concretized his ideas from 1955 into a book for moral education teachers in elementary and middle school. One of the key things I noticed reading this book is that more than half of it is examples—from his direct experiences teaching morality to elementary and middle school students, extracts of their class work, stories shared by veteran school teachers, and even from parents sharing worries or arguing with him during parent-teacher conferences!

In this chapter, we will continue with *The Moral Education We Do Together* (1959), another practical book for school teachers, and three volumes of *New Life* (1962), textbooks written for *middle school students* by a panel that includes Mori Akira himself. (It also includes Katsube Mitake, Watsuji's disciple who founded the moral education association.) There are a number of chapters in these volumes that Mori directly references, suggesting that he was heavily involved in writing them, perhaps drafting them himself.

These books form a precious opportunity to think about the philosophy of awakening in a genuinely pragmatic way. Mori takes seriously the Deweyan point that thinking begins from actual problems experienced in life, where it develops in tandem with thinking toward "meaningful action." With these books, we can see those actual problems as he faced them, and consider the process of how one actually learns to live, to walk this path of becoming human.

We will begin with Mori's view of life guidance (informal moral education) found in his 1959 book for teachers, and how it transforms into moral ideals. Then, we will examine formal moral education via four sample classes from *New Life* of how students are given opportunities to consider the ethics of self, communication, the group, and creativity. Finally, we end with the question of evidence-based education.

Life Guidance

For Mori, education is a primarily ethical process of becoming human, wherein we grow in responsibility for our existence as *ningen*, learning our place and awakening to ourselves. However, looking at the realities of psychological development, students do not start out as capable of taking charge of this process of becoming. In *The Moral Education We Do Together*, Mori writes,

> Children need to eventually become "an existence that ought themselves to be responsible for their personal becoming." It is our responsibility as adults to create the foundation for them to be able to fulfill this responsibility [for their own becoming].[4]

Children need to *learn* to become responsible for their becoming. Mori understands moral education as the process wherein parents and teachers momentarily shoulder responsibility for the becoming of children—not to take this burden away from them, but to help them learn to shoulder this responsibility themselves.

We see here that Mori defines moral education very broadly. In his book for moral education teachers, he writes:

> A world where anyone can live fully (*sei ippai ikite yukeru* 精一杯生きてゆける), where anyone can think, "I'm glad I was born." A world where valuing oneself is at the same time valuing others. Isn't the goal of moral guidance [for students] to become someone who can build such a world, to build such a world together?[5]

Moral education is about growth in response to the environment and with other people, and making a society that supports this growth. However, in *The Practicality and Inwardness of Education*, which he wrote for philosophy researchers, he writes: "Completing control over nature / Complete human becoming (*ningen seisei*) / People who can build society / Raising (*ikusei* 育成) such people is the ultimate goal of education. This is simultaneously the goal of moral education."[6] Here we see the same elements of collective growth in nature and building such a society—and the direct equation of moral education with the wider process of education and becoming human.

Moral education is thus not one subject in school, or even one function of school itself. *Moral education is a fundamental ethical response from one person to another as fellow wayfarers on the path of becoming human.* As such, I continue to use it in our graduate team, my undergraduate classes, and my mentees and counselees. And given that all people struggle and need to learn how to live life, these ideas can be applied even to one's friends or one's elders, when one is helping them along the path.

However, Mori's idea of moral education was in conflict with many forces in 1960s Japan. During that time, there was a push in the Ministry of Education (which included some members of the Kyoto School)[7] to re-establish moral education as a separate "moral hour"—a move that pushed through and has progressed recently into moral education becoming a separate subject with its own fixed curriculum. However, Mori felt that this would result in separating moral education from other academic subjects and the broader process of education. Additionally, he felt that many ethics professors in universities who were involved in this would talk about the ideals of moral education but knew nothing of the actualities of educating students in schools, coming up with mere abstractions.[8] The Ministry of Education had the advantage of having ears on the ground, but it had its own political vision of what society needed and sought to impose the values and virtues of this on students via a manualized method of moral education.

However, such a moral education that "enlightens from above" would merely be socialization of generic citizens, not the becoming human of unique people. Mori countered, "My fundamental attitude is not the Ministry of Education's 'top-down ideas' but *considering the lifestyle of children, 'thinking bottom-up'* (*shita kara hassō* 下から発想) about moral education and *proceeding in an autonomous way*."[9] Mori was also concerned with conservative forces—not just politicians but some teachers and parents—trying to use "top-down" moral education to inculcate values like feudal versions of patriotism and filial piety. Therefore, Mori took a bottom-up stance that connected with Miyasaka Tetsufumi's idea of "life guidance" and Ueda Kaoru (Nishida's grandson!) and his view of morality and citizenship as part of all education.

What is a "bottom-up" approach to moral education? Such an approach begins from the reality of children and their *living* (*seikatsu* 生活, also translatable as "way of life").

> Whether adult or child, *ningen* learn through living (*seikatsu*). Human living is broadly "learning lifestyle" [or learning history].... Living means: 1. Living that must connect to the life (*inochi*) of the child.... 2. Individual activities that each child carries out with sincere subjective feeling (*jikkan* 実感), interest, and concern. 3. Group activities that each child participates in with sincere subjective feeling, interest, and concern.... 4. What stipulates (*kitei* 規定) their way of being (way of seeing things, thinking, feeling, living), whether children realize it or not.[10]

"*Seikatsu*" is the key word of this book. And with it, Mori draws attention to the objective world of human action—what we do individually, what we do as groups, and the contexts to which these actions respond. But in addition to this objective life is what it subjectively means:

> Whether we consider individual guidance or general guidance, we need to grasp well the environmental conditions and consciousness of the problem of the children, otherwise we will not really be able to guide them in a way that is fitting to (*micchaku shita* 密着した) their living. I call this undercurrent "lifestyle consciousness." 1. *Gestalt structure*: Lifestyle consciousness can be seen as a form of *psyche*.... 2. *Ego consciousness*.... *Group consciousness*... *Moral consciousness*...[11]

In addition to action-in-context, *seikatsu* includes its meaning. Thus, we see that like Watsuji's two non-dualities, the idea of living includes the individual and the collective agent, as well as their material and ideal conditions. Just as Watsuji sought to begin ethics with the "hermeneutics of everyday expressions," Mori demands that the educator commence ethical education from these four dimensions of living.

However, Mori's understanding is more micro than macro. Rather than looking at a nation (or humankind) and its struggles over decades and centuries of civilization, Mori is examining an individual or a small group in a classroom as they contend with various challenges in a scale of weeks (or at most several years). Thus, his approach is akin to hermeneutic phenomenology of experience (in qualitative research and philosophy) and functional analysis of behavior (in psychology).

We look at what individuals and groups actually *do*, we look at the material context around this action, we look at the thoughts and feelings that give meaning to this action. And in so doing, we understand students and groups as meaningfully acting beings.

In my work, I teach classes on educational counseling and qualitative research, and this kind of observation is foundational in both practice and analysis. For example, as I mentioned in Chapter 4, many in my team struggle with connecting their personal growth to academic work. One major issue we have struggled with is students writing and submitting papers regularly and on time. In our handbook, we clearly state that students should submit a semestral paper of a certain level of academic quality. But students often do not submit without repeated reminders, and some of their submissions are merely repetitions of what we have read, lacking academic insight. Many teachers, faced with a scenario like this, may directly confront the student: "Why aren't you submitting your assignments? This is a class rule! You agreed to this!" But here, "submit," "assignment," "rule" all draw us straight into institutionalized frames of meaning (like requirements) within which the behavior is framed and condemned.

In contrast to this, a more qualitative or counseling approach begins with carefully observing the behavior and its context. "Hey Junko-*san*, I haven't gotten your submission yet. What's up, feeling okay?" "Hey Jin-*kun*, I read your assignment today. Seems like you were struggling a bit. Wanna tell me what's going on for you?" And when I ask questions like these, I often find that non-submission is often far more complicated than simply a lack of self-discipline, and each student has their own particular challenges with it.

For example, Junko-*san* struggled with submitting papers because of a fear that her paper would be less than perfect. She would get very self-critical when deadlines drew near, almost paralyzing her. (If I were to add to that criticism, it would make things *worse*, not better!) Taro-*kun* also struggled with submitting, but his problem was a sense of meaninglessness, a doubt that academic work did not really touch the heart of existential problems. Unlike the other two, Jin-*kun* submitted papers on time, but they tended to lack depth precisely because he was stuck in this role of *capable student*, preventing him from connecting to his learning with a sense of openness and vulnerability.

Only then can we richly unpack what the behavior means to this person and the horizon within which it unfolds. Mori writes, "In order to do moral education—lifestyle guidance and moral guidance—well, the most necessary thing is observing children carefully and understanding them correctly. This is a task that requires the educator's own eyes and hands, no, their entire being."[12]

This is a rather loaded statement. First, like pragmatic approaches to qualitative research and participant observation, "hands" means that knowledge is not theoretical but enactive, coming from a process of trying to help students, rather than simply watching them like lab specimens. Second, "own eyes" means that this is not about objective and generalized forms of data like statistics on development. While Mori included data like these, he insisted that the starting point must be observation of the particular child.[13] After all, when teaching, we are faced with unique individuals, not "average students" or "representatives of populations." Third, "entire being" points out how understanding is not merely a cognitive process but involves being guided by one's perspective-taking (imagining what a student is responding to and what they are trying to do therein) which then allows one to try to feel what the student is feeling, and sense motivations that the student might be having as well. In this way, I can take the student's perspective, in its uniqueness, feeling second hand the emotions and meanings that accompany this behavior.[14]

This observation of *seikatsu* is the base for moral education. Taking their perspective, we see areas wherein the students themselves undergo struggles, where their habits work against them and bring them into a moment of disequilibrium with life.

> The first step is to take the moral problems, broadly speaking ("What should I do?" "How should I live my life?"), which are directly encountered in the everyday actual living and academic learning of children, from a state of being only vaguely seen, *developing* them into

a clear consciousness of the problem. This is what it means to be "bottom-up thinking." Not a supplementation from above but development from below.[15]

Rather than beginning from what the teacher might see as a problem (not submitting papers), one begins from how that might be problematic for the student (ex. being trapped by perfectionism, a sense of meaningless, or a lack of personal engagement). We can then help students become aware of these problems, to clarify the context of the behavior when it is unclear, to help them see both short-term and long-term consequences if they need scaffolding there. This unfolds into "direct guidance,"[16] where we try to help students through the Deweyan process of learning (observing, clarifying a problem, considering alternatives, deliberating on them, trying out different kinds of behavior)—scaffolding them only as much as is necessary for them to work the rest out themselves.

For example, after exploring the struggles of Junko-*san*, Taro-*kun*, and Jin-*kun* and the challenging thoughts and feelings that come up when it becomes time to produce academic output, we usually explore the consequences of their behavior. For example, procrastinating a submission might result in short-term relief and getting away from something that feels heavy or meaningless. But long term, it results in a sense of moving away from what one had originally hoped for in joining our team—the personal questions that they brought into their research, the contribution they hoped to make by engaging these questions. On the basis of this contextual understanding, we usually come up with strategies that are quite customized for each student. For example, Junko-*san* found it very helpful to focus on sharing what she found meaningful in the lesson, writing a bit casually because it helped her distance herself from the weight of perfectionism. But it was the opposite strategy for Jin-*kun*, who had to remind himself about the difference between mere studying and creative research, and go over his work again to deepen it.

Furthermore, because individual problems are usually tied to group problems and because individual problems are repeated within certain objective contexts, a major part of moral education is shaping the group context. Mori refers to this as class building, *gakyū zukuri*. Group context is shaped by modeling how the teacher behaves, how the teacher runs the class, and certain rules that shape the overall behavior of the class.[17]

For example, submission issues were common in almost every member of our team. Sometime after I had discussed with students one-on-one, I also took time to discuss with the group. I shared my own struggles with research, and the students shared (but only to the degree they were comfortable with sharing) a bit about their struggles with writing. We then explored our values connecting personal growth and research (as we saw in Chapter 4). We then explored ways we might better move toward those values as a team, and the rule for semestral papers was actually an outcome of one of these team discussions. But this time, we did not need a new rule, but to remember the spirit and values behind that rule.

Shaping behavior directly and shaping contexts indirectly allow people to learn by doing. But this doing is also directly connected to *feeling*. In pragmatism, feeling is not abstract aesthetics, but is connected to the felt sense of actional life, an excitement that accompanies and primes action, an anxiety that narrows attention and increases focus on threats . . . By learning to do the right thing, one also cultivates *moral emotion*—a felt sense of comfort that grooves more helpful forms of behavior, or a tactile discomfort that warns of unhelpful behavior.[18]

With Mori's focus on moral habits and moral emotion, he was ahead of his time. While everyone was focused on Piaget and Kohlberg's fundamentally cognitive models of moral psychology (moral reasoning causes behavior), Mori was already pre-empting the movements in the 1980s toward non-rational elements like moral sensitivity and character (James Rest), which would develop in the 2000s into an awareness of fast, unconscious moral decision-making that often dominates moral action (Daniel Kahneman, Jonathan Haidt).[19] Mori was already working on the habitual (and emotional) base of morality that shapes most of our moral decision-making long-term.

However, this was not merely a matter of sophisticated moral psychology. For Mori, beginning from lifestyle, behavior, and feeling allowed Mori to be fundamentally democratic. Moral thinking and symbolic ideas in general are shared media and thus tend to abstract from the individual case and person into ways of thinking that are generalized—a tendency highlighted even further when moral thinking is governed by a whole nation's value system. Thus, starting from ideas results in a fundamentally generalizing and totalizing approach, which collides with Dewey's idea of democracy as a *way of life* wherein people intelligently find their way through their own experience. Therefore, Mori starts from the process of experiencing life and acting within it, including both technical and moral challenges together. This allows him to begin from the most immediate and unique part of experience, after which he then slowly builds higher levels of abstraction "bottom-up."

Toward Moral Ideals

The previous section highlights dealing with particular contextual problems. However, Mori builds from this pragmatic base toward clarifying ideals. "Directly via living (*seikatsu*), human beings (*ningen*) face problems of 'How should I/we live?' 'How should one live as *ningen*?'"[20]

On one hand, "How should I live" is a basic process of decision-making in life, including what Mori calls the "non-moral base of the personality" and our various habits. But as *should*, this decision-making takes a symbolic form and begins to form one's moral ideals, the moral side of personality. The school-age child begins to have reasons—of varying degrees of sophistication—that serve to guide behavior and justify the behavior to others.

This brings us to the second question, "How should one live as *ningen*?" Humans are not only becoming, they are becoming *human*—humanity here exerts a normative force on becoming. What kind of becoming, as manifest in what kind of behavior, is worth standing up for before humanity? As we become more symbolic, the ideas we use to guide our own behavior becomes justifications to others and thus something we stand up for before others. One's dismissive attitude toward research may inadvertently become a stance, "It doesn't matter if I do the work anyway. Academic work doesn't really matter existentially." And that stance is not a private stance but one that is held before others.

With this, we need more than merely spontaneous lifestyle guidance and require formal moral education—an opportunity to think through our ideas in order to make sure that individual action and group action are guided in ways that are helpful rather than harmful. The first method for Mori is informal group discussions where students can talk about actual problems in class.[21] Our team discussion gave students an opportunity to articulate their struggles and values to others and thus clarify them—by expressing and also by listening to others.[22]

Mori stresses how these discussions should be relaxed and authentic. It is important that the teacher be *curious* rather than judgmental about experience so that student can think about the situation bottom-up rather than from abstract self-criticism, allowing for a sense of psychological safety. The goal is not to impose moral values on students but to get students to clarify and refine their symbolic networks themselves, and they need to have a sense of safety (rather than defensiveness) for that. For example, in discussing the mentality that "Academic work doesn't matter existentially" (and seeing that not only Taro-*kun*, but even I had moments where I struggled with that), students were less defensive and more willing to see how this mentality connects to other tendencies—Jin-*kun*'s tendency to read superficially, Junko-*san* seeing papers merely as something she will be judged by—and how it clashes with what they themselves had hoped to learn in university.

Discussions can also be more structured and make use of some material to stimulate thinking about certain topics. In *The Moral Education We Hope For*, Mori designed a basic framework to help teachers cover the full range of challenges of human becoming. He discussed four types of ethics: ethics of the self, creativity, communication, and groups. He also presented a list of virtues[23]—but he eventually became critical of this focus on virtues because he realized it detracted from a more bottom-up approach that began from the actual lives of the students. But it is possible for a teacher to be grounded on a lifestyle-centered approach, while at the same time using the four types of ethics and the list of virtues to prepare materials—stories, essays, films—to expand the awareness of students and get them to consider real experiences that are a step removed from their direct experience. We will see actual examples of these materials in the following sections.

Through both informal and formal discussions, we build moral understanding and moral judgment—what we saw as the "conscious layer" of the human being. Students can clarify the reasons that buttress their behavior—both helpful and unhelpful. They can become more conscious of their reasons and other possible reasons by conversing with others and with the material. And by examining these reasons pragmatically together with the consequences of behavior in their actual lives, they can build judgment toward actions that sustainably are more helpful in their lives.

In the process of these discussions, however, we come up with deep moral dilemmas, where different ways of thinking may not be resolvable pragmatically but are rooted in a deep sense of personal choice of how to engage life. Mori writes,

> Solving problems like these through discussion (*ketsugi* 決議) is bizarre. Even if you solve them [through platitudes] ... it is meaningless. Worse, stipulating matters (rules) that relate with the internal awakening (*naimenteki jikaku*) of individuals is in a way a method of closed (totalitarian) states. Problems like these should be raised in moral guidance, given to individual students to think about and attain self-awareness about.[24]

With this, moral education shifts from the conscious layer to the self-aware layer where ideas are not merely shared forms but are turned in toward the self in self-understanding. But as seen in the quote above, this process requires special care. One's budding self-understanding (identity) is not a generalizable phenomenon but is unique to the individual. As such, it is difficult to justify it rationally in front of an unsympathetic crowd. It needs a method that allows it some space to form.

For this, Mori turned to methods like journaling and narrative essays. Mori particularly stressed journaling, even dedicating a chapter to it in his moral education textbooks. Journaling presents a safe space where one can express one's thoughts away from the judgment of others. Mori writes, "By *essaying about one's living* (*seikatsu*), what was once simply living life gives rise to an opportunity to better *consider* (*omoimiru*) one's living experience—to reconsider it, and rethink it."[25] By giving it an objective form, one allows oneself to grasp the subject behind it and *re-flect* upon oneself. In a sense, we are teaching them to look at their own *seikatsu* carefully and reflexively, just as the teacher was in trying to understand them.

While most journaling remains private, there were cases where Mori asked for certain journal entries as submissions, and occasionally got the permission of the student to discuss the journal entry in class, taking care not to subject it to judgment but to openly think about it together.

When we give students space to make sense of themselves and their personal values, we find that they are dealing with moral problems in a way that is essentially the same as the adult teacher. Mori writes,

> "What should I (we) do?" "As *ningen*, how should I (we) live?" Particularly in the present day when the system of values is in chaos, it has become incredibly difficult to know correctly about our behavior and way of life. Rather than teaching children, we [educators] need to first learn. And there will be many instances where we learn while we teach.[26]

Mori repeatedly stresses how real moral dilemmas children face are, taking children seriously rather than using the Heinz dilemma merely to measure levels of moral development. Children are actually trying to find their way forward in life, not just for themselves but for humankind. And thus, moral education needs to be "a time when teachers and students think together / a time when we can discover opportunities for reflection for fathers and mothers / a time when we can genuinely pursue the truth of good and evil."[27] In their self-awareness, we are not transmitting pre-existing ethics to children—we are walking the path of moral philosophy *together*.

As fellow wayfarers, generativity is not the exclusive domain of the teacher. Interestingly, Mori made a diagram of methods in moral education in increasing levels of self-awareness/awakening: shaping the social context, guiding life and behavior, discussions, dramatization, essays/journals ... At the very top of this was survey research (*chōsa kenkyū* 調査研究) and project essays (*kadai sakubun* 課題作文)![28] This may seem bizarre from the point of view of self-awareness as mere identity, but when we consider intimacy, generativity, and integrity, the focus on research makes sense. In surveys, a student goes beyond their own subjectivity to look at the reality they share with others as *ningen*.[29]

Thus, when the student does a "project essay," the student is building upon discussions (conscious self), journaling (self-awareness1), and a sense of social generativity in social research (self-awareness2) in order to express, in a public form, what they want to contribute to the world. These are submitted to the teacher, shared with the class, and can be the subject of class discussion, allowing opportunities not only for fellow students to learn, but for the teacher to learn from students as well.[30]

Mori had written this primarily for students up to middle school. But as we see in my examples above, the questions of how we ought to live continue for university and graduate students. In many ways, I see the graduation thesis as a kind of "project essay." It is not just about fulfilling an academic writing or showing off one's intelligence. In the process of working hard on a single topic, one deepens one's understanding of a certain domain in life, one builds certain skills and habits, and one shapes oneself in the direction of certain *personal values*. And that is given public form in the graduation thesis—a way of generatively standing before the world to give voice to the values that one realized through one's academic journey.

Awakening in the Classroom

Above and in the previous chapter, we have seen a "moral education" that cultivates the awakening of students to their values in the midst of the various crises of human development. But perhaps some are wondering, is this kind of education really possible? And how can this be done if you have to deal with a whole classroom of thirty to forty students?

In the next four sections, I will look at sample chapters from *New Life*, a textbook series for students co-authored by Mori Akira. I will present these as stories, as if Mori were the teacher, including the activities that he has students do. Hopefully you can read this while imagining Mori, in a classroom with several dozen middle school students, trying to actually realize an education for awakening.

1. Ethics of the Self

"How the Self has Grown" was written for third year middle school students—around 14 years old.[31]

> Mori begins with the story of the British clergyman Joseph Singh in Godamori near Calcutta, India. In 1920, he found what seemed to be strange animals living with wolves, who turned out to be two female humans who had been raised by wolves. He named them Kamala (8 years old) and Amala (18 months old). They were momentarily placed in an orphanage. But they behaved like wolves, walking on all-fours, licking water from their bowls and carrying things in their mouths. They did not mix well with the other children and eventually ran away. But Singh and his wife found them and tried to raise them with love, consoling Kamala after the unexpected death of Amala.
> With this parental kindness, Kamala slowly began to grow. After three years, she learned how to sign yes and no, and her vocabulary

gradually expanded. She slowly gave up her nocturnal habits. When she was 14, she was walking upright and accustomed to wearing clothes. By 17, she was even caring for other children. She died at 17, with the mental age of a 4-year-old child.

Mori asks the students, "What did you think of Kamala's story?" He points out that becoming human is not an automatic thing, but something that requires a human environment, love, a family. Furthermore, this story makes us think about what traits are "human." Walking upright, using your hands to grasp things, making things, learning language, and feeling complex emotions.

So, what do we need in order to grow in a human way? Unlike animals, humans are born completely helpless. The one thing we are sensitive to is the signs of love from our mothers and caregivers, from whom we learn to trust the world. This trust opens us up to cooperate with others in communal life. Then toddlers try to do things themselves. Their imagination grows through their life of play. With school, we learn group life by learning together, playing together, even fighting with each other. We learn about rules and cooperation, and we learn academic things too. This is how we become full-fledged members of society. Around middle school, adolescents like you try to find their individuality, their own strengths, and how they might be useful in society.

Mori then breaks up the students into small groups where they share their impressions of the story. They also discuss the characteristics of human beings and what is needed to for development. After discussing, he asks them to journal privately about two things: First, how do the different stages of development connect to their own experience—how did they experience love, autonomy, imagination, becoming a full-fledged member? Second, he asks them to make a simple autobiography—their family tree, the town one was from, who influenced them, an experience that left a strong impression on them, and a book that deeply moved them.

As we see above, Mori begins not with abstractions but with stories that awaken the imagination and encourage the students to take a different perspective. Through the stories of Kamala and Amala (a common story in the field of education of disputed authenticity), he encourages imagining a situation where the developmental support human beings are usually afforded has been completely denied. As such, it draws into relief that human becoming is not something one can take for granted.

This narrative allows Mori to transition to more academic matters—the psychology of development of identity of Erik Erikson—with a sense of realness. Students are able to think about what someone like Kamala might have been needing, as seen through the eyes of Singh.

The questions at the end show the separation between what can be discussed as a group and what is best left to personal reflection. Group discussion is for generalizable matters, the conscious layer of *ningen*. But when matters shift to the self-aware layer, Mori shifts to private work. Here, the student is able to make a personal connection between their own experience and the various developmental needs of childhood. I do this in my "Introduction to Education" class, and some students do mention trauma and other psychological issues here—something about which one does not want to expose the student to public ridicule. The autobiographical exercise is also interesting, and I will turn to an example of that at the end of this chapter.

2. Ethics of Communication

"Feeling Defeated" is a story written for second year middle school students, usually around 13 years old.

> Mori begins this chapter with the short story by the writer Kunikida Doppo (1871–1908). This story is of an adolescent boy, Okamoto (probably modeled after Kunikida himself), who loved drawing and was very talented. Okamoto was a confident boy but also a bit of a troublemaker, who spent his days drawing (and making trouble).
>
> Okamoto's struggles began with another boy, Shimura, who was a bit dull but incredibly talented in drawing. However, unlike the arrogant, rambunctious Okamoto, Shimura was mild-mannered, fair, with almost feminine features. As a result, all the students loved him,

and all the teachers praised his drawings. But all the praise was all for Shimura and none for Okamoto.

One day, there was a school art exhibition. Determined to show his skill, Okamoto put days of effort into a large, lifelike pencil drawing of a horse. He had drawn it excellently and submitted the drawing confident of securing the win. On the day of the exhibition, he went to the hall and saw people gathered around two large drawings. One was his. The other was Shimura's, a portrait of Columbus made in chalk—a medium they had yet to be taught in class. There was no way his pencil's gray could compete with the colors and the energy of the Columbus portrait. "The horse is nice, but that Columbus..." he heard his classmates say.

Okamoto fled from the school to a nearby river and collapsed by the bank. Flailing his legs, screaming, throwing stones... When his feelings had subsided, he bought chalk and brought his new art materials beyond the river, eager to paint the steam engine. But when he arrived, there was Shimura—already sketching the locomotive.

Okamoto decided to draw Shimura instead. Shimura turned around and smiled. "What are you drawing?" "I'm drawing you." "Well, I'm done with drawing the train." "Really? I'm not done yet." "Oh okay." And Shimura returned to his original position. "Go ahead, draw. I'll fix my drawing while you're at it." As Okamoto drew him, his anger softened, and he saw Shimura differently. "You did good with Columbus, I was quite surprised."

After, Okamoto and Shimura became close friends. They often walked the mountains and meadows sketching. Eventually, Okamoto graduated and went to Tokyo to study. When he was twenty, he returned and asked about Shimura—only to find out that Shimura had died 3 years ago. Okamoto walked around the mountains and meadows like they used to and found himself in tears.

After sharing this story, Mori presented the students with notes from previous middle school students talking about their problems.

One girl had problems talking in front of others. She would blush and panic. She tried to improve it in smaller groups, but still she found that she could not talk in front of the whole class. She would be so afraid of having to talk in front of the class that she could not eat.

Another girl had very bad scores. She would work hard on it but could not seem to make progress. Her father said she was hopeless, that it was the fault of her laziness. He compared her to her big brother and her little sister and said that she was the only one who was no good. It made her furious and want to lash out.

One boy had no friends and nobody seemed to like him. He felt envy every time he saw people show fondness to their friends. He had friends he played with but felt that nobody really knew him or understood him. Even his mom preferred his sister to him. And somehow, it made him feel so lonely . . .

After sharing these letters, Mori explains that we all have something we're insecure about. People are insecure about various things, from their looks to their abilities to their financial situation . . . Some insecurities we don't even know about then they pop out of nowhere. But why are people insecure? It's because we live in society. And society now is more competitive than cooperative: those who lose feel inferior, and those who win feel superior. Thus, insecurity is not just our fault, but something caused by outside factors too, much like getting ill.

But like sickness, this is something that we have to help ourselves recover from. One can work on improving things that one is objectively bad at. But sometimes, there are things that we feel inferior about, but we actually are not inferior! And some get so focused on this inferiority that they fall into despair—even suicide. It is important that we overcome this sickness of feeling inferior. Rather than getting caught up in one's inferiority, one good way is to talk to others or one's teacher about it. Inferiority comes from a sense of *isolating* oneself, and so connecting to others can really help.

Mori then groups up students, asking them to discuss the following: Where does Okamoto's sense of inferiority come from? Why do inferiority and superiority complexes exist? Why did Okamoto's relationship to Shimura change? Privately he also asks students to think both about times that they feel proud and times they feel down. Finally, he has students discuss what the class can do to reduce people getting isolated in their worries, and has each student write an essay about it.

Reading this, I could not help but remember Jin-*kun* from Chapter 1. Above, Mori uses stories to allow students to experientially access times when they compared themselves to others and felt inferior. The detailed description of Okamoto flying into a rage after his defeat allows students to emotionally resonate with this experience. The examples from students then broadens the experience to allow students to catch different ways they might be feeling insecure.

Mori then turns to build understanding and judgment, seeing the nature of inferiority and its relation to a competitive, measuring society—the degreeocracy and profit-society that Watsuji critiqued. Combined with his questions about Okamoto and Shimura's turning point, we see that Mori is trying to get students to see the possibility of reframing their self-isolation and self-comparison by genuinely seeing other people, not just as people to be compared to, but as a Thou which the I stands before. In this relation, it is not a matter of inferiority or superiority but a genuine sense of existential relation and connection with others.

Finally, in the discussion, students are given an opportunity to think generatively about this problem, seeing even existential connection (and its opposite in self-isolation) as something that can be addressed not merely individually but in the structure of a community like one's homeroom.

In a sense, we see a tension here between Watsuji's tendency for "relation without an other" in a static society and the self-criticism found in his version of Confucianism where one is always reflecting if one has been virtuous enough. In contrast to this, Mori is trying to build an ethics of communication where we see other people as *other*, not through roles but through perspective-taking, genuinely connect with them, and try to shape our communities together.

3. Ethics of the Group

"An Open Heart" is also for second year students.[32]

> Mori tells the students about the difficulty of Japanese students becoming self-aware of Japanese traits. The Japanese have lived for thousands of years on a small island and with its own culture. But in

the past century, Japan westernized. Western culture was developed over thousands of years, but Japan had a rushed modernity. As such, many Japanese traits are half-cooked, and there are many old traits that remain, blocking the progress of contemporary society.

Since the Meiji period, Japan quickly developed into a modern nation-state, but feudal ways of thinking still remain. For example, fathers tend to lord it over the rest of the family and women are treated as inferior to men. Because Japanese are used to submitting to feudal authorities, we still have the tendency to suck up to those in power and bully those who are weaker than us. We see this in sayings like "*Gomuri gomottomo*," where we follow people even if we know the command is unreasonable.

Feudalism also lingers in how we build cliques, *batsu*, that tend to cover-up wrongs of the ingroup and exclude those in the outgroup. Perhaps this comes from a long history of living in tight feudally-controlled groups, and we find these cliques all over society. But students do this too. For example, one might ignore an old person who needs a seat on the train, but quickly yield one's seat for a member of one's clique. Thus, the right people don't get what they need because people are caught up in a narrow perspective. We also tend to be easily swayed by what other people are doing, becoming envious of others, copying how others dress, chasing fads. This comes at the cost of considering the needs of one's own way of life.

Another trait we tend to have is that we tend to get excited very quicky, but only to give up just as fast. Perhaps this comes from monsoon weather and how rice farming has a fixed annual process. But beyond natural conditions, it was feudalism that tended to prevent people from changing their fates, resulting in a Japanese "selfless resignation."

Another tendency we have is to be quite intuitive but to the contrary lacking in rational consideration. We have sayings like "*Rikutsu wa yame ni shite* (stop with all the theory)" or "*Riron to jissai wa chigau* (theory and practice are different)," showing how we fail to use theory and reason to actually guide our behavior and instead simply rely on intuition. This tends to make us lack planning and increases chances of failure.

Perhaps it is painful for you to hear these criticisms of Japan. But good and bad traits come together. For example, while we may tend to be overeager to keep up with others, that helped us learn a lot from other countries during the Meiji restoration. If we could progress like this but also autonomously create our own culture, this would really help us as a country. Similarly, our resignation can be turned into resilience, and our intuition can be turned into an attention to the wisdom of everyday practice. Japan does have its old traditions and strengths. But at the same time, it has these feudal traits that get in the way of autonomy, and we would do well to challenge those. We should try to modernize Japan and broaden our narrow-mindedness to consider broader society, international society, and universal truth.

Mori also included a letter from a French missionary talking about the strengths and weaknesses of Japan as well as some sayings both from feudal thinking and modernity. He ends with a discussion of the various sayings and what they mean, and group reflection on our tendency to build cliquish groups. He asks both boys and girls to see if they put down girls simply for their gender. He asks people to consider times when they fell to submissive compliance, mindless keeping up with groups, give up too easily . . . He ends with homework for individuals to write an essay about "The Japanese from now on."

While this chapter includes much of Mori's ideas, my guess is that it was drafted by Katsube, because the method is more idealistic and the content connects directly to Watsuji (Katsube's mentor). For example, the idea of Japanese traits like resignation being shaped by Japan's milieu as an archipelago with monsoon rains (*Climate and Culture*) and the idea of a more intuitive culture learning from more rational cultures (*Ethics III*) come from Watsuji.

Despite this, the chapter connects to main ideas highlighted by Mori. From his first book, Mori was deeply critical of Japan's "half-modernity," where superficial changes hid a deeply feudal way of thinking that remained unquestioned. He also deliberately critiqued the tendency of students to form cliques and hierarchies. More importantly, unlike Watsuji's tendency to criticize this merely from ideal demands like the balance of *ningen* or the pursuit of truth, this chapter follows Mori's pragmatic approach of pointing out *consequences* to learn from—like how cliques and hierarchies result in failure to cooperate with broader society or an inability to make decisions in response to the needs of one's own lifestyle.

Furthermore, the idea that "Theory ought to be useful in actuality, our actual [behavior] should be guided by theory"[33] shows Mori's pragmatic union of theory and practice directly taught to students. Theory and practice should form a healthy back-and-forth movement—as found in the experimental method of Dewey—and this contrasts with merely going by ideal intuitions (*kan*), in what might be Mori's indirect critique of the tendencies of other members of the Kyoto School.[34]

4. Ethics of Creativity

"The Path I Walk" is for third year middle school students.[35] It talks about two real boys about to graduate from middle school. During the 1960s, education was only required until middle school and many chose to go directly to work. In the present, this is closer to the situation in high school, where poorer students choose to work directly. (Okano Kaori[36] has excellent ethnographic work detailing this process.)

Mori begins by reading a letter from Ryūichi to Masao:

Masao-*kun*,

It might seem strange that I'm writing you even though we talk every day. But there's something I want to clear up with you, so I thought it would be better if I write.

Today, during lunch break, you said, "Good for you man. When I finish middle school, it's the peasant life (*hyakushō*) for me. Guess we're parting ways huh." You probably didn't mean anything by it, but I hated hearing that, from the bottom of my heart.

Do you remember, on one rainy day, they told us our Civics teacher wasn't coming and that we were to study on our own. Everyone started bouncing off the walls, but I said, "Hey, we should be studying even if our teacher isn't around." And you backed me up and said, "The true measure of your smarts is what you do when the teacher isn't around!" And we got everyone to straighten up.

But these days, you don't stop people from goofing off, and somehow, I can't bring myself to do so either. During self-study time, I was staring out the window and you said in a hushed voice, "I'm only going as far as middle school. You're going to high school, yeah?" I nodded and asked you why. "I'm poor, I'm a peasant, what can I do? I'm going to farm." Six years of elementary, three of middle school, and you never said anything about poverty. We were just always together, inseparable, a tag-team. Remember when we won the three-legged race? Everyone knew we'd be so in synch that we'd be unstoppable.

Okay so I guess you're the eldest son of five kids in a farming family. We have a store and it's just me and my sister. It's plain as day that our backgrounds are different. But what do you mean this is it for us?

I never thought we were going our separate ways. Sure, you might start farming, and I'll be in high school. We might be apart for a bit. It won't be like it is these days, sitting side-by-side. But if we believe in each other, nobody has to give up on anything. What, are you saying you're embarrassed about farming? It doesn't make me better than you. You're smart. You have to see why your work matters, just like *Sensei* told us. Your job is useful too. What's so different about business? I'm the eldest too so I'll probably take over dad's store. But if you're farming and helping the community, and I'm doing my best for our village by doing good business, there's nothing different about us. We aren't going to change.

So stop saying things like "this is it for us." Maybe I'm overthinking it, if I am, I'm sorry. I've written a lot and it's getting late. I'll stop here. But stop saying crap like we're going our separate ways, Masao-*kun*.   – Ryūichi

Ryūichi-*kun*,

Thanks for writing. Really. I read your letter a few times, and it cheered me up.

I didn't realize you cared for me that much, so I guess I whined a bit. I'm sorry I worried you. Before we entered 3rd year, my dad talked to me. "Take over," he said. I knew this was coming. I didn't even think they'd be able to get me as far as middle school. It's that bad. My mom is sick a lot, and she can't work. I have to do something. Mom tries to work the fields sometimes, even in her state. It really messes me up, and I tell her to lie down, that I'll take a day off from school and work. That's why I was absent every now and then.

So I knew I had to help out. I'm quite resigned to becoming a farmer. I don't hate it. I like working the fields, sitting with the cows and watching the sky. I like this life.

But somehow the thought of going straight to the fields after graduating middle school makes me so lonely. I'm not sure why. I'm thinking of being stuck on the farm and I look at you and you look cheerful. And I end up saying stuff like, "Oh good for you."

But I know now. We're going to be friends even after graduation. I wonder why I didn't realize that sooner. Maybe I wasn't thinking things through, sorry. It cheers me up thinking, maybe we'll even be closer than before. Our teacher used to say that you should learn from life. I should remember that when I work the fields, try to be useful, try to have some pride in it. I'm going to work hard, just like you.

I still have your letter on my desk. I'm sorry I worried you. Ryūichi-*kun*, we'll be friends, and keep moving forward in this life. – Masao

After sharing these two letters, Mori has the students discuss the motive behind Ryūichi's and Masao's letters, also examining their attitudes toward studying and work. Individually, he has students consider what they need to make their future paths meaningful, considering the relationship of study and work, between work and their own individuality, work and their personal circumstances, and work and community. He then asks them to develop their ideas into an essay on "The Path I Walk."

In this chapter, we see Mori's attitude to study, work, and society, a key element of Dewey's philosophy of education. Like Dewey, Mori sees study as something that should be continuous with the rest of one's growth in life. Not a "preparation" that precedes work, studying is a way of learning how to respond more effectively to the challenges of life, a path that continues even when teachers are not around, and even when students have left the school.

However, while Mori sees that work should be connected to one's own desires and abilities, he does not reduce work to an "expression of one's authentic desires" or identity. Instead, he sees work as a back-and-forth between one's inner world of meaning and one's outer world, both with its immediate demands (like that of one's family circumstance) and with the needs of society. Just as Mead saw the "me" as something constructed in the interaction between the "I" and the rest of society, Mori takes an interactionist view rather than essentializing the self and its path.

I also remembered Junko-*san* and Taro-*kun* from Chapters 2 and 3 in this activity. Here, Mori was also showing us the existential relationship that transcends mere roles dictated by position or class, and how one person reaches out to another to create an encounter between personality to personality, as we saw in Dōgen's idea of face-to-face transmission (*menju*).

*

Above, we have seen the process of learning to live—starting from receiving guidance in one's everyday living to learning to build moral ideals both socially and introspectively. We also saw four chapters—with moving stories, letters, essays—starting from experiences and progressing into learning to build one's moral ideals.

What I hope to show here is that because of how Mori built his philosophy co-constructively with teachers and students, his ideas were *doable*. The person-to-person relationship does not require that you spend all your time one-on-one with students counseling them daily or that you be a paragon like Dōgen. This consciousness that students are people and this attentiveness to their lifestyle can manifest even in a large classroom via the examples you give, how you share your own real engagement with what you teach, how you encourage and engage the questions of students, the opportunities you give them to digest what they learned and share that with others . . . As we have seen in Chapter 1, there is much that is already present in active learning and collaborative learning that can be appropriated *philosophically* toward an education as human becoming.

Pragmatic Evidence

Observing one's way of life, clarifying the problems therein, finding one's way forward, scaffolding this path meaningfully through intelligence and ideas—we have seen this in Chapter 4 as the very process of pragmatic learning championed by Dewey and Mori. However, allow me to end with a short discussion of one final step essential to pragmatism—learning via consequences.

Just as students need to learn about themselves, communication, the dangers of closed community, and so on, not merely looking at ideal factors but at practical consequences, educators too—school teachers, professors, parents—need to consider consequences. The stories may be moving, you may be thoroughly convinced by the dynamic between individuality and totality, but if you do not track the consequences of this education and adjust your teaching accordingly, the process is reduced to idealism and not the non-duality of subject and object. And the danger here is that ideal education may be beautiful but have absolutely no positive effect on students.

However, just as many tend to see science as mechanism and positivism, many tend to see "evidence" in a superficial way. Philosopher of education Gert Biesta's "Evidence-Based Education between Science and Democracy" introduces "evidence-based education" which sees that "... evidence should be the *only* basis for our decisions about the conduct of education."[37] He then talked about how this resulted in an obsession with positivist statistical measures of the effectivity of education (pre- and post-tests, competitive league tables), which then were used by the markets and by the state within "measurement-centered" education. Indeed, this "evidence-based education" would reduce a unique individual's way of becoming to a generic measure of developmentalist growth—the very thing Mori criticized.

However, like the assertion of contextual psychology in Chapter 4, "evidence" can be *contextualist* instead of mechanist causation or formist statistics. For example, I have done a class that is based on Mori's ideas, particularly on the module on "How the Self has Grown."

In "Core-Curriculum Education Seminar," an introduction to university life required in Kyushu University, I give students opportunities to think about various stories in their lives—various challenges they faced, various moments of overcoming they find personally meaningful, their personal values—and have them use these stories to get to know themselves and think about how they want to plan their future career. I have published an article explaining the design of this class.[38] What I want to highlight here, however, is how I track the outcomes of such a class.

In this class, their final project is a presentation and an essay about their lives, their stories, and how it connects to what they study and where they want to take their careers. How should the teacher evaluate this final project? There is a temptation to look merely at compliance ("Did the student complete the tasks on time with the requisite format?") and the surface content ("Did the student talk about their stories and their future plans?"). However, what I try to do is read the stories sympathetically and look for what is happening on the level of the life (*seikatsu*) of the student.

When one looks closely at these stories, one finds that it reveals much more than surface content. For example, in my qualitative research on this class,[39] I discussed the case of "Ms. A." Her stories exhibit a certain "persona"—a "me," a role that tends to do certain things, think certain things, and feel a certain way. In most of her stories, she had a "good girl" persona, joining the student council, trying to do well in school, trying to be good at foreign languages. This good girl had a tendency to define herself by comparison to others and often was afraid of failure and inferiority. However, in other stories, you could see her author self ("I") shift outside this good girl persona to question it. "I want to become a kind of person who doesn't compare myself with others and who always has confidence but does not look down on others."

This is a crucial outcome for this class. This shifting of the persona suggests that her stories are not just about presenting a stable "image" to her teacher. Instead, you see certain dominant images start to waver, to be questioned, a process of negotiation between "I" and "me." (In other students in my article, you see multiple developed personas competing for space in the stories of students!) This is *evidence*. Not formist statistics or mechanistic analysis of causation but contextualist evidence. By paying close attention to the final project of my students as a way of understanding their lifestyle (*seikatsu*), I can already see that something real is at stake in my class, and at least some students are using the class as an opportunity to think deeply about their identities in a real and constructive way. This tells me that this Mori-inspired narrative class is not just a "good idea" that makes sense philosophically, it has *consequences* that show me they are worth the effort.

In my paper, I used a fairly complex system of narrative analysis from the psychologist Dan P. McAdams.[40] But the core of it is simple: About any academic requirement that has some degree of personal expression—a book report, a presentation on a social problem, a reflection on political issues, a thesis—we can ask, "What is this telling me about the *experience* of my students, their personal interests and values, their struggles? Was my class able to help them deal with something real?" In doing this, we can know beyond mere wishful thinking and see if we are indeed contributing to the process of human becoming.

Conclusion

Thank you for taking this journey with me. I began this book with a suggestion that these two Japanese philosophies of education might help us as we face the complications of life. As we have seen, rather than simplifying life into a single principle, Watsuji Tetsurō and Mori Akira began with paradox: The mutual negation of individuality and totality, and the tensional unity of subjectivity and objectivity. Starting from paradox shows us that life is difficult not because we or our students "*suck* at it" (to borrow a phrase from my young students), but it is because it is *innately hard*, and life requires a constant process of emptying and letting go. Let me briefly summarize the path of this "education for emptiness," but with a different order, more in resonance with the rhythm of life.

As we have seen in "Chapter 6. Learning to Live," life, awakening, the very dynamic of emptiness is happening *right now*, in the classroom and at home, for every student. Students have real challenges. Education for emptiness starts with "life guidance," engaging students where they are, helping them face their situations well, and helping them build and share meaning in the process. In "Chapter 4. The Practical-Pragmatic Nexus," Mori explained the spirit of this approach via pragmatism. Pragmatism highlights the foundational process of encountering the world, engaging it in action, and learning from consequences, both as individuals and as groups. Emptiness is first manifest in letting go of mere reactivity to intelligently respond to the world.

However, at the same time, action in the long-term and with other people demands more from us than just personal response. Thus, we need the world of symbols and meaning, shared via communication. This world of meaning is where Watsuji Tetsurō is most helpful. In

"Chapter 1. Confucianism and Finding Your Place," we saw the process of real learning, grounded in *ningen* finding their way in life, in community, where students learn by deeply connecting to their teachers and classmates, supported by the call-response of the virtues of the teacher and the student. Here, emptiness is manifest as letting go of isolated ego to engage our roles and institutions in a real way.

However, in "Chapter 2. Relation without an Other?," we saw the danger that emptying individuality might lead to a loss of uniqueness and a stagnation on the level of roles and institutions. We explored the process of further emptying social self in "Chapter 3. Buddhism and Awakening to Self." In Watsuji's reading of Zen Master Dōgen, we see how people can negate totality and its calcified roles and rules, letting go of social self in encountering a master person-to-person, and awakening to one's unique and critical *Existenz*.

These different movements come together in "Chapter 5. The Rhythm of Life." Life is a process of becoming human. But this becoming is all about learning to face paradox and contradiction via a constant process of emptying oneself. The challenges of adapting to the environment, the crisis of the transition to symbolic life, the tension between social harmony and personal meaning all call us beyond the stasis of dualistic thinking. These tensions and crises call us to emptying, letting go, in hopes that we might move with the rhythm of life. And we do not go through this alone—it is our journey as human beings, a journey that connects teacher and student, from one generation to the next.

My hope for this book is that this vision of education for emptiness be worthwhile to you, at least in some ways. I hope reading it brought back your memories of being educated by your parents, teachers, and other role models, and also your experiences as an educator. Perhaps you found that these insights are not brand new but *already present*, in varying levels of clarity, within your own experiences.

I also tried to share different ways to actualize these insights into education and life. With the various examples, I tried to show ways that you can engage the experience of your students, help them come to terms with themselves, and also help them actualize themselves within communities. I did not intend these examples to be fixed ideals but merely a mood board to show how these ideals might exist in reality.

While I shared the examples that I thought might be most helpful, behind what I presented is a whole history of trial-and-error-and-some-more-error, struggling with how to deal with the insecurities of students, confounded by how Japanese students engage groups, and wondering if I was even meant to be in education at all! I got through these struggles by learning a lot of things outside philosophy—active learning, collaborative learning, psychotherapy (both as a client and a practitioner), group therapy, ProSocial group facilitation—and if you find that these particular modalities might help you, I left links in the comments to various helpful sources.

However, I am certain one found parts that one disagreed with or found lacking. Some of these are simply a matter of my current limitations as a human being and a thinker, and I look forward to continuing to learn. (For example, I am completely drawing a blank on the problem of *institutional* change.) But one of these deficiencies I am very conscious of, and I wish to turn to that now as this book ends.

The Unfolding of Emptiness

Looking at the previous chapters, it seems that emptying and becoming are things you *do*—learning to face the environment, negating that to explore symbolic life, finding your place, awakening to yourself. And as students *do* these things, educators *do* things in order to assist this process—helping people engage their context, encouraging thinking, fostering connections, and calling out from personality to personality. Learning, negating, helping, encouraging—all of these are transitive verbs, things we do from subject to direct object.

However, is emptying really something you *do*? If we are ignorant, is it the ignorant self that seeks to learn? If we slumber, how can the slumbering self even consider becoming awake? Is the ego self even capable of journeying on this path toward emptiness?

In the Introduction, I situated Watsuji and Mori among the Kyoto School of Philosophy. However, within the Kyoto School, Watsuji and Mori were, given their focus on ethics and moral education, relatively more focused on the doing, the striving that comes on the path of pure experience and awakening to absolute nothingness. (There are small exceptions, like when Watsuji speaks about art, or Mori speaks about generativity.) However, the more you find your place in relationships, the more you awaken to your own creativity, the very sense of agency, of the I doing-things-in-the-world, starts to change.

Halfway through writing this book, I read the book of Nishida scholar Takaya Shōko, a mentee of Nishihira Tadashi, who I had also taught when I was just starting teaching. *The Philosophical Anthropology of Education of* I and Thou—*Arriving at and Departing from Nishida Philosophy* (2024, in Japanese)[1] is framed as a response to Mori Akira's critique of the philosophy of awakening from the point of view of Nishida Kitarō. She highlights key pedagogical themes in Nishida—the unity of intellect, emotion and the will via self-negation, how awakening happens in the call-response between the I and Thou, the unity of forming-another with self-formation, and how this is all emplaced within history. The whole book develops how awakening unfolds in education. And what was most moving for me was how she explored not merely Nishida's ideas but the letters between Nishida and his disciple, Kimura Motomori, showing how the process of education for awakening *actually happens*. (Part of this book is available in English.[2]) I was so moved by reading this that I revised my drafts to respond to Takaya-*san* and Nishida.

However, the interesting thing is that while the content of my book seems to greatly overlap with hers, my book focuses on what you can *do* to support human becoming. Her book includes doing but does not focus on it, rather highlighting how human becoming is something that *unfolds*, the ontological conditions that make possible such an awakening. As Nishida says in "On Education,"

> [T]his world determines itself in the unity of subject and object. Herein is the significance of truly formative activity in socio-historical

determination. Education (*kyōka*, 教化) must be seen as joining in this formative activity. In this sense, I think that the educator's mission is "assisting in the creation of heaven and earth" (*tenchi no kaiku o tasuku*, 贊天地之化育).

Here, education as doing is put in the service of a creation, a becoming, that unfolds. At first, I was confused, faced with something very different from what I see, but something I could not ignore.

This little crisis in the middle of my writing brought me back to the writings of Nishihira Tadashi. He was my teacher, instrumental in my shift to Clinical Pedagogy. (In my mind, he is Nishihira-*sensei*, my "master/*shishō*," but you should see him squirm when I say this.) In *The Philosophy of No-Mind*, he discusses "no-mind" (*mushin* 無心), a way of radically flexible thinking, of using the mind without being used by it or becoming attached to it. On one hand, he develops this by connecting it to the philosophies and spiritual traditions of no-mind in Japan—examining D. T. Suzuki and Izutsu Toshihiko who connected no-mind to Zen, to the swordsmanship of Takuan where no-mind is an "unfettered mind" that never gets stuck, and to the Noh theater of Zeami. But at the same time, he connects it to students' everyday experiences, like playing the piano and completely losing yourself in the music (*mushin ni hiiteita* 無心に引いていた).[3] He even talks about the tension of social order and social critique in Ishida Baigan, similar to how I spoke of Watsuji. The fundamental insights of this book directly connect to education, as one can see in Japanese in *The Philosophy of the Lifecycle*.[4]

However, one key feature of no-mind is its constant reversion between the active and the receptive, movement and stillness, deliberately *emptying* mind and mind *being emptied*. Nishihira highlights this as a tension between Bodhidharma's severe practice of negating mind versus Mazu's "If one seeks the true Way, ordinary mind, as it is, is the way."[5]

For the educator, perhaps the most concrete way to arrive at some sort of answer is to ponder the question: "In the face of life, its mysterious rhythms, and the challenges of awakening, should we prepare for it, or must we simply wait?" Drawing from Noh theater genius Zeami, Nishihira writes,

> "In the state of *mushin*, the experiences learned during practice disappear from consciousness..." ... However, Zeami reverses his position in the next sentence: "The state of having not a single thing in mind is itself felt to be the result of one's efforts in practice." ... in reality, it is an art that is realized as a result of repeated training.[6]

The practices of understanding students, engaging them, helping them past experiential blocks, and helping them collaborate in genuine ways all need to be learned and repeatedly practiced. But at the same time, if one only has in mind, "Oh we need to have person-to-person engagement," "We need to become a more ProSocial team," we are responding to ideas, not real people, and we are being used by mind in a most unfree way. The *happening* of education for emptiness cannot be contrived, but it comes, as if by grace.

Nishihira ends his chapter on Zeami with a question: "In *mushin*, does one wish for a successful performance?" Can we aim at education for emptiness, or not? He writes,

> *Mushin* includes "wishing for the fulfillment of a performance." But this "wishing" is not the wishing that is in opposition to "not wishing." One can hope; one can not hope.... Having once completely negated the desire to seek for the success of a performance, as if thoroughly resolving to "not wish for" it, hope is reborn in a different phase.... In that moment, "hoping" (*negau* 願う) and "praying" (*inoru* 祈る) are inseparable.[7]

On one hand, Nishihira's book has many resonances with mine—the idea of paradox, social order and change, flexibility and letting go—and I realized just how much I had deeply absorbed from Nishihira-*sensei*. In a way, my book is my own way of taking up this "generational cycle" from my teacher, and perhaps Takaya-*san*'s book was her way of taking it up. But I feel we took quite different sides of this paradox: Like Bodhidharma, I took the side of doing, hoping that people would rage against the status quo and awaken their efforts. And like Mazu, Takaya-

san took the side of being, praying that people would let go of the poisoned excesses of effort (that are born from a competitive educational system).

Behind the paradox of individual and community, subject and object, is another paradox: Emptying is something you do and something that happens. Emptying unfolds in both activity and stillness. I can find no better way to end this book by pointing to Nishihira-*sensei*'s and Takaya-*san*'s work as a way of shining light on the dynamism, the zero-point that makes the striving I have written about possible.

Notes

Introduction

1 For more on this, see James W. Heisig, *Philosophers of Nothingness* (Honolulu: University of Hawaii Press, 2001), 13–17.
2 James W. Heisig, Thomas P. Kasulis, John C. Maraldo, *Japanese Philosophy: A Sourcebook* (Honolulu: University of Hawaii Press, 2011), 646.
3 Nishida Kitarō, *An Inquiry into the Good*, trans. Masao Abe and Christopher Ives (New Haven: Yale University Press, 1990).
4 Agustín Jacinto Z., "Nishida Kitarō's Views on Education: 1895-1935," *Nishida tetsugakkai nenpō* 13 (2016): 171–191.
5 Michiko Yusa, *Zen & Philosophy: An Intellectual Biography of Nishida Kitarō* (Honolulu: University of Hawaii Press, 2002), 271–277.
6 I am indebted to the insights of Prof. Monzen for the part on Kimura. See Anton Sevilla-Liu and Monzen Ayaki, "Nihongata kyōiku o tetsugaku suru kokoromi," in Takii Kazuhiro ed. *Nihongata kyōiku o kangaeru* [Forthcoming].
7 Nishida Kitarō, "Kyōikugaku ni tsuite," in *Nishida Kitarō zenshū* [hereon NKZ] vol. 12 (Tokyo: Iwanami shoten, 1966), 87–88.
8 Nishida scholar Takaya warns that this image could be criticized from theories like those of Otto Bollnow, and clearly argues why Nishida does not fall into this critique.
    Takaya Shōko, *"Watashi to nanji" no kyōiku ningengaku: Nishida tetsugaku e no ōkan* (Kyoto: Kyōto Daigaku Shuppankai, 2024).
9 Yano Satoji, "The Philosophical Anthropology of the Kyoto School and Post-War Pedagogy," in *Education and the Kyoto School of Philosophy*, ed. Paul Standish and Naoko Saito (Dordrecht: Springer, 2012), 30.
    Takaya points out that this was not a one-way call from Nishida to Kimura, but part of a continuing dialogue with Nishida on the problem of free will and awakening. As Nishida himself suggested, if education is

merely an application of theory, it becomes a mere *techne* and loses its proper independence.

Takaya, *"Watashi to nanji."*

10 Yano, 30. Translation amended.

11 Kimura Motomori, *Kokka ni okeru bunka to kyōiku* (Tokyo: Iwanami Shoten, 1946), 127.

12 Yano, 31. Translation amended.

13 One can understand more of this idea of "historical life" by examining Nishida's accessible essay, Nishida Kitarō, "The Historical Body," in *The Sourcebook for Modern Japanese Philosophy: Selected Documents*, trans. David A. Dilworth and Valdo H. Viglielmo (Westport, CT: Greenwood Press, 1998).

14 Standish and Saito, *Education and the Kyoto School*.

15 Yano Satoji, *Kyōto gakuha to jikaku no kyōikugaku: Shinohara Sukeichi, Osada Arata, Kimura Motomori* (Tokyo: Keisō Shobō, 2021).

16 Takaya, *"Watashi to nanji."*

17 Monzen Ayaki, *Kimura Motomori no "hyōgen ai": "hyōgen," "keisei," "tsukuru koto" no shintairon* (Tokyo: Minerva, 2019).

18 I credit Monzen for this information. Kimura Motomori, *Hana to shi to unmei* (Tokyo: Kōbundō Shobō, 1948), 4.

19 Watsuji Tetsurō, Yamamoto Seisaku (trans.), and Robert E. Carter (trans.), *Watsuji Tetsurō's* Rinrigaku (Albany: State University of New York Press, 1996), 9.

20 Ibid., 15.

21 Ibid., 23.

22 Watsuji Tetsurō, *Watsuji Tetsurō zenshū* (hereon WTZ) vol. 10, edited by Abe Yoshishige et al. (Tokyo: Iwanami Shoten, 1991–1992), 526.

23 Anton Luis Sevilla, *Watsuji Tetsurô's Global Ethics of Emptiness: A Contemporary Look at a Modern Japanese Philosopher* (Cham: Palgrave Macmillan, 2017).

24 Yusa, *Zen & Philosophy*, 268–270.

25 Ministry of Education, *Kokutai No Hongi: Cardinal Principles of the National Entity of Japan*, trans. John Owen Gauntlett, ed. Robert King Hall (Cambridge; Harvard University Press, 1949).

26 Graham Mayeda, "Permeating each Other's Hearts: Natsume Sōseki and Watsuji Tetsurō on Ethics and the Unity of Self and Other," *European Journal of Japanese Philosophy* 6 (2021): 35–74.

Kyle Michael James Shuttleworth (trans.), Sayaka Shuttleworth (trans.), "Watsuji Tetsurō: Middle School," *European Journal of Japanese Philosophy* 6 (2021): 267–322.

27 Yamaguchi Yukio, "Ningen oyobi ningen shakai no sonzai no fūdosei-kūkansei ni kansuru chiri kyōikuronteki kōsatsu," *Shin Chiri* 54, no. 4 (2007): 34–42.

Takamiya Masaki, "'Aidagara' to 'sonkei' no rinrigaku: Watsuji Tetsurō to Kanto kara miru dōtoku no naiyō kōmoku," *Kindai kyōiku fōramu* 30 (2021): 50–55.

28 Tanaka Tsunemi, "Mori Akira o yomu: Kyōikuteki kōkyōsei kara sedai keishōteki kōkyōsei e," in *Nihon kyōikugaku no keifu*, ed. Ogasawara Michio et al. (Tokyo: Keisō Shobō, 2014).

29 Ibid.

30 Mori Akira, *Shinpen Mori Akira chosakushū* (hereon SMAC) vol. 1 (Tokyo: Gakujutsu Shuppankai, 2015), 25.

31 *SMAC1*, 134.

32 *SMAC3*, 3–4.

33 Ibid., 23.

34 Ibid., 31.

35 Ibid., 32.

36 *SMAC4*, 246.

37 Yano, "Philosophical Anthropology," 34.

38 *SMAC8*, 62.

39 Ibid., 103.

40 Tanaka Tsunemi, *Rinshōteki ningen keisei ron e: raifu saikuru to sōgō Keisei* (Tokyo: Keisō Shobō, 2003).

Tanaka Tsunemi, *Rinshōteki ningen keisei ron no kōchiku* (Tokyo: Tōshindō, 2012).

Tanaka Tsunemi, *Keimō to kyōiku: rinshōteki ningen keisei ron kara* (Tokyo: Keisō Shobō, 2021).

41 Kawakami Hideaki, "Tanabe Hajime to Mori Akira no keikenshugi hihan ni okeru ninshikiron no mondai: Kyōto gakuha kyōikugaku ni okeru 'kōiteki jikaku' no keifu," *Kindai kyōiku fōramu* 30 (2021): 147–157.

Kawakami Hideaki, "Tanabe Hajime to Mori Akira ni okeru gūzensei no mondai: Sengo kyōikugaku no hattatsuron ni tomonau hitsuzensei o sōtaika suru tame," *Kyōikugaku kenkyū* 88, no. 4 (2021): 610–621.

Chapter 1

1 These cases were built both from informal observations and formal qualitative research. The latter included action research on narrative classes, analysis of academic submissions, and interviews. Participation in analysis and interviews was voluntary and under informed consent, under a project approved by the Research Ethics Committee of the Faculty of Arts and Science, Kyushu University ("Narativu jugyō jissen no shitsuteki kenkyū").
2 Watsuji, *Rinrigaku*, 29.
3 Ibid., 30.
4 Ibid., 50.
5 Ibid., 54.
6 Ibid., 57.
7 *WTZ10*, 572.
8 Ibid., 575.
9 My ideas on Watsuji and Confucianism were first developed in the following article, which was substantially revised for this book:
   Anton Sevilla-Liu, "Learning your Place: Watsuji on Education, Bildung, and Negotiating Tradition," *Journal of Philosophy of Education* 58, no. 5 (2024): 710–727, https://doi.org/10.1093/jopedu/qhae060
10 See Sevilla, "Chapter 4. Universality vs. Particularity," in *Global Ethics*.
11 *WTZ10*, 574–575.
12 Ibid., 575.
13 Emile Durkheim, *The Rules of Sociological Method*, 2nd edn. (Basingstoke: Palgrave Macmillan, 2013), 23.
14 *WTZ11*, 380.
15 This book is partially translated: Watsuji Tetsurō, *Who was Confucius? A Critical Analysis of Sources*, trans. Avery Morrow (Boston: Avery Morrow's Printing and Bagels, 2012).
   However, I directly refer to the original in *WTZ6*.
16 Kyle Michael James Shuttleworth, "Confucianism, Nationalism, and *Nihonjinron* in Watsuji Tetsurō's *Climate*," in *Confucianism at War: 1931-1945*, ed. Shaun O'Dwyer, (London: Routledge, 2025), 268–273.
   Andrew Ka Pok Tam, "On the Relation between Watsuji Tetsurō's *Ningen Rinrigaku* and Mencius' Five Relationships. A Critique from the

Perspective of Mou Zongsan's Moral Metaphysics," *Taiwan Journal of East Asian Studies* 17, no. 2 (2020): 135–182.
17 *WTZ6*, 264.
18 Ibid. Watsuji was consistently averse to this idea of abstract cosmopolitanism, which he associated with a mere attempt to legitimize empires and as a major source of ethical individualism. See Sevilla, *Global Ethics*, Chapter 4.
19 Roger T. Ames, Henry Rosemont Jr. *The Analects of Confucius: A Philosophical Translation* (Ballantine Books, 1999), [For ease, I cite by the book and analect number:] 1.1.
20 *WTZ6*, 312.
21 Ibid.
22 Ames and Rosemont, *Analects*, 1.15.
23 Ronald Dore, *The Diploma Disease: Education, Qualification and Development* (Berkeley, CA: University of California Press, 1976).
24 L. Dee Fink, *Creating Significant Learning Experiences: An Integrated Approach to Designing College Courses* (San Francisco, CA: Jossey-Bass, 2003), 30.

 I also compare Watsuji, active learning, and cooperative learning in: Sebiria Anton, "Akutibu rāningu to mushin no kea," in *Kea no kongen o motomete*, by Nishihira Tadashi, Nakagawa Yoshiharu, Sakai Yuen, Sebiria Anton (Tokyo: Kōyō Shobō, 2017).
25 Ames and Rosemont, *Analects*, 1.16.
26 David W. Johnson, Roger T. Johnson, Edythe Johnson Holubec, *Circles of Learning: Cooperation in the Classroom* (Edina, MN: Interaction, 2009), 8–9.
27 Ibid., 6–7.
28 David Baruch Gordon, *Self-Overcoming as the Overcoming of Modernity: Watsuji Tetsuro's A Study of Nietzsche (1913) and its Place in the Development of His Thought* (Honolulu: University of Hawaii Dissertation, 1997), 60.
29 Ibid., 60.
30 Shuttleworth and Shuttleworth, "Middle School."
31 For further explanation, see Sevilla, *Global Ethics*, "Chapter 3. Individuality vs. Community."
32 Ibid., 91.

33 Kyle Michael James Shuttleworth, "Virtues and Ethics within Watsuji Tetsurō's *Rinrigaku*," *Asian Philosophy* 30, no. 1 (20): 57–70, https://doi.org/10.1080/09552367.2020.1736746
34 Okuda Kazuhiko as cited in Shuttleworth, "Virtues."
35 Ames and Rosemont, *Analects*, 1.8.
36 Ibid., 5.9.
37 Ibid., 1.2.
38 *WTZ6*, 316.
39 Ames and Rosemont, *Analects*, 1.8.
40 Ibid., 1.6.
41 *WTZ6*, 315.
42 This idea of crises in generational care is explained by: Nishihira Tadashi, Nishihira Tadashi, *Raifusaikuru no tetsugaku* (Tokyo: Tokyo Daigaku Shuppankai, 2019), ch. 4–5.

   I discuss this both philosophically and practically in the following two articles:

   Anton Sevilla-Liu, "Schema Care Ethics: The Philosophy and Psychology of Caring amidst Woundedness," in *Care Ethics and Beyond: Moral, Epistemological, and Cross-Cultural Perspectives*, ed. Seisuke Hayakawa and Michael Slote (Forthcoming).

   Anton Sevilla-Liu, "Potential Applications of Schema Pedagogy in Japanese University Education," *Bulletin of KIKAN Education* 9 (2022), 33–52. https://doi.org/10.15017/6769087
43 Ames and Rosemont, *Analects*, 1.10.
44 *WTZ6*, 324.
45 Ames and Rosemont, *Analects*, "Introduction."
46 *WTZ6*, 311.
47 Ames and Rosemont, *Analects*, 2.4
48 *WTZ6*, 324.
49 Hoshi Kaoru, *Shōgai hattatsu shinrigaku kenkyū* (Tokyo: Hōsō Daigaku, 2011).
50 Ames and Rosemont, *Analects*, 1.12.
51 Shuttleworth, "Virtues."
52 Watsuji, *Rinrigaku*, 276.
53 Nel Noddings, *Starting at Home: Caring and Social Policy* (Berkeley: University of California Press, 2002)

I further explain connections between care ethics and Watsuji in Sevilla, *Global Ethics*, "Chapter 2. Relationality vs. Singularity."
54 Watsuji, *Rinrigaku*, 276.
55 *WTZ10*, 399.
56 Ibid., 402-403.
57 Nel Noddings, *Philosophy of Education*, 3rd edn. (Boulder: Westview Pressi, 2012).
58 *SMAC4*, 246.
59 Gert J. J. Biesta, *Good Education in an Age of Measurement: Ethics, Politics, Democracy* (Oxon: Routledge, 2010), 19–21.
60 *SMAC4*, 30.
61 Inaga Shigemi. "Japanese Philosophers Go West: The Effect of Maritime Trips on Philosophy in Japan with Special Reference to the Case of Watsuji Tetsurō (1889-1960)." Japan Review, no. 25 (2013): 113–44. http://www.jstor.org/stable/41959188
62 Watsuji, *Rinrigaku*, 43.

Chapter 2

1 Ames and Rosemont, *Analects*, 11.12.
2 *WTZ6*, 339.
3 Ibid., 344.
4 Ibid., 348.
5 Ibid., 350.
6 I am an educational counselor, not a licensed psychotherapist. But I am extensively trained in Acceptance and Commitment Therapy (ACT) and Contextual Schema Therapy, and I do research in those fields as well. I will not raise these directly in this book, but perhaps you will find traces of my psychological training here and there.
7 Ames and Rosemont, *Analects*, 7.3.
8 See Matthieu Villatte, Jennifer L. Villatte, Steven C. Hayes, *Mastering the Clinical Conversation: Language as Intervention* (New York, NY: Guilford Press, 2016), 211.
9 Anton Sevilla-Liu, "Understanding Self-Compassion within Narrative Identity: The Struggles of Japanese Students with Measuring Up," *The*

Qualitative Report 27, no.10 (2022): 2230–2250. https://doi.org/10.46743/2160-3715/2022.5602

10 Ministry of Education, *Kokutai No Hongi: Cardinal Principles of the National Entity of Japan*, trans. John Owen Gauntlett, ed. Robert King Hall (Cambridge: Harvard University Press, 1949).

11 Anton Luis Sevilla, "Educational Ideals in Pre and Post-War Japan: From Imperial Subject to Deweyan Democratic Citizen," *Budhi: A Journal of Ideas and Culture* 21.2 (2017): 75–119.

12 *SMAC4*, 73.

13 Nel Noddings, *Caring: A Relational Approach to Moral Education* 2nd edn. (Berkeley: University of California Press, 2013), 15.

14 Michael Slote, *The Ethics of Care and Empathy* (London: Routledge, 2007).

15 Noddings, *Caring*, 30.

16 Slote, *Ethics of Care*, 13.

17 Emmanuel Levinas, *On Thinking-of-the-Other: Entre Nous*, trans. Michael B. Smith, Barbara Harshav (New York, NY: Columbia University Press, 1998).

18 Ames and Rosemont, *Analects*, 4.15.

19 Ibid., 2.11.

20 *WTZ6*, 277–278.

21 Watsuji, *Rinrigaku*, 57.

22 Steve Odin, "The Social Self in Japanese Philosophy and American Pragmatism: A Comparative Study of Watsuji Tetsurō and George Herbert Mead," *Philosophy East and West* 42, no. 3 (1992): 475–501.

23 George Herbert Mead, *Mind, Self and Society* (Chicago: University of Chicago Press, 1962), 175.

24 Carl Johnson (trans.), "Watsuji Tetsurō's *Mask and Persona*," *Japan Studies Review* 15 (2011), 147–158.

25 Ibid., 152.

26 Ibid., 154.

27 Ibid., 154–155.

28 Emmanuel Levinas, *Otherwise than Being or Beyond Essence*, trans. Alphonso Lingis (The Hague: Martinus Nijhoff Publishers, 1981), 5.

29 *WTZ10*, 527.

30 *NKZ6*, 348. For its significance in education, see Takaya, "*Watashi to nanji*."

31 *WTZ10*, 528–529.
32 One can see clear examples of this in the autobiography of Watsuji, when he talks about a village that is shifting from wheat to rice farming. Watsuji Tetsurō, *Attempt at an Autobiography*, trans. Kyle Michael James Shuttleworth and Sayaka Shuttleworth (Honolulu: University of Hawaii Press, Forthcoming).
33 Ibid., 529.
34 Ibid., 532.
35 Mead, *Mind, Self*, 42.
36 Ibid., 47.
37 *WTZ9*, 176.
38 Watsuji, *Rinrigaku*, 43.
39 Erving Goffman, *The Presentation of Self in Everyday Life* (Garden City, NY: Doubleday Anchor Books, 1959).
40 Sakai Naoki, *Translation and Subjectivity: On "Japan" and Cultural Nationalism* (Minneapolis: University of Minnesota Press, 1997), 96.
41 *SMAC1*, 96.
42 Mead, *Mind, Self*, 176.
43 Ibid., *Mind, Self*, 154–155.
44 *SMAC6*, 629.
45 Ibid., 196.
46 *NKZ6*, 352.
47 *WTZ11*, 59.
48 Ibid., 72.
49 Ibid., 349–354.
50 Ibid., 379.
51 Ibid., 380.
52 Ibid., 64.

Chapter 3

1 Anton Sevilla-Liu, "ACT and the Kyoto School of Philosophy: Interdisciplinary Dialogues on Personhood, Ethics, and Becoming," *Journal of Contextual Behavioral Science* 26 (2022): 173–180. https://doi.org/10.1016/j.jcbs.2022.09.008

2 Watsuji Tetsurō, *Pilgrimages to the Ancient Temples in Nara*, trans. Hiroshi Nara (Portland, Maine: Merwin Asia, 2012).
   For research on how this book connects to Watsuji's later philosophies on milieu and ethics, see Graham Mayeda, *Japanese Philosophers on Society and Culture: Nishida Kitarō, Watsuji Tetsurō, and Kuki Shūzō* (Lanham, MD: 2020), Chapter 2.
3 Watsuji Tetsurō, *Purifying Zen: Watsuji Tetsurō's Shamon Dōgen*, trans. Steve Bein (Honolulu: University of Hawaii Press, 2011), 5, 117.
4 Abe Masao, *A Study of Dōgen: His Philosophy and Religion* (Albany: State University of New York Press, 1992), 1–3.
5 *WTZ9*, 35.
6 *WTZ10*, 312.
7 Watsuji, *Purifying Zen*, 36.
8 Ibid., 35.
9 Ibid., 38.
10 Ibid., 71.
11 Ibid., 52.
12 A much more technical formulation of doubts very similar to these have been articulated in the following: James Reveley, "School-Based Mindfulness Training and the Economisation of Attention; A Stieglerian View," *Educational Philosophy and Theory* 47, no. 8 (2014): 804–821.
13 Watsuji, *Purifying Zen*, 44.
14 Ibid., 56.
15 Ibid., 106.
16 I am not a certified ACT instructor, but I underwent the training, practice, and group supervision for it. I do not consider myself qualified to teach *therapists*, but rather educational counselors whose job is between education and therapy.
17 Watsuji, *Purifying Zen*, 53.
18 Ibid., 57.
19 Steven C. Hayes, Kirk D. Strosahl, Kelly G. Wilson, *Acceptance and Commitment Therapy: The Process and Practice of Mindful Change* 2nd edn. (New York, NY: The Guilford Press, 2012), 77.
20 Ibid.
21 Willard Day, *Radical Behaviorism: Willard Day on Psychology and Philosophy*, ed. Sam Leigland (Reno, Nevada: Context Press, 1992).
22 Watsuji, *Purifying Zen*, 96–97.

23 Dōgen, "*Fukanzazengi*: Universal Guide to the Standard Method of Zazen," in *Shōbōgenzō: The True Dharma-Eye Treasury* vol. 1, trans. Gudo Wafu Nishijima, Chodo Cross (Berkeley, CA: Numata Center for Buddhist Translation and Research, 2007).
24 Watsuji, *Purifying Zen*, 111.
25 Ibid., 54.
26 Anton Sevilla-Liu, Honda Teruhiko, Mizokami Atsuko, Nakayama Hiroaki, "Experiences of Mindful Education: Phenomenological Analysis of MBCT Exercises in a Graduate Class Context," *The Journal of Contemplative Inquiry* 7, no. 1 (2021): 195–221.
27 Daniel P. Barbezat, Mirabai Bush, *Contemplative Practices in Higher Education* (San Francisco, CA: Jossey-Bass, 2014), 67.
28 Watsuji, *Purifying Zen*, 57. We remember that in *Ethics I*, "imitation" was the essence of learning itself. This was a profound idea for Watsuji.
29 Ibid., 87.
30 For the literature surrounding this fascicle, see: Anton Luis Sevilla, "Founding Human Rights within Buddhism: Exploring Buddha-Nature as an Ethical Foundation," *Journal of Buddhist Ethics* 17 (2010): 213–252.
31 Watsuji, *Purifying Zen*, 93.
32 Ibid., 95.
33 Ibid., 96.
34 Dōgen, *Treasury* vol. 1, 42.
35 Sevilla, "Founding Human Rights."
36 Ibid., 57.
37 Watsuji, *Purifying Zen*, 86.
38 Ibid., 92.
39 Ibid.
40 Ibid., 93.
41 Ibid., 94.
42 Ibid., 113.
43 Ibid., 113.
44 Ibid., 114.
45 Ibid., 115.
46 Ibid., 26.
47 Ibid., 28.
48 Ibid., 26.
49 Shuttleworth and Shuttleworth, "Middle School."

50 Kyle Michael James Shuttleworth, "Watsuji Tetsurō's Memory of Natsume Sōseki: A Translation of 'Until I met Sōseki' and 'Sōseki's Character,'" *The Journal of East Asian Philosophy* 4 (2024).
51 Ibid. Pagination not available.
52 Mayeda, "Permeating," 40–41.
53 Ibid., 37–38.
54 Watsuji, *Purifying Zen*, 65.
55 Ibid., 29–30.
56 Ibid., 85.
57 *NKZ6*, 357.
58 Nishitani Keiji, *Religion and Nothingness*, trans. Jan Van Bragt (Berkeley, CA: University of California Press, 1982), 138.
59 Takaya, *"Watashi to nanji"*, Introduction.
60 *SMAC1*, 118.

My ideas for the pedagogic relationship were first developed in the following article that has been substantially revised for this book: Anton Sevilla-Liu, "The Pedagogic Relationship in Existential Education," in *The Dialectics of Absolute Nothingness: The Legacies of German Philosophy in the Kyoto School*, ed. Gregory S. Moss, Takeshi Morisato (Ithaca, NY: Cornell University Press, 2025), 268–291.

61 *SMAC1*, 31.
62 Ibid., 218.
63 Ibid., 270.
64 Karl Jaspers, *Philosophy* vol. 2, trans. E. B. Ashton (Chicago: University of Chicago Press, 1970), 178.
65 This is what Biesta criticizes as "humanism," which he means in a critical sense as "the idea that it is possible to know and express the essence or nature of the human being, and also that it is possible to use this knowledge as the foundation for subsequent action." Biesta, *Good Education*, 78.
66 *SMAC1*, 273–274.
67 Karl Jaspers, *The Idea of the University* (Boston: Beacon Press, 1959), 50.
68 *SMAC1*, 27.
69 Ibid., 108–109.
70 Tanabe Hajime, *Philosophy as Metanoetics*, trans. Takeuchi Yoshinori (Berkeley: University of California Press, 1986), 276.
71 Watsuji Tetsurō, "Japanese Literary Arts and Buddhist Philosophy," trans. Hirano Umeyo, *The Eastern Buddhist* 4, no. 1 (1971): 112.

72 Ibid.
73 Ibid., 112–113. Translation amended. For more on this, see Sevilla, *Global Ethics*, "Chapter 5. Ethics of Emptiness."

Chapter 4

1 Sakai, *Translation and Subjectivity*.
   Bernard Bernier, "Transcendence of the State in Watsuji's Ethics," *Essays in Japanese Philosophy* 2 (2008); 94–100.
2 File is free for use. https://pixabay.com/vectors/yin-yang-yin-yang-taoism-34549/
3 For example, see Sueki Fumihiko, *Philosophy Live: A Perspective from Japan* (Kyoto: Nichibunken, 2018), 35–38.
4 Sevilla, *Global Ethics*, Chapter 3.
5 Ibid., Chapter 5.
6 Watsuji Tetsurô, *Climate and Culture: A Philosophical Study*, trans. Geoffrey Bownas (Tokyo: Yushodo Co., 1961), v. Translation amended.
7 Augustin Berque, "Offspring of Watsuji's Theory of Milieu (Fûdo)," *GeoJournal* 60 (2004): 389–396.
8 Watsuji, *Climate*, 1. Translation amended.
9 Ibid., 5.
10 Ibid., 3.
   For more concrete examples of this, see Mayeda, *Japanese Philosophers*, Chapter 2–3. Mayeda also suggests that this way of thinking was already present as early as Watsuji, *Pilgrimages*.
11 Wilhelm Dilthey, *The Formation of the Historical World in the Human Sciences*, ed. Rudolf A. Makkreel, Frithjof Rodi (Princeton, NJ: Princeton University Press, 2002), 102.
12 *WTZ9*, 120.
13 Watsuji, *Ethics*, 43.
14 John C. Maraldo, "Between Individual and Communal, Subject and Object, Self and Other: Mediating Watsuji Tetsurô's Hermeneutics," in *Japanese Hermeneutics: Current Debates on Aesthetics and Interpretation*, ed. Michael F. Marra (Honolulu, University of Hawaii Press, 2002), 76–86.
15 *NKZ6*, 346.
   Nishida, "Historical Body," 44.

16 Steve Odin, *The Social Self in Zen and American Pragmatism* (Albany: State University of New Yori Press, 1996), 10–11.
17 *WTZ11*, 194–195.
18 Ibid., 195.
19 Ibid., 195.
20 Ibid., 63–64.
21 Ibid., 348.
22 Ibid., 378–379.
23 *SMAC3*, 4.
24 Ibid., 42.
25 *SMAC4*, 121.
26 John Dewey, *How we Think* (Boston: D.C. Heath & Co., 1910), 72.
27 *SMAC6*, 692–698.
28 Dewey, *How we Think*, 77–78.
29 The Kyoto School was already aware of Darwinism, as is seen in Nishida's writings. Yusa, *Zen & Philosophy*, 269.
30 According to the research of Kawakami, this experimentalism was not absent in the Kyoto School but was present in Tanabe's philosophy of science, which deliberately highlighted Galileo's and Heisenberg's experimentation as knowing-by-doing.
    Kawakami, "Tanabe to Mori no keikenshugi," 149.
    However, strictly speaking, Mori's contribution was expanding this to the domain of human sciences and morality and actually carrying out this experimentation (rather than merely spectating about it).
31 Watsuji Tetsurō, Kyle Shuttleworth (trans.), Sayaka Shuttleworth (trans.), "America's National Character" *Philosophy East and West* 71, no. 4 (2021): 1005–1028.
32 *SMAC4*, 46.
33 Ibid., 137.
34 *SMAC3*, 343–344. Mori's main criticism of Dewey was that Dewey focused so much on the individual's inquiry that he did not sufficiently stress how that inquiry is situated in a larger context of social inquiry, by which the individual contributes to a body of knowledge that exceeds the individual.
35 *SMAC4*, 121.
36 *SMAC5*, 442–443. Mori developed this idea of systematic knowledge beyond individual inquiry in his later works. While thoughts begin as

pragmatic inquiry, they acquire a degree of freedom from immediate context and can be organized conceptually—a form of idealism built on top of a pragmatic base.
37 *SMAC5*, 544.
38 *SMAC4*, 145–146.
39 Given that Mori had already referred to Mead's idea of "me," it is unfortunate that he did not refer to Mead's idea of "I," which would have allowed him to better reconcile the Kyoto School and pragmatism.
40 Ibid., 149–150.
41 Kawakami writes that Tanabe saw the inability to grasp reality deterministically as a form of "nothingness." Furthermore, the ability to grasp reality but only probabilistically was a form of the "self-negation of nothingness."

   Kawakami, "Tanabe to Mori no keikenshugi," 150.
42 Tanaka, *Kōchiku*, 40.
43 John Dewey, *Democracy and Education* (New York, NY: The Macmillan Company, 1916), 5.
44 *SMAC6*, 593.
45 William A. Haviland, Harald E. L. Prins, Bunny McBride, Dana Walrath, *Cultural Anthropology: The Human Challenge* 13th edn. (Belmont, CA: Wadsworth, 2011), 35–37.
46 Bernard Bernier, "National Communion: Watsuji Tetsurô's Conception of Ethics, Power, and the Japanese Imperial State," *Philosophy East and West* 56, no. 1 (2006): 84–105.

   Sakai, *Translation and Subjectivity*.
47 Paul W. B. Atkins, David Sloan Wilson, Steven C. Hayes, *ProSocial: Using Evolutionary Science to Build Productive, Equitable, and Collaborative Groups* (Oakland, CA: Context Press, 2019).
48 Watsuji, *Rinrigaku*, 86.
49 Ibid., 58.
50 Yuasa Yasuo, *Watsuji Tetsurō: Kindai Tetsugaku no Unmei* (Tokyo: Chikuma Shobō, 1995).

   Kimura Bin, *Hito to Hito no Aida* (Tokyo: Kōbundō, 1972).
51 Inukai Yuichi, *Watsuji Tetsurō no Shakaigaku* (Tokyo: Yachiyo, 2016).
52 Odin, *The Social Self*.

   Joel Krueger, "Watsuji, Intentionality, and Psychopathology," *Philosophy East and West* 70, no. 3 (2020): 757–780.

53 Dean Anthony Brink, *Philosophy of Science and the Kyoto School: Nishida Kitaro, Tanabe Hajime, and Tosaka Jun* (Bloomsbury Academic, 2021).
54 Yano, "Philosophical Anthropology," 34.
55 *SMAC4*, 94.
56 Stephen C. Pepper, *World Hypotheses: A Study in Evidence* (Berkeley: University of California Press, 1942).
57 Robert D. Zettle, Steven C. Hayes, Dermot Barnes-Holmes, and Anthony Biglan, *The Wiley Handbook of Contextual Behavioral Science* (Malden, MA: Wiley Blackwell, 2016), 19.
58 Dewey, *How we Think*, 87, 117–118.

Chapter 5

1 Nishitani, *Religion and Nothingness*.
2 Tanabe, *Philosophy as Metanoetics*.
3 Ames and Rosemont, *Analects*, 2.4.
4 Nishihira Tadashi, *The Philosophy of No-Mind: Experience Without Self*, trans. Catherine Sevilla-Liu, Anton Sevilla-Liu (London: Bloomsbury Academic, 2024), 30.
5 Yano Satoji, *Kyōto gakuha to jikaku no kyōikugaku* (Tokyo: Keisōshobō, 2021).
6 *SMAC4*, 246.

An early version of my discussion of Mori's views on human becoming and moral education are found in the following: Anton Sevilla-Liu, "Japanese Philosophy of Moral Education: From Watsuji Tetsurô to Mori Akira," *Budhi: A Journal of Ideas and Culture* 23, no. 3 (2019): 95–142.

However, ideas from this article have been substantially revised for this publication.
7 There is evidence that Mori was directly using the idea of becoming to critically expand on Watsuji's ethics of human existence, when Mori writes, "Ethics (*rinri*) is the fundamental principle (*rihō*) of human becoming," drawing on Watsuji's key word use and ideas of dual-structure without naming him.

SMAC6, 821.
8 *SMAC4*, 248.

9 *SMAC4*, 248–249.
10 The principle behind this becoming remains unclear in the 1950s, but in his *Philosophical Anthropology of Education*, he expounds on this via the idea of "superstasis"—an idea he was beginning to play around with in *The Moral Education We Want*. If human beings were homeostasis-seeking beings, disruptions (of our bodies for example) would merely lead to a return to equilibrium, meaning that everything would be reducible to development, and there would be no real qualitative shifts. But because we seek a *higher* level of equilibrium, then disruptions (ex. limitations in conscious control of things) can result in higher forms of complexity (ex. self-awareness). He takes the idea from personality psychologists Henry Murray and Clyde Kluckhohn.
   SMAC5, 317.
11 https://www.erikson.edu/about/history/erik-erikson/
12 Erik H. Erikson, *Childhood and Society* (London: Paladin, 1977), 37.
13 Mori Akira, *Minna no negau dōtoku kyōiku* (Nagoya: Reimei Shobō, 1958), 37.
14 Ibid., 43.
15 Ibid., 53.
16 *SMAC5*, 340–341. German terminology is from Mori.
17 Nishihira, *Raifusaikuru*.
18 *SMAC4*, 30.
19 Ibid.
20 Ibid., 125.
21 Ibid.
22 Ibid., 130–134. Mori directly draws from Jaspers's *Psychologie der Weltanschauung* in *Practicality and Inwardness*.
23 *SMAC5*.
24 *SMAC4*, 260.
25 Itō Ayako, "Jidōki seinenki no shinriteki tokuchō," in *Jidō seito shidô no riron to jissen* (Tokyo: Hōsō Daigaku, 2011).
   However, whether this problem is a developmental one or a result of other social and psychological factors is a matter of debate.
26 *SMAC4*, 118.
27 Ibid., 145–146.
28 Ibid., 25–26.

29 Erikson, *Childhood and Society*, 237.
30 Ibid., 247.
31 Nishihira, *Raifusaikuru*.
32 I address developmental crises via another contextual therapy, schema therapy. Schemas are traumas that come from unmet developmental needs. This therapy has also been directly applied to educational contexts as "Schema Pedagogy" by Marcus Damm. See Anton Sevilla-Liu, "Potential Applications of Schema Pedagogy in Japanese University Education," *Bulletin of KIKAN Education* 9 (2022): 33–52. https://doi.org/10.15017/6769087
33 Erikson, *Childhood and Society*, 224.
34 *SMAC5*, 479. I have greatly simplified this for ease of viewing. The original has vertical lines and further detail on developmental tasks for each age.
35 *SMAC6*, 590.
36 Ibid., 600.
37 *SMAC4, Practicality and Inwardness*, 185.
38 Ibid., 186–187.
39 *SMAC6*, 604.
40 *SMAC4*, 188–189.
41 *SMAC6*, 629.
42 Paul Standish, Saito Naoko. *Education and the Kyoto School of Philosophy*. Dordrecht: Springer, 2012, 26. For a discussion of the responses to this critique, see the following: Anton Luis Sevilla, "Education and Empty Relationality: Thoughts on Education and the Kyoto School of Philosophy," *Journal of Philosophy of Education* 50, no. 4 (2016): 639-654.
43 Naoko Saito, Tomohiro Akiyama, "On the Education of the Whole Person" *Educational Philosophy and Theory* 56, no. 2 (2024): 153–161.
44 Naoko Saito, *The Gleam of Light: Moral Perfectionism and Education in Dewey and Emerson* (New York, NY: Fordham University Press, 2005).
45 One can see a theory of development in contextual psychology in the following:
    Steven C. Hayes, Dermot Barnes-Holmes, Bryan Roche, *Relational Frame Theory: A Post-Skinnerian Account of Human Language and Cognition* (New York, NY: Kluwer, 2002), 157–180.
46 *SMAC1*, 134.
47 *SMAC8*, 103.
48 Early versions of the ideas in this section were discussed in Anton Sevilla-Liu, "Mori Akira's Education for Self-Awareness: Lessons from the

Kyoto School for Mindful Education," *Journal of Philosophy of Education* 55, no. 1 (2021): 243–262.
    SMAC8, 201.
49 Ibid., 202.
50 Ibid., 209.
51 Ibid., 230–231.
52 Ibid., 213–214.
53 Erikson, *Childhood and Society*, 242.
54 *SMAC8*, 218.
55 Tanaka, "Mori Akira o yomu," 356.

Chapter 6

1 *SMAC3*, 29–30.
2 Takaya, "*Watashi to nanji*."
3 Tanaka, "Mori Akira o yomu."
4 Mori Akira, *Minna de susumeru dōtoku shidō* (Nagoya: Reimei Shobō, 1959), 25–26.
    I first discussed moral guidance in the following article, which has been substantially revised for this book: Sevilla-Liu, "Pedagogic Relationship."
5 Mori, *Minna no negau*, 33.
6 *SMAC4*, 39.
    Some may be uncomfortable with his use of the word "complete," and this is a stance Mori would revise in his last book, as explained in Chapter 5.
7 Kawakami suggests that Amano Teiyu and Kōsaka Masaaki were leading this push.
    Kawakami, "Tanabe to Mori no keikenshugi," 155.
8 Mori, *Minna de susumeru*, 53
9 Ibid., 1.
10 Ibid., 69–70.
11 Ibid., 93–94.
12 Ibid., 95.
13 Ibid., 152.

14 This qualitative attitude toward students is developed in Van Manen's phenomenological approach to "pedagogic tact." See Max van Manen, *The Tact of Teaching: The Meaning of Pedagogical Thoughtfulness* (Albany: State University of New York Press, 1991).
15 Mori, *Minna de susumeru*, 56.
16 Ibid., 219.
17 Ibid., 160.
18 Ibid., 73, 163.
19 Elizabeth C. Vozzola, *Moral Development: Theory and Applications* (New York: Routledge, 2014).
20 Mori, *Minna de susumeru*, 49.
21 Ibid., 192.
22 Ibid., 105.
23 I have explained these types of ethics and their virtues in the following: Sevilla-Liu, "Japanese Philosophy of Moral Education," 110–112.
24 Mori, *Minna de susumeru*, 196.
25 Ibid., 200.
26 Ibid., 257.
27 Ibid., 258.
28 Ibid., 254.
29 Ibid., 215.
30 Ibid., 202-208.
31 Atarashii seikatsu henshū iinkai (ASHI), *Atarashii seikatsu 2 nen* (Tokyo: Tokyo Shoseki, 1962), 86–93.

   These are not direct quotes but loose partial translations re-rendered as a story as if Mori were teaching.
32 ASHI, *2 nen*, 86–95.
33 Ibid., 90.
34 See Chapter 4 for the discussion on Tanabe and Mori's critique of Nishida's enactive intuition.
35 ASHI, *3 nen*, 60–69.
36 Kaori H. Okano, *Young Women in Japan: Transitions to Adulthood* (Oxon: Routledge, 2009).
37 Biesta, *Good Education*, 28.
38 Anton Sevilla-Liu, "From Mori Akira to Narrative Education: Weaking the Tapestry of Narrative Philosophy, Analysis, Therapy, Pedagogy, and Research." *Human Arenas* 6 (2023): 82–101.

39 Sevilla-Liu, "Understanding Self-Compassion."
40 Dan P. McAdams, *The Stories we Live By: Personal Myths and the Making of the Self* (New York: The Guilford Press, 1993).

Conclusion

1 Takaya, *"Watashi to nanji."*
    Anton Sevilla-Liu, "Book Review: Takaya Shōko, '*Watashi to nanji*' no kyōiku ningengaku," *European Journal of Japanese Philosophy* [in-press].
2 Takaya Shōko, "Historical Nature in Nishida and Kimura Motomori," *European Journal of Japanese Philosophy* 7 (2022): 171–190.
3 Nishihira, *No-Mind*, 2. For a connection of these ideas to western thinkers like Bateson, the following is also available in English: Tadashi Nishihira, Jeremy Rappleye, "Unlearning as (Japanese) Learning," *Educational Philosophy and Theory* 54, no. 9 (2021): 1332-1344.
4 Nishihira, *Raifusaikuru*.
5 Nishihira, *No-Mind*, 174.
6 Ibid., 102.
7 Ibid., 110.

Bibliography

Author Bibliography in Support of this Book

Sebiria Anton. "Akutibu rāningu to mushin no kea," in *Kea no kongen o motomete*, by Nishihira Tadashi, Nakagawa Yoshiharu, Sakai Yuen, Sebiria Anton. Tokyo: Kōyō Shobō, 2017.

Sevilla, Anton Luis. "Founding Human Rights within Buddhism: Exploring Buddha-Nature as an Ethical Foundation," *Journal of Buddhist Ethics* 17 (2010): 213–252.

Sevilla, Anton Luis. "Education and Empty Relationality: Thoughts on Education and the Kyoto School of Philosophy," *Journal of Philosophy of Education* 50, no. 4 (2016): 639–654.

Sevilla, Anton Luis. *Watsuji Tetsurô's Global Ethics of Emptiness: A Contemporary Look at a Modern Japanese Philosopher*. Cham: Palgrave Macmillan, 2017.

Sevilla, Anton Luis. "Educational Ideals in Pre and Post-War Japan: From Imperial Subject to Deweyan Democratic Citizen," *Budhi: A Journal of Ideas and Culture* 21.2 (2017): 75–119.

Sevilla-Liu, Anton. "Japanese Philosophy of Moral Education: From Watsuji Tetsurô to Mori Akira," *Budhi: A Journal of Ideas and Culture* 23, no. 3 (2019): 95–142.

Sevilla-Liu, Anton. "Mori Akira's Education for Self-Awareness: Lessons from the Kyoto School for Mindful Education," *Journal of Philosophy of Education* 55, no. 1 (2021): 243–262.

Sevilla-Liu, Anton. "ACT and the Kyoto School of Philosophy: Interdisciplinary Dialogues on Personhood, Ethics, and Becoming," *Journal of Contextual Behavioral Science* 26 (2022): 173–180. https://doi.org/10.1016/j.jcbs.2022.09.008

Sevilla-Liu, Anton. "Potential Applications of Schema Pedagogy in Japanese University Education," *Bulletin of KIKAN Education* 9 (2022): 33–52. https://doi.org/10.15017/6769087

Sevilla-Liu, Anton. "Understanding Self-Compassion within Narrative Identity: The Struggles of Japanese Students with Measuring Up," *The Qualitative Report* 27, no.10 (2022): 2230–2250. https://doi.org/10.46743/2160-3715/2022.5602

Sevilla-Liu, Anton. "From Mori Akira to Narrative Education: Weaving the Tapestry of Narrative Philosophy, Analysis, Therapy, Pedagogy, and Research." *Human Arenas* 6 (2023): 82–101.

Sevilla-Liu, Anton. "Learning your Place: Watsuji on Education, *Bildung*, and Negotiating Tradition," *Journal of Philosophy of Education* 58, no. 5 (2024): 710–727. https://doi.org/10.1093/jopedu/qhae060

Sevilla-Liu, Anton. "The Pedagogic Relationship in Existential Education," in *The Dialectics of Absolute Nothingness: The Legacies of German Philosophy in the Kyoto School*, edited by Gregory S. Moss, Takeshi Morisato. Ithaca, NY: Cornell University Press, 2025. 268–91.

Sevilla-Liu, Anton. "Book Review: Takaya Shōko, '*Watashi to nanji' no kyōiku ningengaku*," *European Journal of Japanese Philosophy* [Forthcoming].

Sevilla-Liu, Anton. "Schema Care Ethics: The Philosophy and Psychology of Caring amidst Woundedness," in *Care Ethics and Beyond: Moral, Epistemological, and Cross-Cultural Perspectives*, ed. Seisuke Hayakawa and Michael Slote [Forthcoming].

Sevilla-Liu, Anton. "Watsuji's Ethics of Education," in *The Springer Companion to Watsuji Tetsuro*, edited by Hans Peter Liederbach. Cham: Springer [Forthcoming].

Sevilla-Liu, Anton, Honda Teruhiko, Mizokami Atsuko, Nakayama Hiroaki. "Experiences of Mindful Education: Phenomenological Analysis of MBCT Exercises in a Graduate Class Context," *The Journal of Contemplative Inquiry* 7, no. 1 (2021): 195–221.

Sevilla-Liu, Anton, Monzen Ayaki. "Nihongata kyōiku o tetsugaku suru kokoromi," in Takii Kazuhiro *Nihongata kyōiku o kangaeru*, ed. Takii Kazuhiro [Forthcoming].

Primary Sources of Watsuji and Mori

Atarashii seikatsu henshū iinkai (ASHI), *Atarashii seikatsu 2 nen* (Tokyo: Tokyo Shoseki, 1962).

Mori Akira. *Minna no negau dōtoku kyōiku*. Nagoya: Reimei Shobō, 1958.

Mori Akira. *Minna de susumeru dōtoku shidō*. Nagoya: Reimei Shobō, 1959.

Mori Akira. *Shinpen Mori Akira chosakushū* (hereon SMAC) vols. 1–8. Tokyo: Gakujutsu Shuppankai, 2015.

Watsuji Tetsurô. *Climate and Culture: A Philosophical Study*, translated by Geoffrey Bownas. Tokyo: Yushodo Co., 1961.

Watsuji Tetsurō. "Japanese Literary Arts and Buddhist Philosophy," translated by Hirano Umeyo, *The Eastern Buddhist* 4, no. 1 (1971).

Watsuji Tetsurō. *Watsuji Tetsurō zenshū* (hereon WTZ) vols. 4–11, edited by Abe Yoshishige et al. Tokyo: Iwanami Shoten, 1991–1992.

Watsuji Tetsurō. *Watsuji Tetsurō's* Rinrigaku, translated by Yamamoto Seisaku, and Robert E. Carter. Albany: State University of New York Press, 1996.

Watsuji Tetsurō. "Watsuji Tetsurō's *Mask and Persona*," translated by Carl Johnson. *Japan Studies Review* 15 (2011), 147–158.

Watsuji Tetsurō. *Purifying Zen: Watsuji Tetsurō's Shamon Dōgen*, translated by Steve Bein. Honolulu: University of Hawaii Press, 2011.

Watsuji Tetsurō. *Pilgrimages to the Ancient Temples in Nara*, translated by Hiroshi Nara. Portland, Maine: Merwin Asia, 2012.

Watsuji Tetsurō. *Who was Confucius? A Critical Analysis of Sources*, translated by Avery Morrow. Boston: Avery Morrow's Printing and Bagels, 2012.

Watsuji Tetsurō. "America's National Character," translated by Kyle Shuttleworth, Sayaka Shuttleworth. *Philosophy East and West* 71, no. 4 (2021): 1005–1028.

Watsuji Tetsurō. "Watsuji Tetsurō: Middle School," translated by Kyle Shuttleworth, Sayaka Shuttleworth. *European Journal of Japanese Philosophy* 6 (2021): 267–322.

Watsuji Tetsurō. "Watsuji Tetsurō's Memory of Natsume Sōseki: A Translation of 'Until I met Sōseki' and 'Sōseki's Character,'" translated by Kyle Shuttleworth. *The Journal of East Asian Philosophy* 4 (2024).

Watsuji Tetsurō. *Attempt at an Autobiography*, translated by Kyle Shuttleworth, Sayaka Shuttleworth. Honolulu: University of Hawaii Press [In press].

Other References

Abe Masao. *A Study of Dōgen: His Philosophy and Religion*. Albany: State University of New York Press, 1992.

Confucius. *The Analects of Confucius: A Philosophical Translation*, translated by Roger T. Ames, Henry Rosemont Jr. Ballantine Books, 1999.

Atkins, Paul W. B., Wilson, David Sloan, Hayes, Steven C. *ProSocial: Using Evolutionary Science to Build Productive, Equitable, and Collaborative Groups*. Oakland, CA: Context Press, 2019.

Barbezat, Daniel P., Bush, Mirabai. *Contemplative Practices in Higher Education*. San Francisco, CA: Jossey-Bass, 2014.

Bernier, Bernard. "National Communion: Watsuji Tetsurô's Conception of Ethics, Power, and the Japanese Imperial State," *Philosophy East and West* 56, no. 1 (2006): 84–105.

Bernier, Bernard. "Transcendence of the State in Watsuji's Ethics," *Essays in Japanese Philosophy* 2 (2008): 94–100.

Berque, Augustin. "Offspring of Watsuji's Theory of Milieu (Fûdo)," *GeoJournal* 60 (2004): 389–396.

Biesta, Gert J. J. *Good Education in an Age of Measurement: Ethics, Politics, Democracy*. Oxon: Routledge, 2010.

Brink, Dean Anthony. *Philosophy of Science and the Kyoto School: Nishida Kitaro, Tanabe Hajime, and Tosaka Jun*. Bloomsbury Academic, 2021.

Day, Willard. *Radical Behaviorism: Willard Day on Psychology and Philosophy*, edited by Sam Leigland. Reno, Nevada: Context Press, 1992.

Dewey, John. *How we Think*. Boston: D.C. Heath & Co., 1910.

Dewey, John. *Democracy and Education*. New York, NY: The Macmillan Company, 1916.

Dilthey, Wilhelm. *The Formation of the Historical World in the Human Sciences*, edited by Rudolf A. Makkreel, Frithjof Rodi. Princeton, NJ: Princeton University Press, 2002.

Dore, Ronald. *The Diploma Disease: Education, Qualification and Development*. Berkeley, CA: University of California Press, 1976.

Durkheim, Emile. *The Rules of Sociological Method*, 2nd edn. Basingstoke: Palgrave Macmillan, 2013.

Dōgen. *Shōbōgenzō: The True Dharma-Eye Treasury* vol. 1, translated by Gudo Wafu Nishijima, Chodo Cross. Berkeley, CA: Numata Center for Buddhist Translation and Research, 2007.

Erikson, Erik H. *Childhood and Society*. London: Paladin, 1977.

Fink, L. Dee. *Creating Significant Learning Experiences: An Integrated Approach to Designing College Courses*. San Francisco, CA: Jossey-Bass, 2003.

Goffman, Erving. *The Presentation of Self in Everyday Life*. Garden City, NY: Doubleday Anchor Books, 1959.

Gordon, David Baruch. *Self-Overcoming as the Overcoming of Modernity: Watsuji Tetsuro's A Study of Nietzsche (1913) and its Place in the Development of His Thought*. Honolulu: University of Hawaii Dissertation, 1997.

Haviland, William A., Prins, Harald E. L., McBride, Bunny, Walrath, Dana. *Cultural Anthropology: The Human Challenge* 13th edn. Belmont, CA: Wadsworth, 2011.

Hayes, Steven C., Barnes-Holmes, Dermot, Roche, Bryan. *Relational Frame Theory: A Post-Skinnerian Account of Human Language and Cognition.* New York, NY: Kluwer, 2002.

Hayes, Steven C., Strosahl, Kirk D., Wilson, Kelly G. *Acceptance and Commitment Therapy: The Process and Practice of Mindful Change* 2nd edn. New York, NY: The Guilford Press, 2012.

Heisig, James W. *Philosophers of Nothingness.* Honolulu: University of Hawaii Press, 2001.

Heisig, James W., Kasulis, Thomas P., Maraldo, John C. *Japanese Philosophy: A Sourcebook.* Honolulu: University of Hawaii Press, 2011.

Hoshi Kaoru. *Shōgai hattatsu shinrigaku kenkyū.* Tokyo: Hōsō Daigaku, 2011.

Inaga Shigemi. "Japanese Philosophers Go West: The Effect of Maritime Trips on Philosophy in Japan with Special Reference to the Case of Watsuji Tetsurō (1889-1960)." *Japan Review*, no. 25 (2013): 113–44. http://www.jstor.org/stable/41959188

Inukai Yuichi. *Watsuji Tetsurō no Shakaigaku.* Tokyo: Yachiyo, 2016.

Itō Ayako. "Jidōki seinenki no shinriteki tokuchō," in *Jidō seito shidô no riron to jissen*, by Sumida Masaki, Okazaki Tomonori. Tokyo: Hōsō Daigaku, 2011.

Jacinto, Z. Agustín. "Nishida Kitarō's Views on Education: 1895-1935," *Nishida tetsugakkai nenpō* 13 (2016): 171-191.

Jaspers, Karl. *The Idea of the University.* Boston: Beacon Press, 1959.

Jaspers, Karl. *Philosophy* vol. 2, translated by E. B. Ashton. Chicago: University of Chicago Press, 1970.

Johnson, David W., Johnson, Roger T., Holubec, Edythe Johnson. *Circles of Learning: Cooperation in the Classroom.* Edina, MN: Interaction, 2009.

Kawakami Hideaki. "Tanabe Hajime to Mori Akira ni okeru gūzensei no mondai: Sengo kyōikugaku no hattatsuron ni tomonau hitsuzensei o sōtaika suru tame," *Kyōikugaku kenkyū* 88, no. 4 (2021): 610–621.

Kawakami Hideaki. "Tanabe Hajime to Mori Akira no keikenshugi hihan ni okeru ninshikiron no mondai: Kyōto gakuha kyōikugaku ni okeru 'kōiteki jikaku' no keifu," *Kindai kyōiku fōramu* 30 (2021): 147–157.

Kimura Bin. *Hito to Hito no Aida.* Tokyo: Kōbundō, 1972.

Kimura Motomori. *Kokka ni okeru bunka to kyōiku.* Tokyo: Iwanami Shoten, 1946.

Kimura Motomori. *Hana to shi to unmei.* Tokyo: Kōbundō Shobō, 1948.

Krueger, Joel. "Watsuji, Intentionality, and Psychopathology," *Philosophy East and West* 70, no. 3 (2020): 757–780.

Levinas, Emmanuel. *Otherwise than Being or Beyond Essence*, translated by Alphonso Lingis. The Hague: Martinus Nijhoff Publishers, 1981.

Levinas, Emmanuel. *On Thinking-of-the-Other: Entre Nous*, translated by Michael B. Smith, Barbara Harshav. New York, NY: Columbia University Press, 1998.

Maraldo, John C. "Between Individual and Communal, Subject and Object, Self and Other: Mediating Watsuji Tetsurō's Hermeneutics," in *Japanese Hermeneutics: Current Debates on Aesthetics and Interpretation*, ed. Michael F. Marra. Honolulu, University of Hawaii Press, 2002. 76–86.

Mayeda, Graham. *Japanese Philosophers on Society and Culture: Nishida Kitarō, Watsuji Tetsurō, and Kuki Shūzō*. Lanham, MD: 2020.

Mayeda, Graham. "Permeating each Other's Hearts: Natsume Sōseki and Watsuji Tetsurō on Ethics and the Unity of Self and Other," *European Journal of Japanese Philosophy* 6 (2021): 35–74.

McAdams, Dan P. *The Stories we Live By: Personal Myths and the Making of the Self*. New York: The Guilford Press, 1993.

Mead, George Herbert. *Mind, Self and Society*. Chicago: University of Chicago Press, 1962.

Ministry of Education, *Kokutai No Hongi: Cardinal Principles of the National Entity of Japan*, trans. John Owen Gauntlett, ed. Robert King Hall. Cambridge; Harvard University Press, 1949.

Monzen Ayaki. *Kimura Motomori no "hyōgen ai": "hyōgen," "keisei," "tsukuru koto" no shintairon*. Tokyo: Minerva, 2019.

Nishida Kitarō. *Nishida Kitarō zenshū* [hereon NKZ], vols 6–12. Tokyo: Iwanami shoten, 1966.

Nishida Kitarō. *An Inquiry into the Good*, translated by Masao Abe and Christopher Ives. New Haven: Yale University Press, 1990.

Nishida Kitarō. "The Historical Body," in *The Sourcebook for Modern Japanese Philosophy: Selected Documents*, translated by David A. Dilworth and Valdo H. Viglielmo. Westport, CT: Greenwood Press, 1998.

Nishihira Tadashi. *Raifusaikuru no tetsugaku*. Tokyo: Tokyo Daigaku Shuppankai, 2019.

Nishihira Tadashi. *The Philosophy of No-Mind: Experience Without Self*, translated by Catherine Sevilla-Liu, Anton Sevilla-Liu. London: Bloomsbury Academic, 2024.

Nishihira Tadashi, Rappleye, Jeremy. "Unlearning as (Japanese) Learning," *Educational Philosophy and Theory* 54, no. 9 (2021): 1332–1344.

Nishitani Keiji. *Religion and Nothingness*, trans. Jan Van Bragt. Berkeley, CA: University of California Press, 1982.

Noddings, Nel. *Starting at Home: Caring and Social Policy*. Berkeley: University of California Press, 2002.
Noddings, Nel. *Philosophy of Education*, 3rd edn. Boulder: Westview Press, 2012.
Noddings, Nel. *Caring: A Relational Approach to Moral Education* 2nd edn. Berkeley: University of California Press, 2013.
Odin, Steve. "The Social Self in Japanese Philosophy and American Pragmatism: A Comparative Study of Watsuji Tetsurō and George Herbert Mead," *Philosophy East and West* 42, no. 3 (1992): 475–501.
Odin, Steve. *The Social Self in Zen and American Pragmatism*. Albany: State University of New Yori Press, 1996.
Okano, Kaori H. *Young Women in Japan: Transitions to Adulthood*. Oxon: Roudledge, 2009.
Pepper, Stephen C. *World Hypotheses: A Study in Evidence*. Berkeley: University of California Press, 1942.
Reveley, James. "School-Based Mindfulness Training and the Economisation of Attention; A Stieglerian View," *Educational Philosophy and Theory* 47, no. 8 (2014): 804–821.
Saito Naoko. *The Gleam of Light: Moral Perfectionism and Education in Dewey and Emerson*. New York, NY: Fordham University Press, 2005.
Saito Naoko, Akiyama Tomohiro. "On the Education of the Whole Person," *Educational Philosophy and Theory* 56, no. 2 (2024): 153–161.
Sakai Naoki. *Translation and Subjectivity: On "Japan" and Cultural Nationalism*. Minneapolis: University of Minnesota Press, 1997.
Shuttleworth, Kyle Michael James. "Confucianism, Nationalism, and *Nihonjinron* in Watsuji Tetsurō's *Climate*," in *Confucianism at War: 1931-1945*, edited by Shaun O'Dwyer, London: Routledge, 2025. 268–273.
Shuttleworth, Kyle Michael James. "Virtues and Ethics within Watsuji Tetsurō's *Rinrigaku*," *Asian Philosophy* 30, no. 1 (2020): 57–70. https://doi.org/10.1080/09552367.2020.1736746
Slote, Michael. *The Ethics of Care and Empathy*. London: Routledge, 2007.
Standish, Paul, and Saito Naoko. *Education and the Kyoto School of Philosophy*. Dordrecht: Springer, 2012.
Sueki Fumihiko. *Philosophy Live: A Perspective from Japan*. Kyoto: Nichibunken, 2018.
Takamiya Masaki. "'Aidagara' to 'sonkei' no rinrigaku: Watsuji Tetsurō to Kanto kara miru dōtoku no naiyō kōmoku," *Kindai kyōiku fōramu* 30 (2021): 50–55.

Takaya Shōko. "Historical Nature in Nishida and Kimura Motomori," *European Journal of Japanese Philosophy* 7 (2022): 171–190.

Takaya Shōko. *"Watashi to nanji" no kyōiku ningengaku: Nishida tetsugaku e no ōkan*. Kyoto: Kyōto Daigaku Shuppankai, 2024.

Tam, Andrew Ka Pok. "On the Relation between Watsuji Tetsurō's *Ningen Rinrigaku* and Mencius' Five Relationships: A Critique from the Perspective of Mou Zongsan's Moral Metaphysics," *Taiwan Journal of East Asian Studies* 17, no. 2 (2020): 135–182.

Tanabe Hajime. *Philosophy as Metanoetics*, translated by Takeuchi Yoshinori. Berkeley: University of California Press, 1986.

Tanaka Tsunemi. *Rinshōteki ningen keisei ron e: raifu saikuru to sōgō keisei*. Tokyo: Keisō Shobō, 2003.

Tanaka Tsunemi. *Rinshōteki ningen keisei ron no kōchiku*. Tokyo: Tōshindō, 2012.

Tanaka Tsunemi. "Mori Akira o yomu: Kyōikuteki kōkyōsei kara sedai keishōteki kōkyōsei e," in *Nihon kyōikugaku no keifu*, ed. Ogasawara Michio et al. Tokyo: Keisō Shobō, 2014.

Tanaka Tsunemi. *Keimō to kyōiku: rinshōteki ningen keisei ron kara*. Tokyo: Keisō Shobō, 2021.

Villatte, Matthieu, Villatte, Jennifer L., Hayes, Steven C. *Mastering the Clinical Conversation: Language as Intervention*. New York, NY: Guilford Press, 2016.

Vozzola, Elizabeth C. *Moral Development: Theory and Applications*. New York: Routledge, 2014.

Yamaguchi Yukio. "Ningen oyobi ningen shakai no sonzai no fūdosei-kūkansei ni kansuru chiri kyōikuronteki kōsatsu," *Shin Chiri* 54, no. 4 (2007): 34–42.

Yano Satoji. *Kyōto gakuha to jikaku no kyōikugaku: Shinohara Sukeichi, Osada Arata, Kimura Motomori*. Tokyo: Keisō Shobō, 2021.

Yano Satoji. "The Philosophical Anthropology of the Kyoto School and Post-War Pedagogy," in *Education and the Kyoto School of Philosophy*, ed. Paul Standish and Naoko Saito. Dordrecht: Springer, 2012.

Yuasa Yasuo. *Watsuji Tetsurō: Kindai Tetsugaku no Unmei*. Tokyo: Chikuma Shobō, 1995.

Yusa, Michiko. *Zen & Philosophy: An Intellectual Biography of Nishida Kitarō*. Honolulu: University of Hawaii Press, 2002.

Zettle, Robert D., Hayes, Steven C., Barnes-Holmes, Dermot, and Biglan, Anthony. *The Wiley Handbook of Contextual Behavioral Science*. Malden, MA: Wiley Blackwell, 2016.

van Manen, Max. *The Tact of Teaching: The Meaning of Pedagogical Thoughtfulness*. Albany: State University of New York Press, 1991.

Index

abuse 47, 88
Acceptance and Commitment
 Training/Therapy (ACT) 81,
 86, 128, 131–2, 135
 process of training in, 88–103
 teaching, 106–7
active learning 38, 40, 193, 199
alienation 19, 41, 76, 121, 156
alterity 63–4, 66, 69, 74, 113
arched bridge (*tsuzumi hashi*) 19–20,
 22, 163–5

Buddha. *See* Buddhism
Buddhism 3, 5, 11–2, 14, 17, 21,
 33–4, 58–9, 81–3, 111–3, 117,
 123, 165, 198
 Buddha-nature, 91–95, 99–100
 master-disciple relationship in,
 84–89, 104–6
 practice, 89–91

call-response 49, 165, 198, 200
cases
 explanation of the use of,
 2, 28
 Jin-*kun*, 2, 8, 10, 21, 27–8, 35–48,
 117, 130, 146, 162, 173, 175,
 178, 186
 Junko-*san*, 2, 8, 11, 21, 61–74,
 117, 123, 130, 134, 146, 162,
 173, 175, 178, 193
 Taro-*kun*, 2, 8, 11, 22, 81, 86–9,
 96, 103, 106, 117, 123, 127,
 130, 134, 152, 162, 173, 175,
 178, 193
 team, 2, 22, 39, 41–4, 49, 52, 65,
 90, 127, 130–4, 157–8, 173–8,
 202
cognition 14, 29–30, 61, 71, 73, 118,
 146

collaborative learning 27, 40, 48,
 193, 199
communication 23, 41, 52, 70, 117,
 123, 128–30, 194, 197
 ethics of, 169, 179, 184, 187
Confucianism 3–4, 14, 21, 27–8, 31,
 33–5, 37–8, 41–3, 46–9, 52–55
Confucius. *See* Confucianism
consequences 17, 22, 119–22,
 125–135, 137, 149, 160, 175,
 179, 190, 194–7
conservativism 17, 57–60, 79,
 112, 171
contextualism 81, 89, 117, 134–5,
 160, 165, 175, 177, 194, 196
continuity and discontinuity 22,
 69–70, 76, 141, 150–1,
 164, 168
cooperation 65, 70, 72–3, 106, 114–8,
 123, 130, 142, 155, 168, 183,
 186, 190
 in education, 12, 28–9, 35, 38–40,
 43, 47–8
counseling, 1–2, 46, 59, 81, 86, 90,
 107, 127, 130–1, 171, 173, 193
creativity, 12, 19–22, 33, 64, 80–1,
 83–4, 93–6, 106, 113, 118, 139,
 144, 165, 200
 and tradition, 5, 7
 ethics of, 23, 169, 175, 179, 190
crisis 16, 22, 83, 125–6, 141, 149,
 151–3, 156, 161, 165, 198, 201
critical thinking 89, 101, 119

data and evidence 18, 42, 23, 134–5,
 160, 169, 174, 194–6
degreeocracy 35–7, 42, 141, 187
democracy 17, 31, 36, 38, 42, 50,
 52, 60, 128, 130, 155–6, 161,
 177, 194

development 170, 174, 194
  Confucian moral, 47–8
  in psychology, 61, 75, 139, 141
  of identity, 18, 22, 142–163, 181–4
Dewey, John 31, 135, 190, 192, 194
  and democracy, 52–3, 60, 155, 177
  and Mori, 16–7, 119–21, 150, 169
  learning and self-awareness, 122–8, 163, 175
Dilthey, Wilhelm 16, 53–5, 60, 101, 106, 115–6
discipline 27, 46, 143–4, 149, 173
Dōgen 21, 82–99, 113, 119, 164, 193, 198
Dore, Ronald 36
Durkheim, Emile 32, 55, 132

egoism 33–4, 42–3, 57, 81, 83, 85, 139–41
empathy 21, 63–8, 71, 91, 98
emptiness (*kū*) 16, 20, 23, 159, 161, 165, 167–8, 199, 202
  in Japanese philosophy, 3, 4, 81, 93–5, 100, 106, 137–40,
  of individual and totality, 11–4, 29, 52, 81–6, 112, 137, 198
  of subject and object, 127, 137, 197
enlightenment 22, 58, 85, 87, 95, 159, 162, 168, 171
Erikson, Erik 4, 18, 22, 142–5, 151–3, 160, 164, 184
evolution 18–19, 85, 118, 121–2, 151, 156
existentialism 74–6, 82–6, 96, 99, 152, 198
  and pragmatism, 119–28, 160–165
  existential communion, 22, 31, 155–6, 187, 193
  existential education, 15–22, 53, 102–5
Existenz. See Existentialism

feudalism 17, 36, 156, 171, 188–9
flexibility 88, 102, 123, 130, 135, 159, 202
friends 34, 38, 41, 43–4, 59, 83, 107, 128, 150, 185–6, 192
  and development, 145, 155–7
  virtue of friendship, 31

Gemeinschaft and *Gesellschaft* 32, 35–6, 156, 187
generalized other 66, 75, 80
generational care and crisis 152, 164–5, 202
generativity 19, 141, 145–7, 151, 156, 162–4, 181–2, 187, 200
Goffman, Erving 73
guidance 23, 95, 124, 169–179, 193, 197

Herbart, Johann Friedrich 5–6, 52–3
hermeneutics 54–5, 68, 71–3, 115–7, 133, 172
human becoming (*ningen seisei*) 107, 168, 170, 179, 184, 193, 196, 200
  and development, 151–4, 159–60
  Mori's philosophy of, 15–18, 53, 139–41
human existence (*ningen sonzai*) 68, 102, 114, 134, 167–8
  and becoming, 18–9, 53, 139–40
  Watsuji's philosophy of, 11–3, 30, 71, 82
human relations (*jinrin*) 12, 43, 58, 118

I and me 66, 73–6, 80, 96, 105, 124, 193, 195–6
identity 66, 74, 122–8, 193
  in Erikson, 18, 143–58, 160–1, 184
  narrative, 60, 180–1
institution 19, 30, 39, 75–7, 80, 96, 107, 113, 153, 156–8, 173, 198–9

I and Thou (*watashi to nanji*) 31, 46, 69–78, 80, 96, 100, 105, 117, 156, 187, 200

Kant, Immanuel 5, 16, 53, 103, 120, 125
Katsube Mitake 15, 169, 189

leader 32–3, 45, 49, 57, 60, 80, 118, 128–9
Levinas, Emmanuel 61, 63–8

Marx, Karl 16, 53, 116, 156
Mead, George Herbert 4, 55, 61, 80, 135
  and Watsuji, 117–120
  theory of self, 65–6, 70–7, 96, 193
mechanism 134–5, 142, 194, 196
meritocracy 36, 38, 44, 85
milieu (*fūdo*) 9, 13, 22, 72, 78, 114–5, 155, 189
mindfulness 81, 90–1, 102, 105, 131
Ministry of Education 5, 14, 60, 171
moral education 14–5, 18, 20, 23, 87, 139, 200
  and development, 143–7
  practice and textbooks, 168–182

narrative 20, 60, 83, 102, 131, 135, 142, 180–1, 184, 196
Natsume Sōseki 41, 97–9
negation (*hitei*) 11, 22, 50, 79–80, 86, 89–95, 100, 111–3, 120, 127, 139, 141, 197, 200
Nishida Kitarō 11, 20, 117, 120, 167, 171
  and education, 4–9, 69–70, 80, 100–1, 200
  influence, 14–7, 126, 141
Nishihira Tadashi 139, 146, 152, 164, 200–3
Nishitani Keiji 4, 15, 82, 92, 100, 137–8, 159, 162

Nitobe Inazō 40–1, 97
Noddings, Nel 4, 21, 50, 52, 61–4, 67
non-duality 5–12, 17–20, 114, 122, 127, 137, 167, 172, 194
nothingness (*mu*) 3, 5–6, 9, 12, 100, 126–7, 138, 159, 167, 200

phenomenology 64, 67–8, 71–2, 82, 115, 125, 172
philosophical anthropology (*ningengaku*) 53, 114, 149
  in the Kyoto School, 8, 139–40
  Mori's book on, 18, 120, 124, 129, 133, 143, 146, 153–4, 200
practical nexus (*jissenteki kōiteki renkan*) 12, 16, 21–2, 52–4, 61, 77, 101, 111, 115–23, 126, 133, 197
pragmatism 15–8, 22, 114, 139, 159–60, 176, 194, 197
  and contextualism, 89, 126–131, 134–5, 165
  theory of learning, 117–23
ProSocial 131, 135, 199, 202

qualitative research 53, 130, 132, 172–4, 195

role model 87–88, 91, 198

Saitō Naoko 8, 159
Sakai Naoki 73–4, 96, 111, 130
self-awareness (*jikaku*) 6, 103, 134, 137–9, 167, 179
  endless, 16, 19, 160–2
  generative, 162–5
  in ethics, 11, 80
  in personality, 22, 124, 149–50, 181
  on a pragmatic base, 119–27
social coherence 66, 71, 77, 81, 113, 123–4, 130
social self 65–8, 76–7, 96, 117, 125, 145, 198
social sorting 35–8, 42

socialization 19, 22, 32, 53, 75–76, 96, 150, 154, 171
Socrates 33, 52, 58–9, 141
Socratic teacher/midwife 104, 107, 162
Standish, Paul 8, 158–9

Tanabe Hajime 4, 9, 15, 20, 82, 105, 127, 138, 141, 159, 160, 162
Tanaka Tsunemi 15, 20, 164, 168

teacher-student relationship 22, 39–40, 73, 91, 101–7
totalitarianism 19, 61, 82, 121, 130, 159, 179
trauma 45, 47, 81, 101, 184

values, personal 29, 127, 145, 158, 180–1, 195

Yano Satoji 8, 19, 133, 139